CW00972443

WORLD FLY

FINDER

WORLD FLY FINDER

ALL THE FLIES YOU NEED TO FISH ALL THE WATERS OF THE WORLD

Peter Cockwill

Photography by Peter Gathercole and Terry Griffiths

COLLINS & BROWN

First published in Great Britain in 2004
by Collins & Brown Ltd, The Chrysalis Building
Bramley Road London W10 6SP

An imprint of **Chrysalis** Books Group

Distributed in the United States and Canada by
Sterling Publishing Co., 387 Park Avenue South
New York NY 10016

10 9 8 7 6 5 4 3 2 1

British Library Cataloguing-in-Publication Data: A catalogue record for this title is available from the British Library.

ISBN 1-85585-077-7

Senior Editor: Nicola Hodgson
Editor: Claire Wedderburn-Maxwell
Designer: Anthony Cohen

Reproduction by Anorax Imaging
Printed by Times Offset, Malaysia

This book was typeset in Optima

Contents

Introduction

WORLD FLY FINDER WILL HELP YOU to locate the best fly patterns for all the most likely fly-caught species of fish wherever they occur throughout the world, be it in fresh- or saltwater, Arctic or tropical regions.

The rapidly expanding boundaries of fly fishing coupled with new tackle technology now mean that there is virtually nowhere that prohibits the adventurous angler from taking sport with the fly. My intention is to stretch your fly fishing imagination and let you see that the vastly complex world of fly fishing can indeed be reassembled into a relatively small number of flies which can be used with confidence wherever you are.

It's a fact that the fly fishing fraternity is quite small, and almost everyone either knows each other or has common contacts. If you add the experience of my worldwide fishing travels and my years in the fishery business and tackle trade to the encyclopaedic knowledge of flies and materials shared by the many names mentioned throughout this book, then we have between us a whole world of friends whose views and information are packed into this book.

Some fly patterns are truly original, while others have been created quite independently by many individuals but from a similar base, and yet others are time-honoured classics whose origins are long lost. Wherever possible I have credited originators, but in the pattern's research I found so many that had been re-invented and given new names that I have always tried to go back to the first probability. Often there are minor variants, which are known and respected, but without creating confusion I have kept to as wide a tying option as possible to cover every likely situation while leaving the individual colour choices to you – the angler.

Fly tying involves the use of fur, feather, thread, tinsel and synthetics to create something that can be either truly realistic or solely impressionist. Maybe the fly is suggestive either by movement, shape or colour, or perhaps it just combines certain qualities that fish find acceptable. There is literally no limit to the ingenuity of the fly tier, and although we all strive for the ultimate pattern there really is no such thing. A successful fly may be the simplest of scraps applied to a hook, or it may be a carefully crafted construction requiring much skill and patience. Anyone can tie a successful fish-catching fly, and in the following pages the basic concepts of fly tying are covered which will get you started.

Accept that fish see colour and that the many food items they choose can have a wide range of colours depending on the species, environment and time of year, and then use your own observations to select the pattern and colour that will best serve you at the particular location and time. Most of the flies are either easy to tie (if you don't tie then use a fishing buddy or go to evening classes to learn), or they are readily available from a variety of commercial sources. I believe that the interplay of ideas and skills through being part of a group tying class is probably the best way to learn the art and thoroughly recommend that you don't rely forever on commercially available patterns but strike out and try your own creations. There is nothing more satisfying in fly fishing than the first capture on a fly of your own making.

Whenever I travel I meet anglers who have strong views against some aspects of fly fishing. For example, there are those who believe that the use of sight indicators makes the sport more akin to the use of a bobber and dough balls, while others feel that anything other than a dry fly on a chalk stream is just not proper fly fishing. Some think that flies should only be imitative, while there are those who would look down on the angler who enjoys his sport with a 2-weight rod and small stream trout.

A fish does not have to be big or glamorous to make it a favoured target with a fly rod, and I very much hope that this book will spur you into trying a new branch of the sport. There are areas within fly fishing that I personally simply don't enjoy, but have absolutely nothing against anyone who does, providing it is fair and does not impinge on anyone else's sport or the welfare of wild stocks.

Fly fishing should be fun, although much of its literature can be very dry to read. This book is different, and is the compilation of my lifetime spent doing what I most enjoy, and combining the experiences and knowledge of my many friends and colleagues to condense a vast subject into a commonsense and invaluable guide.

GETTING STARTED

How to use this book

THROUGHOUT THE WORLD there is an incredibly diverse range of fish species in both fresh- and saltwater. Many are unique to an area, while others have been successfully introduced to new habitats. Literally hundreds of varieties can be caught on fly, but in this book you will find the principal target species from each area of the world. These are grouped into salmonids, freshwater and saltwater fish to illustrate the wealth of fishing available to the travelling angler.

The initial charts for salmonids, freshwater and saltwater on pages 16–27 give an approximate location of each chosen species for the three groupings and here you can see where they occur so that you choose a new location to pursue your favourite species. You may then use the cross reference under each chart to find out which flies can be used to fish that particular species. Here you will find the page number and name of the relevant fly within the fly directory section of the book.

For example, you may wish to catch the Redfish. From the saltwater chart on page 25 you will discover that this fish can be caught in Mexico. Then using the information underneath that chart you will discover that this fish can be caught using Danny's Redfish Special or Go to Joe, which can be looked up on pages 237 and 249. This part of the book is not exhaustive however, there are many other flies that can be tied for each fish, this section is designed as a starting point only.

Alternatively, if you really don't mind what you fish for, then you can look up a particular country that your travels may take you to and check out the available species and again cross refer to fly choice. Another way of using the book is to use the index to look up the name of the fly.

The flies included in the book are chosen to provide a wide selection to cover all the principal food forms available to the many species of fish, and also include many, proven attractor patterns. Some food forms have a number of representative patterns because of their importance to a wide range of habitats and species. Others are prey or species specific. Most are widely-recognized patterns which have more than proven their worth and are easily available through major commercial fly tying outlets. Some are 'one-off' tyings and may be very new to even experienced anglers.

Check the patterns through the book and you will see how even a minor variation might suit your particular home water, or another might inspire you to try a new technique. It may even tempt you into trying a new species, in which case this book has been successful in broadening your outlook and expanding your fly fishing horizons.

Salmonid species

THERE IS MORE IN-DEPTH ANGLING LITERATURE devoted to the pursuit of the salmonids than any other group of fish. This is largely because many of this group, which includes salmon, whitefish, grayling and char, will freely feed on the surface to adult or hatching insects or can be induced to take a surface-presented fly. This habit alone led to the initial development of fly tying, from which evolved a separate art form where close copy or dexterity of construction with natural materials (the classic salmon flies) became almost as important as the actual fishing. The salmonids are good-looking fish with strong fighting ability and have been very successfully introduced to many new habitats, as well as providing the basis of stocked waters which have led to many more anglers having access to game fishing.

Fish Finder

SALMONIDS

	Austria	Australia	Africa	Argentina	Canada	Chile	Denmark	France	Falkland Islands	Germany	Greenland	Iceland	Ireland	India
Atlantic Salmon					●	●	●	●			●	●	●	
Brook Trout				●	●	●								
Brown Trout	●	●	●	●	●	●	●	●		●		●	●	●
Char	●				●		●				●	●		
Cherry Salmon														
Chinook Salmon					●	●								
Chum Salmon					●									
Coho Salmon					●									
Grayling	●				●		●	●		●				
Huchen										●				
Humpback Salmon					●									
Lake Trout	●				●									
Lennox Trout														
Marbled Trout														
Rainbow Trout	●	●	●	●	●	●	●	●		●			●	
Sea Trout				●		●	●	●	●			●	●	
Sockeye Salmon														
Steelhead				●	●	●								
Taimen														

Either select your destination and then find what you can fish or choose your quarry and discover where you should be headed. The charts on these pages only suggest one or two of the flies that may be used for a particular fish – in most cases there are other flies that could be used.

ATLANTIC SALMON Elver Fly p282
BROOK TROUT Mouse Rat p70, Whit's Sculpin p392
BROWN TROUT Blue Winged Olive p383, Watson's Fancy p408
CHAR Roe Bug p317, Alaska Mary Ann p48
CHERRY SALMON Polar Shrimp p167, Russian River Coho p134
CHINOOK Alaskabou p191, Egg Sucking Leech p375

Fish Finder

SALMONIDS

	Italy	Japan	Lapland	Mongolia	New zealand	Norway	Paraguay	Russia	Spain	Sweden	United kingdom	USA	Yugoslavia
Atlantic Salmon						●		●	●	●	●	●	
Brook Trout							●				●	●	
Brown Trout	●		●		●	●	●	●	●	●	●	●	●
Char		●	●			●		●			●		
Cherry Salmon												●	
Chinook Salmon					●							●	
Chum Salmon												●	
Coho Salmon												●	
Grayling	●		●	●		●		●		●	●	●	●
Huchen													
Humpback Salmon													●
Lake Trout												●	●
Lennox Trout				●									
Marbled Trout													●
Rainbow Trout	●	●			●		●	●	●	●	●	●	●
Sea Trout						●	●			●	●		
Sockeye Salmon												●	
Steelhead								●				●	
Taimen				●				●					

CHUM Showgirl p127, Palmered Bunny p277
COHO Flash Fly p369, Pink Pollywog p108
GRAYLING Czech Nymph p91, Klinkhammer p84
HUCHEN Dredger p116, Black Nosed Dace p80
HUMPIE Pink Floozy p193, Fonzie Fly p79
LAKE TROUT Fry Feeder Tandem p338, Mickey Finn p216
LENNOX Prince p314, Bitch Creek Nymph p313
MARBLED TROUT Peeping Caddis p260, Mayfly Cripple Callibaetis p394
RAINBOW TROUT Elk Hair Caddis p243, Cat's Whisker p335
SEA TROUT Sunk Lure p409, Teal, Blue and Silver p397
SOCKEYE Green Eyes p174, Grey Sockeye Nymph p316
STEELHEAD Freight Train p342
TAIMEN Articulated Leech p75, Clint's Lemming p177

Salmonids species

Atlantic Salmon
Highly prized by anglers, and yet extensively persecuted by commercial interests, this beautiful fish is the ultimate puzzle as it will rise to take a fly and yet does not feed while in freshwater.

Brook Trout
Beautifully-coloured member of the Salvelinus group, which has adapted to many new environments although it remains a cold water species. A genuine specimen will weigh over 2.7 kg (6lbs).

Brown Trout
An amazingly versatile species, being equally at home in river or lake, the brown trout possibly has more devotees than any other salmonid. All fly fishers say there is something special about a brown.

Char
Can be sea run or landlocked and has many localized forms, from the giants of the arctic rivers, which can exceed 30 lbs to the 0.4 kg (1 lb) fish of the Scottish lochs. The males at spawning time are truly stunning.

Cutthroat Trout
Another fish which can be sea run or landlocked. Man has eliminated the largest of the strains but this pretty fish is a popular fly species and, although some sea runs are threatened, its future is assured.

Chinook Salmon
The mightiest of the salmon and an extremely tough adversary on the fly rod. Can reach 45.4 kg (100 lbs) and is also known as Tyee, King, Springer and Quinnat. Aggressive and strong, it's a challenge.

Chum Salmon
Very much underrated as a sport fish. It colours up quickly but pound for pound it is a very tough customer and will happily take just about anything pink.

Coho Salmon
Unusual in that its kype is on the upper jaw instead of the usual lower jaw and it will take flies on the surface. Also called Silvers, they leap repeatedly when hooked and taste good too.

Grayling
There are two forms of grayling – arctic and European. To thrive, they must have clean, clear water. Grayling are also a much sought after sport fish. The arctic grayling is the more beautiful and also lives to a great age.

Huchen
A very large and entirely freshwater salmonid of limited distribution. Those living in the European Danube are veiled in secrecy to protect them from exploitation.

Lake Trout
A very long lived fish, with a lifespan of perhaps 100 years, this fish spends much of its life under ice and has a number of sub strains. Some can reach almost 45.4 kg (100 lbs) and all are strong fighters.

Lennox Trout
An eastern Asian fish which has a mouth like a grayling and is yet to be recognized as sport fish, often being caught accidentally while persuing taimen.

Marbled Trout
This unique species occurs only in central Europe and has superb body markings. Its lake form can often reach exceptional sizes and much care is needed to ensure its survival.

Rainbow Trout
Originally from the western Pacific and now the major sport fish throughout the world for trout anglers. It is easily farmed and has the potential to reach 22.7 kg (50 lbs) with some interesting colour variants.

Sea Trout
The migratory form of the brown trout which has flourished in many new locations but can be almost reclusive in some rivers. Where protected some multiple spawners can exceed 13.6 kg (30 lbs).

Sockeye Salmon
A very important commercial species, sometimes running rivers by the thousand. A plankton eater and tough to catch by fair means it peaks around 6.8 kg (15 lbs) and is a great sport fish.

Steelhead
The migratory rainbow trout which fly fishers have elevated to almost mystical levels. 20 lbs is huge but it can reach 9 kg (40 lbs). Very successfully transplanted to the Great Lakes of the USA.

Taimen
Closely related to the European Huchen this fish is wholly freshwater and may reach 45.4 kg (100 lbs), but has been extensively exploited in its native waters of the Russian steppes and Mongolia.

Freshwater species

MANY FRESHWATER fish were non intentional fly captures until it was realized by forward-thinking fly fishers that many of these species were indeed a whole new challenge to be taken on fly gear. New patterns have evolved, new locations and techniques explored and in the ever-shrinking world fly fishers have used their skills on species available to them, rather than just dreaming of annual trips for a favourite fish. To some the species may be all important but surely the whole ethos of fly fishing is that we are catching fish on artificial creations and if I can get just as much thrill from catching carp as I can salmon then my needs are met. Many more freshwater species will be added to the fly fishers range as the sport evolves and expands until equal merits will be given to all aspects just so long as the capture is on fly.

Fish Finder

FRESHWATER

	Africa	Australia	Brazil	Canada	Holland	India	Ireland	Europe	Sweden	Spain	UK	USA
Barbel					●			●		●	●	
Barramundi		●										
Bluegill										●		●
Carp		●		●	●			●	●	●	●	●
Dorado			●									
Largemouth Bass	●	●		●						●		●
Mahseer						●						
Nile Perch	●											
Perch		●			●		●	●	●	●	●	●
Peacock Bass			●									●
Pike				●	●		●	●	●	●	●	●
Smallmouth Bass				●								●
Tiger Fish	●											
Walleye				●	●			●	●		●	●
Whitefish				●								●
Yellow Fish	●											
Inconnu				●								●

BARBEL Crayfish p60, Depth Charge Czech Mate p311
BARRAMUNDI Bait Runner p68, Fritz Rabbit p179
BLUE GILL Pearl Bead PTN p199, Marabou Damsel p330
DORADO Black Deceiver p171, Swimming Frog p412
LARGE MOUTH BASS Frog Popper p59, Harewater Pup p138
MAHSEER Yellow Leech p211, Woolly Worm p303
NILE PERCH Fry Feeder Tandem p338, Grey Ghost p166
PEACOCK BASS Dahlberg Diver p326
PERCH Butcher p61, Janssen's Minnow p186
PIKE Black Mohawk p93, Pike Bomber Chartreuse p390
SMALL MOUTH BASS Grasshopper p348, Dawson's Olive p86
TIGER FISH Lefty's Deceiver p54, Thunder Creek Red Fin p419
WALLEYE Appetiser p275, Whit's Sculpin p392
WHITEFISH Gold Bead Mayfly p119, Perla Stonefly p58
YELLOW FISH Mrs Simpson p400, Black Stonefly p256
INCONNU Pearl Zonker p156, Polar Chub Bucktail p322

Freshwater species

Barbel

This rapidly expanding European species is the next target now that pike and carp have their devotees. It's tough, gets really big, eats bugs and crayfish and in summer can be sight cast in shallow water.

Bluegills

Beautiful in their own right and fantastic sport on light gear. All of the crappies and sun fish family are perfect for summer sport and to introduce newcomers to fly fishing. Ever tried a blue gill of 0.9 kg (2 lbs) on a 5 weight rod?

Carp

The mainstay of commercial coarse fisheries throughout Europe and with a huge following. Hated in Australia and becoming a pest in many parts of the USA and Canada. It is nevertheless an amazing fighter and certain to be a top fly rod species.

Dorado

The golden fish of Argentina. Aggressive, a great leaper and very much prized as a fly rod trophy. Thankfully it is now being released in some areas and sizes are increasing. A very pretty fish and often said to be the South American salmon.

Largemouth Bass

More money gets spent in pursuit of this species than any other and it truly is *the* fish of the USA. In many other countries it is now a fantastic fly rod fish especially in summer when it hits surface lures with that huge mouth.

Mahseer

Early Victorian explorers to India sent back home tales of a golden fish of immense power which needed special tackle to subdue. It's much the same now and on the fly is an awesome proposition with individuals weighing up to 36.2 kg (80 lbs) in some rivers.

Nile Perch

Interesting how so many species have the 'bass' type configuration. This African species can reach well over 90.7 kg (200 lbs) but on fly gear a 30 pounder is enough trouble. A true predator and very worthy of more attention from fly fishers.

Perch

This pretty 'basslike' fish gets to 2.3 kg (5lbs) or so and although not a great fighter it takes fly very well and tastes good too. It can be taken at all times of the year and on nymphs as well as lures.

Peacock Bass

This South American group of fishes has been introduced to other warm water locations and is another big-mouthed predator very worthy of the fly rod, with a wonderful habit of striking surface active lures.

Pike
One of the few freshwater fish which can look at you with both eyes at the same time. Sudden, violent takes are its hallmark and a leaping, shallow water summer-caught fish will very quickly make you a pike addict.

Smallmouth Bass
Lakes, ponds, rivers throughout the USA and Canada have vast stocks of this very popular sport fish, which besides being predatory is also an insect eater and just perfect for fly fishers.

Tiger Fish
The toothy beast of the African waterways. Hard to hook on fly gear because of its dentistry, but a spectacular fighter and very good looking too. Maybe someone will go for the Goliath Tiger on fly – now that would be something!

Walleye
Its variant in Europe is the Zander and although topping around 9.1 kg (20 lbs) this fish isn't the greatest fighter but is very much sought after and is excellent eating too.I think it will become as popular as carp on the fly.

Whitefish
I don't suppose many people genuinely target this species but they are great fighters and take nymphs well. Just because they aren't a glamour species doesn't mean they aren't a suitable subject for the fly fisher.

Yellow Fish
Definitely the up-and-coming sport fish in Africa. They fight like carp and take a fly very well. They're good looking too and this is one fish you are going to see being introduced to other parts of the world with great success.

Inconnu
Also called sheefish, this is a species which you have to go north to find but which is a great jumper and sometimes called the tarpon of the north. Seek out its rivers and then bag yourself an unusual trophy.

Saltwater species

FLY FISHING IN SALT WATER really took off when shallow, warm water species began to be successfully targetted, and then as tackle evolved so the horizons expanded until larger and larger species were taken on fly. Today there are many hundreds of species which are regularly taken on fly throughout the world. This has led to a much greater understanding of many species' needs, their food and habits, with anglers being at the forefront of many conservation measures. Fly tying evolved too, and the use of synthetic materials has led to thousands of new patterns. I am sure that we are still only in the developmental stages of saltwater fly fishing. The 'exotic' locations may offer some of the most exciting fishing but closer to home is a developing area where there are many species which can easily be taken on the fly.

Fish Finder

SALTWATER

	Australia	Africa	Bahamas	Cuba	Denmark	Dubai	Madagasgar	Mexico	New Guineaa	New Zealand	Norway	Seychelles	Sweden	UK	USA	Venezuela
Bonefish		●	●	●			●	●				●			●	●
Tarpon		●	●	●			●	●							●	●
Permit			●	●				●							●	
Trevally	●	●	●	●		●	●	●				●			●	●
Kahawai	●								●	●						
Barramundi	●															
Sailfish	●	●	●	●		●		●		●					●	●
Redfish								●							●	
Spotted Sea Trout															●	
Striped Bass															●	
Bluefish															●	
Snook			●	●				●							●	
Mullet														●		
Bass					●						●			●		
Halibut											●		●		●	
Flatfish					●						●		●	●		
Bonito	●	●	●	●		●	●	●	●	●					●	●
Black Bass									●						●	

BONEFISH Gotcha p244, Seychelles Pink p49
BONITO Abel Anchovy p78, Polar Fibre Minnow p263
PERMIT Net Crab p371
TARPON Cockroach p340, Palolo Worm p47
TREVALLY Sar-Mul-Mac Mullet p124, Silver Banger p382
KAHAWAI Platinum Blonde p121, Seducer p228
SAILFISH Reef Demon p125, Sea Habit Green Machine p312
REDFISH, Danny's Redfish Special p237, Go to Joe p249
SPOTTED SEA TROUT Cuba Bonefish p175, Shallow H_20 Fly p184
BLUEFISH Blue White Deceiver p168, Snook Deceiver p66
BARRAMUNDI Pink Thing p426, Flashtail Whistler p152
BARRACUDA Braided Barracuda Fly p344, Cuda Fly p349
BASS Magic Minnow p357, Surf Candy p272
BLACK BASS Everglow Serpent p240
FLATFISH Sand Shrimp p68, Mini Puff p69
HALIBUT Halibut Ghost p309, Epoxy Pearl Squid p380
MULLET Breadcrust p76, Maggot p225

Saltwater species

Bonefish
Truly the ghost of the flats and a very challenging opponent. Over 10lbs in weight, the bone can be exasperatingly smart and has inspired some fascinating new fly development. There are sure to be more developments to come.

Tarpon
An awesome proposition for a fly rod. This fish can weigh more than 200lbs and because it cruises shallow flats is guaranteed to make hearts race when that huge mouth opens on the fly.

Permit
Once thought to be impossible on the fly but development of crab patterns has really helped to make this fish a fly rodder's dream. Over 20lbs and you had better have plenty of backing!

Trevally
There are many species of trevally, from the humble but astonishingly strong jacks to the improbably massive, giant trevally. All are superb sport and fight much better than any freshwater fish.

Kahawai
Just one of many smaller members of the tunny family which occur throughout the world and are fantastic sport to the fly. Fast-moving fish which require precise locating and identification.

Barramundi
Australia's most prized sport fish. It's anadramous and can reach more than 60lbs. Marvellous sport fish and deserves 'fly only' areas to enhance its status. It's aggressive and will hit many types of fly presentation.

Sailfish
Probably the toughest proposition on fly gear and a truly beautiful group of fishes. Teased to within range of a short cast from a boat it's on the limits of fly fishing. IGFA do wonderful work to enhance the status of these endangered fish.

Redfish
Their numbers and size have increased beyond all expectations since inshore commercial fishing restrictions were implemented and it has brought this shallow water species right back into contention as a trophy fly rod target.

Sea trout (spotted)
Tough, voracious, found just about anywhere along the eastern seaboard of the USA and perfect as an introductory species for saltwater fly.

Striped Bass
Not only is this fish beautiful to look at it is also a dream for fly rodders as it can be caught from the shore and often to its maximum weight. Hard to imagine what a 50 lb striper must be like on fly gear. It's on my must list!

Bluefish
Often found in with stripers – a seriously good fighter but with awesome dentristry so be sure to use a wire leader.

Snook
The fish of the mangroves. Like most saltwater species it is a strong adversary and well within the scope of most fly fishers.

Mullet
Don't confuse this with the Falklands 'mullet' which is an entirely different species. Grey, golden and thin lipped, mullet are phenomenal sport on 'trout' fly gear and a four-pounder will seriously test your skills.

Bass
The European bass is a very long lived species and much persecuted by commercial activity, but conservation areas have enhanced its numbers and with its range increasing too it is the ideal fly rod fish for the colder waters of Europe.

Halibut
The Pacific and Californian halibut can most certainly be taken on fly when they are in shallower waters. Off Alaska the 100 lb barrier has been broken and this is one serious flattie on fly, and is very tasty too.

Flatfish
Many, many species of flatfish can be taken on fly in the shallower waters of the world. They eat shrimp and worm and are perfect for weighted fly patterns on sandy bottoms. You will be surprised how well they fight on fly gear.

Bonito
This and the many other species such as albacore, the king and queen mackerel are all supercharged and truly great sport. Mostly found in warmer waters, you had best be sure you have lots of backing on a big reel for this fish.

Black Bass
I have included this species as worldwide travel has made it more available and because everyone who has tangled with this fish reckons that pound for pound it really is the toughest.

Fly Tying Tools

FOR THE BEGINNER FLY FISHER there are a few basic tools that are required to get you started. Without doubt, the best tools are your hands, but the following items will make the task of tying a fly that much easier. The basic toolkit is shown opposite.

A vice is essential for clamping hooks into when tying. The simple lever actioned vice shown (1) is the easiest to use. A pair of fine point scissors (2), preferably with a fine serration on one blade, is also indispensable. Keep a separate cheap pair for use on tinsels and coarse material. A bobbin holder (3) is also useful – the better ones have a ceramic tube which does not get worn by the thread. I like to have a few for different threads (4). Hackle pliers (5) are great for winding hackles on small dries.

On my bench at home will also be a whip finish tool (6), a dubbing twister (7) and a dubbing needle (8), which I also use for applying varnish to the final whipping. Gadgets abound, but keep it simple while you are gaining experience.

Basic Toolkit

1. LEVER ACTION VICE It is important to adjust the action such that the maximum pressure on the hook is at the peak of the cam and to readjust with each change of hook wire diameter.

2. SCISSORS Keep your scissors clean and sharp. Only cut when you are sure what you want to cut, and cut accurately by using the vice as a hand rest.

3. BOBBIN HOLDER This neat tool tensions the thread, avoids wastage and also positions the thread very accurately. Wax from the thread will gradually accumulate inside.

4. THREADS Several different diameters for the range of hook sizes, endless colour choice and always prewaxed so the materials stick to the hook.

5. HACKLE PLIERS Aid accurate winding of hackles and really help with short feathers such as partridge. Slip a short piece of silicone tubing on one jaw to aid grip.

6. DUBBING TWISTER Makes it easy to apply the delicate dubbing material and achieve a really 'shaggy' effect while also blending thread and dubbing colour.

7. BOBBIN THREADER This is a very simple aid for threading the partly waxed bobbin.

8. WHIP FINISH TOOL Clever device which makes it simple to tie a whip finish at the head of a fly to fully secure the tying.

9. DUBBING NEEDLE Primarily for 'picking out' body dubbing for greater effect and invaluable for spearing wing fibres and applying whipping varnish or epoxy.

Choosing a Hook

The range of patterns and shapes of hooks available is mind boggling. As space is limited within these pages the hooks shown are those that are most likely to be used in any situation. The basic features of the hook, shown in the diagram opposite, are shank length, gape, bend, eye and general shape.

A standard shank hook, such as the fine wire trout hook, covers most conventional wet flies and nymphs. A 2X shank is longer and is used for longer-bodied nymphs and many lures. A 4X hook is mainly used for lures and large nymphs. A 6X shank is commonly used for streamers and very large lures. Fine wire, standard shanks are for dry and emerger patterns, which need to be as light as possible.

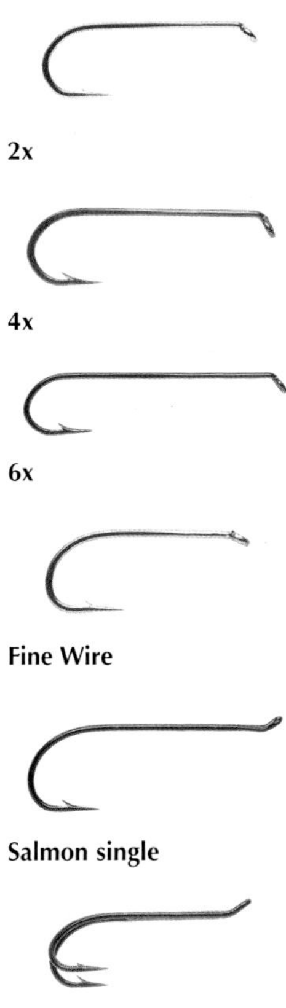

Salmon irons are usually made from heavy gauge wire and are used for large fish in heavy currents or where the particular fighting ability of some species requires greater strength.

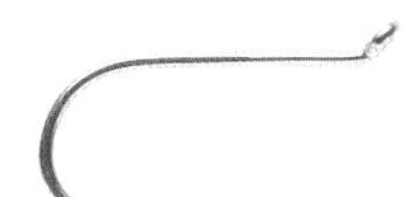

Up eyed dry fly

The gape is the effective width of the hook and bulky tyings require a correspondingly wider gape. Shape, such as the curved shank, can lend itself to the various laral tyings and the incurved point style is increasingly popular for saltwater tyings, as is the requirement of the metal of the hook to be stainless.

O'Shaughnessy salt water hook

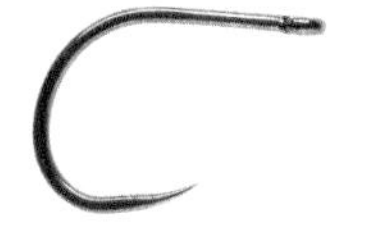

Curved salt water hook

Features of a Hook

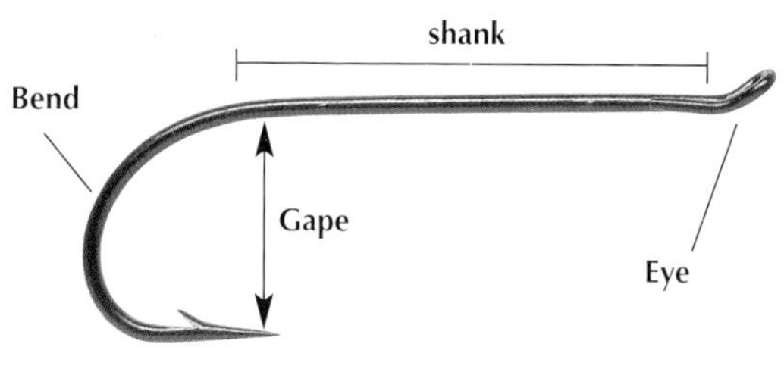

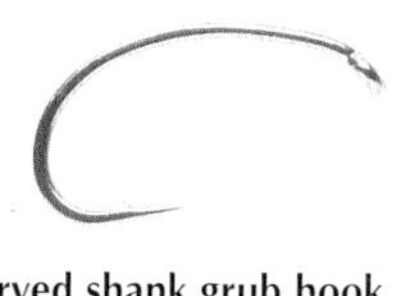

Curved shank grub hook

Waddington shank

Wrapping the thread

IN ORDER TO TIE A ROBUST FLY it is important to know both how to start the fly off properly and, when all the materials have been added, how to cast off the thread securely.

Starting off

The first step when tying most flies, whether they are for freshwater or saltwater, is to build a solid base on which to add all the various materials. This is achieved by laying down close, tight turns of tying thread which will help the finished fly to stay in one piece for as long as possible.

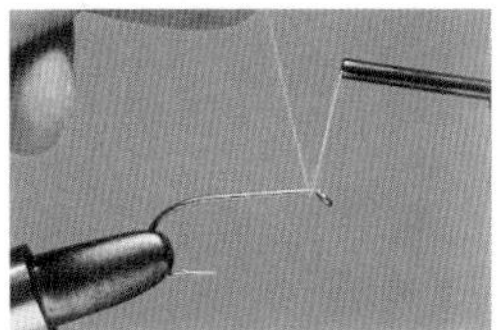

1 First ensure that the hook is fixed firmly and securely in the vice. Next, take hold of the tying thread and holding the loose end taught loop it under the shank so that it forms a V-shape between the fingers and the bobbin holder.

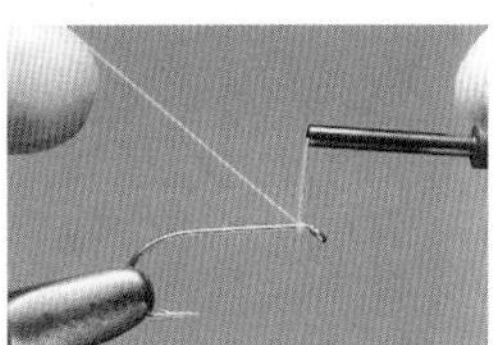

2 Retaining tension on the thread at all times begin to wind the thread down the shank away from the eye. Here a bobbin holder is being used to feed the thread, the aim being to make each turn lock the loose end securely to the hook.

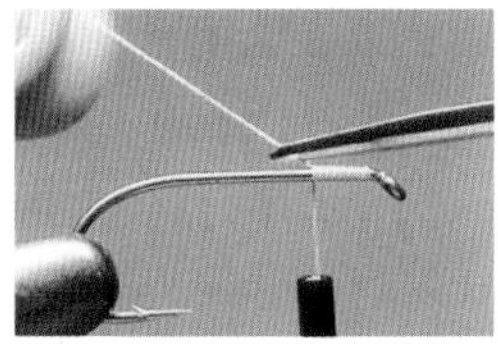

3 Once five or six tight turns have been made the loose end of thread, which the fingers were holding should be secure enough to be released. It can now be removed with scissors.

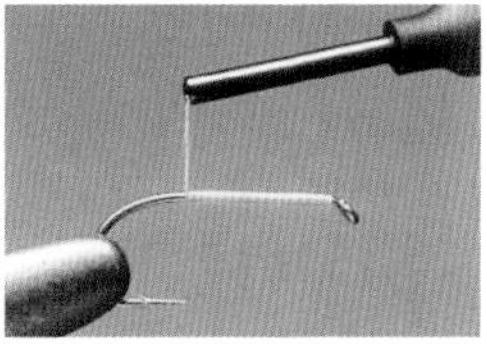

4 Continue winding the thread along the hook shank. Ensure that all the turns are tight and made very close together – they should also never overlap. This will create a very firm base on to which any materials can now be attached.

Finishing off

Once the effort of tying a fly has been accomplished it is very important that the tying thread, which holds everything together, is cast off securely. And the best way of doing this is with a solid whip-finish. The whip-finish is actually a series of loops of thread made over the eye of the hook. Three to five loops are usually created which are then drawn tight locking the thread firmly in place before the loose end is trimmed off.

For clarity, the following steps are shown assuming that the fly has already been tied. Also although a whip-finish can be made with the fingers alone, here a specially designed whip-finish tool is being used.

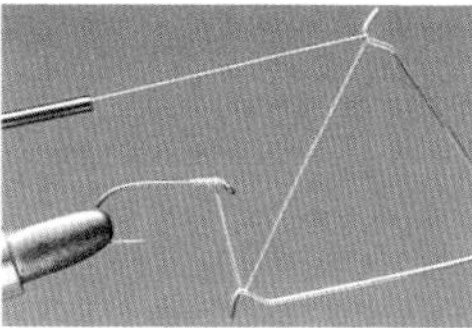

1 Once the eye of the hook has been reached, after all the materials are in place, a small, neat head is built with turns of thread. Next, loop the tying thread over the two, hooked arms of the whip-finish tool. At this stage the arm that comes straight from the handle is positioned below the hook.

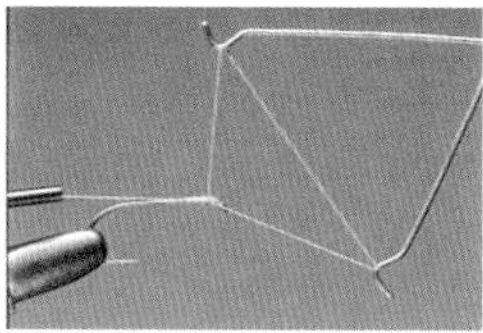

2 Keeping tension on the thread twist the tool so that the arm that was below the hook is now above it. At the same time the thread from the bobbin should lie parallel with the hook shank.

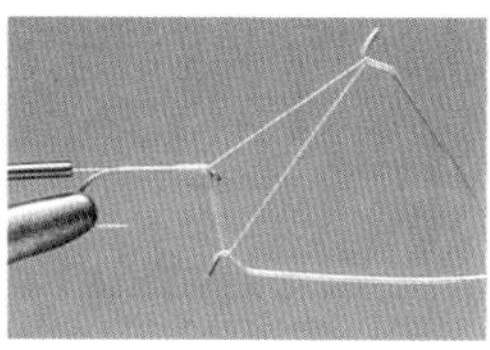

3 Twist the tool another half turn so the arms are in the same position as shot 1 with the arm coming straight from the handle below the hook. This is the first loop of the whip finish.

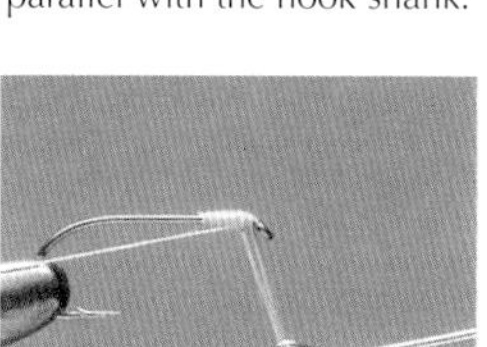

4 Repeat until the required number of loops are wound. Slip the thread from one of the hooked arms, drawing the loop closed by pulling on the thread. Pull until the loop is almost closed.

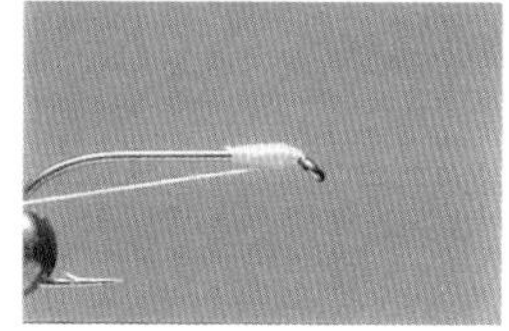

5 With the arm of the tool tight up against the head of the fly slip the loop off the hook. Finally, pull the thread tight so the loop disappears into the head. Trim away the loose thread.

Olive Nymph

THE OLIVE NYMPH IS SHOWN here as a representative fly as it uses many of the techniques used in fly-tying. See Pond Olive Nymph on page 373.

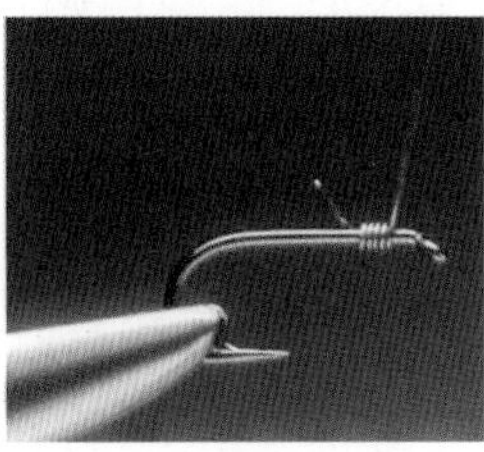

1 Fix the hook securely in the vice and wind on three or four close turns of lead wire just behind the eye.

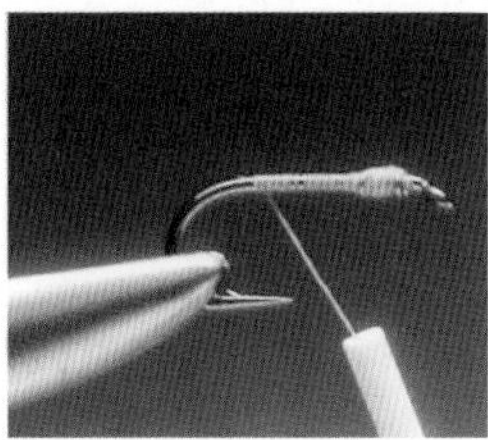

2 Run on the olive tying thread at the eye and wind it in close turns over the lead wire to fix it in place. Carry the thread down the shank to a point opposite the barb.

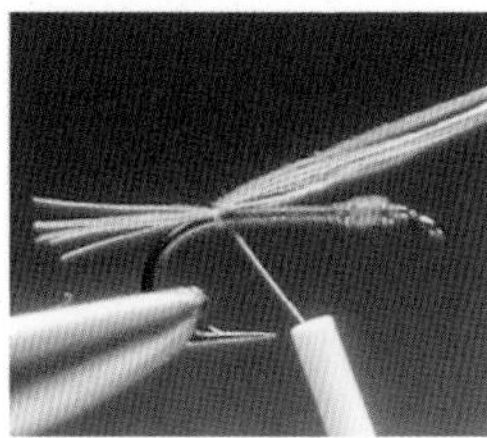

3 Select six to eight fibres of dyed olive pheasant tail, ensuring that the tips are perfect. Catch them in at the hook bend so the tips form the tail.

4 Take two inches of fine copper wire and catch it in place at the same point as the tail. Allow the waste end to lie along the shank and cover with thread.

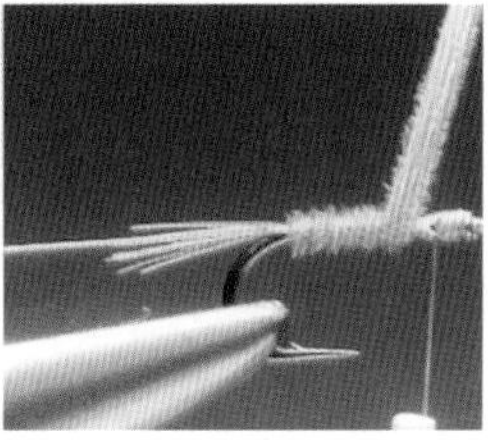

5 Covering the waste end of the copper wire with thread forms an even base for the body. Wind the feather fibres over this base in close turns.

6 With the body in place, secure the loose ends of the pheasant tail fibres with the tying thread. Next, wind on five, evenly spaced turns of wire over the body.

7 Once the copper wire rib has been applied secure the loose end with thread. Remove the excess wire and feather fibre with scissors.

8 Using scissors or a sharp blade cut a strip of olive, translucent plastic strip two inches long and 3/16 of an inch wide. Catch it in dull-side down just in front of the body.

9 Take a small pinch of dyed olive rabbit or muskrat fur. Form a thin rope by dubbing it on to the thread with a simple finger-and-thumb twist. Wind in close turns to create the thorax.

10 Select a small dyed olive hen hackle. Prepare it by removing any broken fibres at the base and catch the hackle in at the eye. Grasp the hackle tip with hackle pliers and wind on two full turns.

11 Secure the loose end of the hackle with thread turns and remove the excess. Stroke the hackle fibres down around the sides of the thorax then stretch the plastic strip over the top.

12 Fix the loose end of the plastic strip at the eye before removing the excess with scissors. Finally, build a small, neat head and cast off the tying thread with a whip finish.

Hackle-point Wing

HACKLE-POINT WINGS ARE USED WIDELY in a number of popular dry fly patterns including the Adams and the Pale Morning Dun. Stripping a pair of equal-sized cock or hen hackles leaving two small tips creates the wings. These are then tied in back-to-back. A range of hackle colours is used with grizzle and browns the two most common.

1 Fix the hook in the vice and run on a solid base of thread just behind he eye. Select two grizzle hackles of equal size ensuring that none of the fibres are damaged.

2 Carefully strip the fibres away from the stems of both feathers to leave two small tips of equal size. These should be approximately the same length as the hook shank.

3 Place the hackle tips together dull-sides out so that the feathers curve naturally away from one another. Catch them in on top of the hook with a couple of turns of tying thread.

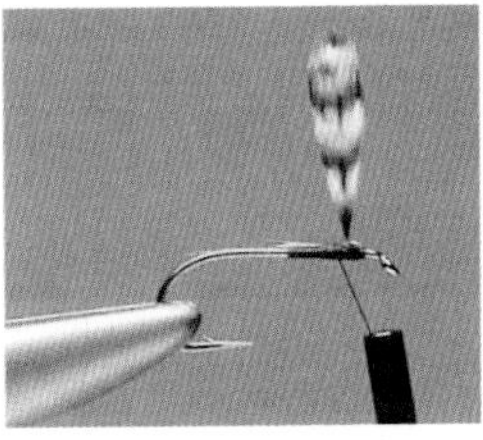

4 Separate the tips then fold the stems back through the gap and secure with thread. Use the thread to fix the hackle tips in an upright position before removing the waste ends of stem. The rest of the materials may now be added.

Muddler Head

MUDDLER HEADS ARE INCORPORATED in a large range of streamer, bucktail and dry fly patterns from the original Muddler Minnow to the Dahlberg Diver plus various imitations of grasshoppers and adult stoneflies. All benefit from the buoyancy of deer body hair, which is spun on to the hook and then clipped to shape. The bulbous Muddler head can either be used simply to help the fly float or to add action to either surface or subsurface patterns. Usually the hair is applied just as a head but in some surface baitfish imitations and highly buoyant dry flies, such as the Bomber, deer hair is applied the entire length of the hook shank.

1 When tying muddlers the first step is to add the body and wing. These should be stopped further back from the eye than normal to leave room for the head. Next take a pinch of deer body and with the tips projecting back along the body wind on two or three loose thread wraps.

2 With the bunch of hair in position the thread should be pulled tight. This causes the soft compressible deer hair to flare around the hook shank. As this occurs further tight turns of thread should be made through the hair to lock it in position.

3 Once this first bunch of hair is locked in place further bunches are added in the same way. Allow each to flare evenly around the hook so that a dense ruff is formed. Once the gap between the wing base and the eye has been filled the thread should be cast off with a whip finish.

4 Finally, with a pair of sharp scissors begin trimming the hair to shape. Work evenly around the hook so that an even shape is formed, ideally this should be slightly flattened beneath the hook and more round above it. Remember to leave the tips sloping back over the body.

Hair Wing

WINGS AND TAILS CONSTRUCTED FROM HAIR are used in many fly patterns both for freshwater and saltwater fish species. Hair has the advantage over softer materials such as feather in that it is far tougher, while still retaining plenty of mobility. The most popular type of hair is bucktail, which comes from the northern white-tailed deer and is easily dyed a variety of colours. Artificial hair is also becoming very popular, being available in a wide range of colours, textures and lengths. For smaller patterns squirrel tail – finer than bucktail– is also useful.

The pattern described here is the Munro Killer, a popular fly for Atlantic salmon (see page 218).

1 Having already tied the body and collar hackle of the fly the winging material is selected. Here it is a combination of black and yellow bucktail. Place the bunches of hair together so that their tips are level.

2 Judge the wing for length. In this pattern the wing is almost twice that of the hook but in other flies it may be only slightly longer. Trim the butts of the hair to length them offer the wing up to the top of the hook. Secure with three or four tight thread wraps.

3 With the wing in position add a few more turns of thread then run a drop of clear lacquer into the wing roots. Hair can be quite slippery and this procedure helps the finished wind to hold in place.

4 Now add further tight wraps of tying thread so that the hair is locked firmly in position. Using the tying thread build a neat tapered head before casting off the thread with a whip finish. The head may then be covered with coats of clear lacquer to give a smooth, glossy finish.

Tinsel Body

TINSELS OF VARIOUS COLOURS ARE USED to add sparkle to the bodies of many flies. Originally metal was used, but today plastics, such as Mylar, are far more popular. They are easier to work with and retain their sparkle longer than real metal, which can tarnish.

With tinsel bodies, it is important that the base on to which they are applied is as smooth as possible. This ensures that the finished body is perfectly flat and has no gaps that can be lead to damage during fishing.

Originally only gold, silver and copper were available but there are now also products that have either a pearl or holographic finish and come in vibrant colours.

1 In this pattern, the Platinum Blonde, the first step is to add a tail of white bucktail and a length of oval silver tinsel, which forms the rib. To create an even base for the tinsel body, the waste ends of the previous materials are bound to the hook with close turns of thread.

2 Continue winding the thread along the hook shank until it is only a short distance from the eye. Remove four inches of medium-width silver Mylar from its spool and cut one end to a point – this helps make the first turn. Catch the tinsel in with a couple of thread wraps.

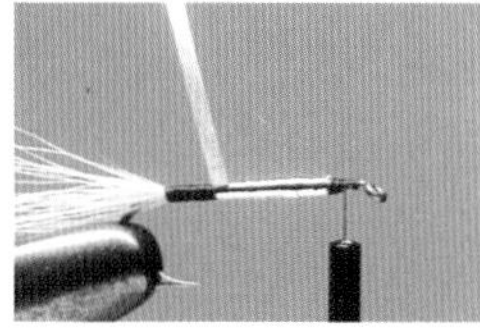

3 Take hold of the tinsel and begin winding it down the shank toward the tail. Ensure that the turns are even and that there are no gaps. If there are simply remove the tinsel and begin winding again.

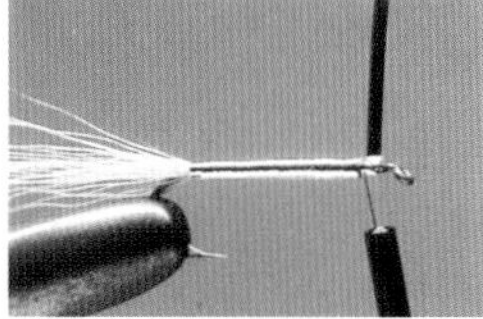

4 This double layer of tinsel helps to ensure that the finished body is nice and smooth. Once the catching-in point has been reached,the loose end of the tinsel is secured with tight thread wraps. The waste end is now removed and the rib and wing added.

WORLD FLY DIRECTORY

Blue Dun

CREATED SOME 300 YEARS AGO, A VARIANT HAS BEEN 'INVENTED' WHENEVER TROUT ARE FISHED FOR. Although not an exact imitation of any of the mayflies, you really can't afford to ignore this old favourite. A wet fly version is also essential for freestone streams, especially early in the season. It used to be very difficult to obtain good-quality, blue dun cock hackles, but now you can purchase genetic feathers. Natural blue dun hen capes are often available.

WHERE: WORLDWIDE IN TEMPERATE AREAS IN FREESTONE STREAMS AND MANY LIMESTONE WATERS

WHEN: SPRING TO EARLY SUMMER

WHAT: TROUT, GRAYLING

HOW: A NON-SPECIFIC MAYFLY IMITATION OR GENERAL-PURPOSE PATTERN

HOOK: 12 TO 18 STANDARD SHANK
TAIL: BLUE DUN COCK HACKLE FIBRES
BODY: MOLE OR MUSKRAT UNDERFUR
WINGS: STARLING PRIMARY OR GREY MALLARD

Silver Corixa

CORIXA (AN AQUATIC BEETLE) ARE SOMETIMES AVIDLY EATEN BY TROUT and I can imagine how trout must enjoy chasing them in the shallows. You should watch corixa as they scuttle around continually and periodically zip up to the surface to collect a bubble of air – this is the stage we are imitating. I like to tie the biots unevenly so that the fly wobbles as it sinks – an action that often brings a take before it reaches the bottom. Shallow margins being warmed by spring sunshine are a perfect place to use this fly. If the water is clear enough you can target individuals.

WHERE: STILLWATER IN TEMPERATE REGIONS IN THE NORTHERN HEMISPHERE

WHEN: ALL YEAR, BUT SPRING AND SUMMER ARE BEST

WHAT: TROUT

HOW: IMITATES THE CORIXA

HOOK: 12 TO 14 STANDARD SHANK
BODY: FLAT SILVER TINSEL WITH FINE PEARL RIB
WING CASE: COCK PHEASANT CENTRE TAIL FIBRES
PADDLES: BROWN GOOSE BIOTS

Hydro

THIS HAIRWING PATTERN IS MUCH USED IN THE WILD RIVERS to the north of Scotland and is at its best when the fish are fresh in from the ocean. Quite why the Atlantic salmon prefers a fly with blue in the tying during its first few days in fresh water is something of a puzzle, as is the reason why it takes a fly at all, as it stops feeding when it enters freshwater. It's an odd thing that sea trout, steelhead and Atlantics, wherever they are in the world, will all take a blue fly when fresh but it has no such fascination for the Pacific salmon.

WHERE: SCOTLAND, ENGLAND, IRELAND, ICELAND, CANADA, FALKLANDS, ARGENTINA, USA

WHEN: SPRING THROUGH SUMMER

WHAT: ATLANTIC SALMON, SEA TROUT, STEELHEAD

HOW: A NON SPECIFIC ATTRACTOR

HOOK: 10–1/0 UP EYE SALMON
TAG: FINE OVAL SILVER
TAIL: GOLDEN PHEASANT TOPPING
BUTT: RED WOOL
RIB: FINE OVAL GOLD
BODY: BLUE LUREX
HACKLE: HOT ORANGE WITH GUINEA FOWL BEARD
WING: NATURAL GREY SQUIRREL WITH PALE BLUE OVER

Palolo Worm

I HAVE WITNESSED THE FABLED PALOLO WORM hatch off Florida where giant tarpon take these creatures from the surface with a sound like small arms fire. Perfectly competent casters become idiots at times like these, and the potential for an immediate hook-up is outstanding – if only you can get a fly in the water.

This worm pattern certainly works but is also worth using in broad daylight to slowly cruising pods of tarpon and for many saltwater species, who seem to home in on these worms as a special treat.

WHERE: TROPICAL REGIONS OF THE OCEANS

WHEN: ALL YEAR, BUT ESPECIALLY AROUND THE HATCH IN SPRING

WHAT: TARPON, REDFISH, SNOOK, BARRAMUNDI

HOW: SPECIFICALLY IMITATES A RED/ORANGE MARINE WORM

HOOK: 3/0 TO 2/0 STAINLESS O'SHAUGHNESSY
TAIL: RED OR ORANGE CALF TAIL FIBRES
BODY: BRIGHT RED OR ORANGE SUEDE CHENILLE
HEAD: GINGER SUEDE CHENILLE

Alaska Mary Ann

I INCLUDED THIS FLY because it embodies the spirit of the last frontier and remains a highly effective streamer pattern. Anyone who has fished in Alaska cannot ever forget this wonderful land and its vast fly fishing riches. The Alaska Mary Ann is the official fly of the Alaska Fly Fishers and I am indebted to Dan Jordan, a highly-gifted tier from Anchorage, who helped me to get to know the traditions of fly fishing in Alaska and who ties such exquisite flies for display. Use this pattern with confidence for any trout or salmon, but make sure you obtain the real material for the wing – there is nothing else like it.

WHERE: WORLDWIDE WHERE MIGRATORY FISH OCCUR, AND IN COLD LAKES

WHEN: BEST IN SPRING AND AUTUMN

WHAT: SALMON, TROUT, CHAR, LAKE TROUT, PIKE

HOW: A GENERAL ATTRACTOR BUT ESSENTIALLY A FRY PATTERN

HOOK: 8 TO 4 2X OR 4X LONG SHANK
TAIL: A FEW BRIGHT RED HACKLE FIBRES
BODY: OFF-WHITE FLOSS WITH A FLAT SILVER TINSEL RIB
WING: NATURAL POLAR BEAR HAIR
CHEEKS: JUNGLE COCK

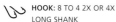

Seychelles Pink

THE SEYCHELLES HAVE BECOME THE 'IN' DESTINATION SINCE 2000, as it is said you don't need to be a competent caster to catch 20 bonefish a day. It won't last, but for now you can expect bonefishing as it must have been in the early days in the Bahamas. Every destination has its colour speciality and the Seychelles is no different with this amazing pink creation coming out best for many anglers. I am a great fan of pink flies for many species, and although I haven't used this one, I am assured by the great UK fly tier, John Goddard, that it works (even though I know that even a bare hook works for this maestro!).

WHERE: TROPICAL SALTWATER FLATS

WHEN: ALL YEAR

WHAT: BONEFISH

HOW: RESEMBLES A SHRIMP

HOOK: 8 TO 4 STAINLESS O'SHAUGHNESSY
BODY: HOT-PINK CHENILLE
WING: PALE PINK BUCKTAIL
EYES: PINK PEARL BEAD CHAIN
HEAD: HOT-PINK TYING THREAD

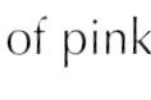

Wingless Wickham

TIED ON A DOUBLE HOOK this fly is very popular in Scotland and as a point fly for competition fishing, which bans weighted flies but permits four hook points to be used on the leader to sink a fly. The Wickham's Fancy has many variants, but omitting the wings and adding a Glo-brite tail certainly makes this one a bit special for summer sport on bright days from a drifting boat on large stillwaters. I think this fly is very attractive to trout feeding on daphnia as those caught on it are invariably stuffed with this tiny little creature.

WHERE: LARGER STILLWATERS, USUALLY THROUGH THE UK AND EUROPE BUT ALSO AUSTRALIA AND NEW ZEALAND

WHEN: DEFINITELY A SUMMER PATTERN

WHAT: BROWN AND RAINBOW TROUT

HOW: A GENERAL PURPOSE WET FLY BUT SPECIFIC TO DAPHNIA FEEDERS

HOOK: 10 TO 16 DOUBLE
TAIL: GLO BRITE FLOSS (NO5)
BODY: PEARL LUREX PALMERED WITH GINGER COCK AND RIBBED WITH FINE SILVER WIRE
HACKLE: BLACK HEN

Sparkler

THE SPARKLER STARTED LIFE AS A TUBE FLY to be towed behind drifting boats on reservoirs to catch fry feeding trout. Often as long as 13 cm (5 inches), it was subsequently found to be very effective for many other predators such as pike, lake trout and landlocked striped bass. It was then adapted to meet International Rules for competition fishing where the reduced fly has been puzzlingly effective for stocked trout in stillwaters. Usually best fished on sinking lines in front of a drifting boat, it can also be good for searching tactics from the bank.

WHERE: WORLDWIDE IN STILLWATER IN TEMPERATE REGIONS

WHEN: ALL YEAR, BUT BEST FROM SUMMER TO AUTUMN

WHAT: BROWN, LAKE AND RAINBOW TROUT, PIKE, NILE PERCH, STRIPED BASS

HOW: THE SHIMMYING ACTION SUGGESTS A PREY FISH SWIMMING RAPIDLY

HOOK: 8 TO 12 STANDARD SHANK (INTERNATIONAL SIZE)
BODY: FLAT GOLD HOLOGRAPHIC TINSEL
WING AND HACKLE: FINE BRAIDED GOLD TINSEL.

Irish Shrimp

THIS IS MORE A STYLE OF FLY with the tying shown being typical to type although colours may vary considerably. The original is attributed to Pat Curry of Coleraine. This type of fly is effective for salmon in so many situations that any Atlantic salmon angler's fly box will contain a range of Shrimps. That wonderful bird the golden pheasant once again contributes its plumage to this fly. One would almost think that the bird was created just to satisfy tier's needs!

Fish the Shrimp Fly with utter confidence, even on loughs as the salmon pass through.

WHERE: RIVERS AND LOUGHS IN THE NORTHERN HEMISPHERE WHERE SALMON OCCUR

WHEN: YEAR ROUND WHEN IN SEASON

WHAT: ATLANTIC SALMON

HOW: SUGGESTS A FOOD ITEM FROM THEIR DAYS IN THE OCEAN

HOOK: SALMON DOUBLE SIZES 6 TO 12
TAG: OVAL GOLD TINSEL
TAIL: GOLDEN PHEASANT RED BREAST FEATHER
BODY: HALF YELLOW FLOSS AND HALF BLACK RIBBED WITH FINE OVAL GOLD TINSEL
HACKLES: MIDWAY IS COCK BADGER WITH A FEW FIBRES OF GOLDEN PHEASANT TIPPET AND ORANGE COCK HACKLE AND THEN AT THE HEAD IS ANOTHER COCK BADGER HACKLE

Holy Grail

CHARLES JARDINE NEEDS NO INTRODUCTION and a great many of his fly patterns are already well-known standards. This one will be another, if only because of its name. All fly tiers hope to find the universal pattern, and Charles has given his ultimate nymph the perfect name for all to remember. It's a fabulous bug for any river situation, especially rough stream fishing. It also works well in stillwater and as a specialized stalking bug in clear water. I love it for my grayling and you have to admit that it just looks edible. Try it – you won't be disappointed.

WHERE: FREESTONE AND LIMESTONE STREAMS WORLD WIDE IN TEMPERATE AND SUB ARCTIC

WHEN: YEAR ROUND

WHAT: TROUT, GRAYLING

HOW: GENERAL PURPOSE NYMPH/PUPA SUGGESTING MANY FOOD ITEMS

HOOK: 10 TO 14 CURVED SHANK
BODY: DUBBED HARES EAR WITH PEARL TINSEL RIB
THORAX: A GOLD OR TUNGSTEN BEAD WITH PHEASANT TAIL FIBRES OVER
HACKLE: BROWN PARTRIDGE

Lefty's Deceiver

WHERE: WORLDWIDE IN FRESH- OR SALTWATER

WHEN: ALL YEAR

WHAT: ANY PREDATORY SPECIES

HOW: CAN SUGGEST ALL MANNER OF BAIT FISH

HOOK: 2 TO 4/0 SALTWATER O'SHAUGHNESSY
WING: SIX TO 12 WHITE SADDLE HACKLES PERHAPS WITH A LITTLE SILVER FLASHABOU
BEARD: TUFT OF RED CRYSTAL HAIR
COLLAR: WHITE BUCKTAIL BOTTOM AND SIDES WITH CHARTREUSE BUCKTAIL TIED LONG ON TOP THEN WITH PEARL AND CHARTREUSE CRYSTAL HAIR FIBRES EACH SIDE
HEAD: CHARTREUSE WITH YELLOW PAINTED EYE AND BLACK PUPIL

THE GREAT MAN, LEFTY KREH, invented this fly, and even when all his many achievements pass into history, this pattern will remain a truly outstanding fly. It is capable of being tied to suggest all manner of bait fish from skinny sand eels to mackerel, and in sizes up to 25 cm (10 inches) you can give great bulk to a fly by using schlappen feathers. Endlessly variable, this version is one of Lefty's favourites, and if you fish in saltwater or for any predatory freshwater fish. I strongly recommend that you read Lefty's book, *Saltwater Fly Patterns*.

Loch Ordie

THIS IS VERY MUCH A GIANT VERSION of a Bivisible but is important because of the way it is fished and for the addition of the flying treble. This fly is tied for the style of fly fishing known as dapping where the fly is skittered across the surface and skipped through the waves. It is used for sea trout in freshwater lochs and loughs of Scotland and Ireland and will also bring up resident browns. It seems to really excite the fish, especially in clear water, where they will often splash mightily at the fly or gently sip it in. Either way gets a pretty poor hook hold, hence the flying treble. Dapping uses very long rods 5 m (18 ft) long with a silk blow line to carry the fly onto the water in front of the drifting boat.

WHERE: LAKES, LOUGHS AND LOCHS IN THE UK

WHEN: USUALLY SUMMER THROUGH TO AUTUMN

WHAT: BROWN TROUT AND SEA TROUT

HOW: IT'S BIG AND FUSSY AND DISTURBES THE SURFACE

HOOK: 6 TO 12 4X SHANK PLUS A NYLON EXTENSION WITH A 14 TO 16 TREBLE HOOK
BODY: A WHOLE SERIES OF RED GAME COCK HACKLES PALMERED ALONG THE SHANK
HACKLE: TWO WHITE COCK HACKLES
THE FLYING TREBLE IS TIED IN NEAR THE HEAD

Fluttering Caddis

I HAVE INCLUDED LOTS OF CADDIS (SEDGE) PATTERNS as they are extremely important for the freshwater angler. This one follows a very familiar style to the others, but is lightweight and hence easy to cast with a 3-weight rod, plus it is simple to tie, which is handy if you need to make one quickly. When travelling, pack enough to tie this fly in black, dun and ginger, and you will cover a wide range of species. As many caddis species have a habit of fluttering over the water while egg laying, this fly works well when given occasional little twitches.

WHERE: WORLDWIDE IN RIVERS IN TEMPERATE AND SUB-ARCTIC REGIONS

WHEN: SUMMER TO AUTUMN

WHAT: TROUT, GRAYLING, CUTTHROAT

HOW: GOOD IMITATION OF SMALLER CADDIS (SEDGE)

HOOK: 14 TO 18 STANDARD SHANK FINE WIRE
BODY: BLACK RABBIT UNDERFUR
WING: BLACK MINK TAIL GUARD HAIR
HACKLE: IRON BLUE COCK OR DARK RUSTY DUN

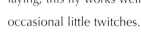

Beacon Beige

INVENTED BY THE LATE PETER DEANE who overcame the disability of a wheelchair to become an inspiration to all fly tiers and fly fishers. This fly was produced for the river Itchen in southern England, a stream much loved by Skues and prized for its wild brown trout. The Beacon Beige has become a standard pattern there, but works on any very clear limestone river where trout become ultra-fussy. You will need fine tippets, a very light rod and the most careful presentation to fish this fly well.

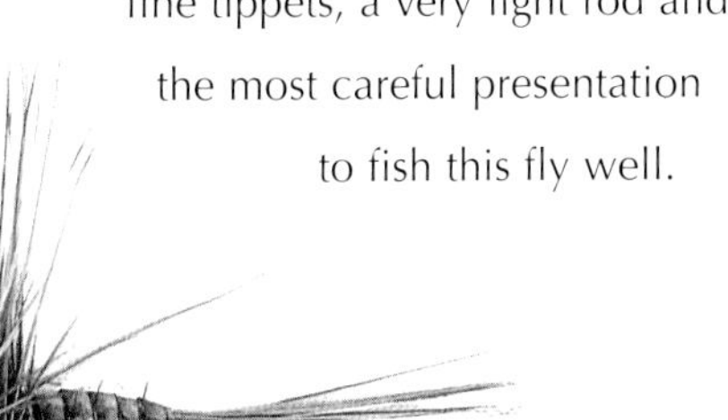

WHERE: WORLDWIDE IN CLEAR LIMESTONE STREAMS, SPRING CREEKS AND RIVERS

WHEN: LATE SPRING TO EARLY AUTUMN

WHAT: TROUT, GRAYLING

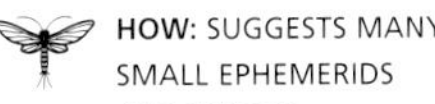

HOW: SUGGESTS MANY SMALL EPHEMERIDS AND MIDGES

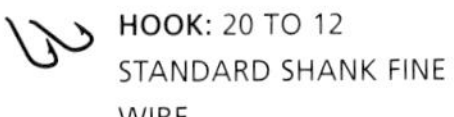

HOOK: 20 TO 12 STANDARD SHANK FINE WIRE
TAIL: GRIZZLE COCK HACKLE FIBRES
BODY: STRIPPED PEACOCK HERL FROM THE EYE
HACKLE: MIXED GRIZZLE AND RED GAME COCK

Perla Stonefly

THIS IMPORTANT STONEFLY PATTERN should be used to match areas where the river or lake bed has soft clay deposits when the natural will have a similar colouration. While I use this one in Canada for grayling and lake trout from the rocky shore of lakes, and in clay-based ponds in the UK, its real home is the freestone rivers of the USA. This 'buggy' fly often works regardless of whether or not the natural stonefly actually occurs in that habitat, and is best fished trickled along the bottom.

WHERE: FREESTONE RIVERS AND MANY LAKES IN TEMPERATE AND SUB-ARCTIC REGIONS

WHEN: ALL YEAR BUT BEST SPRING TO AUTUMN

WHAT: TROUT, LAKE TROUT, GRAYLING, WHITEFISH

HOW: IMITATES A STONEFLY LARVA

HOOK: 6X TO 10 2X SHANK
TAIL: TWO YELLOW GOOSE BIOTS
BODY: YELLOW/AMBER SEAL'S FUR RIBBED WITH CLEAR NYMPH BODY
THORAX: YELLOW/AMBER SEAL'S FUR WITH TWO PRE-CUT GREY GOOSE FEATHERS
HACKLE: BROWN HEN

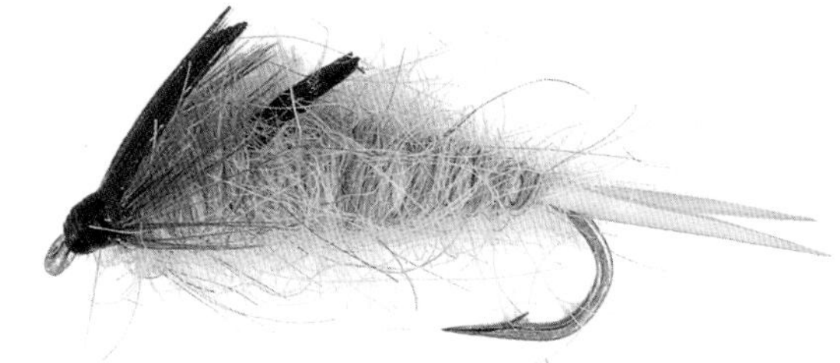

Frog Popper

POPPERS BRING A FLY fisher's dreams to life – crashing takes searing runs and action all the way. The water usually needs to be over 15°C (60°F) to get true top-of-the-water action from bass, and indeed from many other species which will hit this same fly. I got my first largemouth bass on this fly from a lake in central Oregon, and would dearly love to get a really big one. Reservoir rainbow trout are also great fun to fish with poppers, as you get lots of offers and action with a few true takes.

WHERE: WORLDWIDE IN STILLWATER IN TEMPERATE AND SUB-TROPICAL REGIONS

WHEN: AS SOON AS WATER REACHES 15°C (60°F) IN SUMMER

WHAT: LARGEMOUTH AND SMALLMOUTH BASS, TROUT AND SOME INSHORE SALTWATER SPECIES

HOW: CREATES SURFACE DISTURBANCE SUGGESTING A STRUGGLING FISH OR REPTILE

HOOK: 6X 4X SHANK
TAIL: TWO GREEN, TWO WHITE AND TWO YELLOW COCK SADDLE HACKLES
HACKLE: MIXED GREEN AND YELLOW COCK SADDLE
BODY: CORK WITH CONCAVE FACE GLUED TO HOOK THEN PAINTED

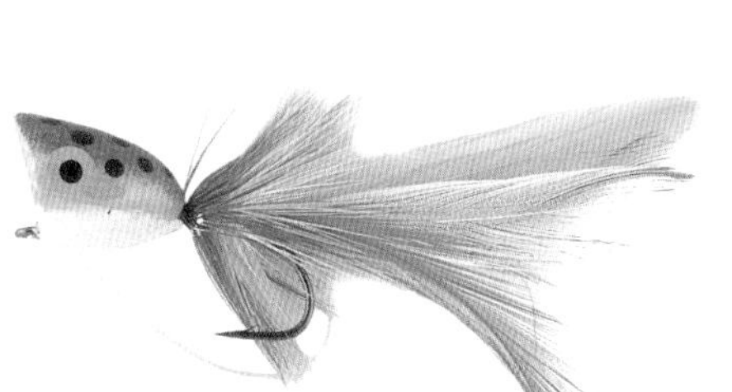

Crayfish

I'M AWARE THAT CRAYFISH PATTERNS are considered essential in Australia and the USA, and yet in many other parts of the fly fishing world they have not really made an impact. I believe that as other non-game fish species are targeted on the fly, the crayfish will become an important fly for fishes such as the European barbel and chub. John Bailey is doing much to further this advance in fly fishing boundaries and I believe there will be specific books on this subject with the crayfish as a dominant pattern.

WHERE: RIVERS AND STILLWATER IN TEMPERATE REGIONS

WHEN: ALL YEAR BUT WARMER MONTHS ARE BEST

WHAT: TROUT, LARGEMOUTH AND SMALLMOUTH BASS, BARBEL, PERCH, PIKE

HOW: CRAYFISH IMITATION

HOOK: 6X TO 4 4X SHANK
TAIL: PINE SQUIRREL OVER DEER HAIR WITH BROWN EYES ON MONO STALKS
CLAWS: HEN PHEASANT BODY FEATHERS TRIMMED
ABDOMEN: OLIVE SUEDE CHENILLE WITH THE SQUIRREL OVER AND LEGS OF BROWN PARTRIDGE
BODY: REST OF THE SQUIRREL TAIL FIBRES TIED DOWN AND THEN ALLOWED TO SPRAY OUT AND BE CLIPPED OVER THE HOOK EYE

Butcher

I WOULD SUGGEST THAT THIS BEAUTIFUL FLY can work for most species, but it's best-known as a trout pattern and with it I caught my first 450 g (1 lb) brown trout from a stream near my home in Cornwall. A well-tied Butcher is a sure sign that a fly tier has mastered the art of winging. Tied in larger sizes or even as a tandem, it is a great sea trout fly and will take salmon in low water. It excels as a trout fly on rivers and lakes. Tied short with a clipped wing, it works best late in the day during a chironomid hatch. On overcast days at fry time it looks just like a little fish, while at other times it has an almost magical ability to charm trout.

WHERE: WORLDWIDE IN LAKES AND RIVERS

WHEN: ALL YEAR

WHAT: TROUT, SEA TROUT, SALMON, STEELHEAD

HOW: A NON-SPECIFIC IMITATION BUT WITH THE ESSENTIAL INGREDIENTS OF BLACK, RED AND SILVER

HOOK: 8 TO 16 OR SOMETIMES AS A TANDEM
TAIL: SCARLET FEATHER FIBRE (RED IBIS SUBSTITUTE)
BODY: FLAT SILVER TINSEL
HACKLE: BLACK HEN TIED FALSE
WING: BLUE MALLARD COVERT FEATHERS

Alexandra

A TRUE WET FLY, which is an attractor rather than a deceiver, and uses red, black and silver in its construction with the amazingly glossy feathers from the peacock sword. Very attractive to migratory trout and a standard pattern for rough streams and lakes. Older fly fishers regard this fly with mystical awe as it was once banned in some locations for being too successful. It looks relatively simple to tie but proportion is important if the fly is to yield its best results.

WHERE: WORLDWIDE IN TEMPERATE REGIONS IN RIVERS AND STILLWATER

WHEN: ANY TIME OF YEAR BUT COOLER MONTHS ARE BEST

WHAT: TROUT INCLUDING CUTTHROAT AND SEA TROUT

HOW: A CLASSIC ATTRACTOR PATTERN

HOOK: 8 TO 12 STANDARD SHANK
TAIL: RED IBIS SUBSTITUTE AND A FEW FIBRES OF PEACOCK SWORD
BODY: FLAT SILVER TINSEL WITH SILVER OVAL OR WIRE RIB
HACKLE: BLACK HEN
WING: PEACOCK SWORD WITH SLIP OF RED IBIS SUBSTITUTE EACH SIDE

Royal Wulff

IT TAKES A SKILLED TIER to build this fly and those who do so at exhibitions leave the audience spellbound. Fortunately, we find that trout think so too, and although it doesn't resemble anything that flies, it is a great pattern and a great catcher of fish. During the bigger mayfly hatch it works extremely well. It can also be effective during the fall of the spent gnat in late evening. It is an excellent search pattern for rough streams, particularly in remote tundra country.

WHERE: WORLDWIDE IN RIVERS AND STILLWATER IN TEMPERATE AND TUNDRA REGIONS

WHEN: ALL YEAR

WHAT: TROUT, GRAYLING, CHAR, LAKE TROUT

HOW: AN ALL-ROUNDER, THIS DRY FLY ATTRACTS RATHER THAN IMITATES

HOOK: 8 TO 14 STANDARD SHANK
TAIL: BROWN BUCKTAIL OR WHITE CALF BODY HAIR
BODY: BRONZE PEACOCK HERL WITH CENTRE SECTION OF RED FLOSS
WINGS: WHITE CALF HAIR TIED VERTICALLY AND THEN DIVIDED
HACKLE: GINGER COCK

Muskrat

THIS SUPER LITTLE CADDIS (SEDGE) LARVA, is simply deadly. I like to use it where streams and lakes have fine gravel areas where I trickle it over the bottom. If you fish Czech Nymph style then make sure you have the Muskrat as your tail fly and it will catch you a lot of fish. Muskrat fur gives us many patterns and it really is a lovely material to use. Some Scandinavian anglers like this fly tied on a big hook for large river brown trout.

WHERE: WORLDWIDE IN STILLWATER AND RIVERS IN TEMPERATE AND ARCTIC REGIONS

WHEN: ALL YEAR BUT SPRING AND SUMMER ARE BEST

WHAT: TROUT, GRAYLING

HOW: SUGGESTS A CADDIS (SEDGE) LARVA

HOOK: 6X TO 14 2X SHANK
BODY: MUSKRAT UNDERFUR
HACKLE: GUINEA FOWL SPECKLED FIBRES
HEAD: BLACK OSTRICH HERL

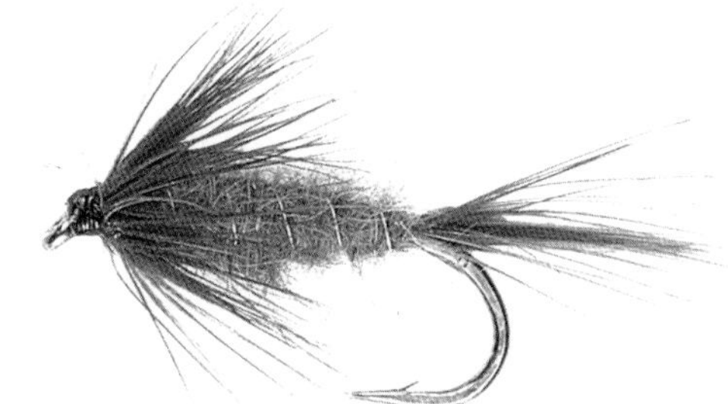

Bonefish Bitters

THERE ARE A NUMBER OF COLOUR VARIANTS of this fly and each will work over certain coloured terrain. It's very important to use patterns that don't look out of place when fishing for elusive fish such as bonefish. They know that hermit crabs on muddy flats are highly unlikely to be bright green, but that around shallow, weedy and rocky areas they may very well be that colour. Bonefish have a real passion for crabs, and finding what they believe to be a hermit crab looking for a new home will often bring an instant take.

WHERE: TROPICAL SALTWATER

WHEN: ALL YEAR

WHAT: BONEFISH, PERMIT, REDFISH

HOW: SUGGESTS A HERMIT CRAB

HOOK: 6 TO 8 O'SHAUGHNESSY
LEGS: CHARTREUSE
WINGS: CHARTREUSE, ANTRON AND DEER
HEAD: GOLD BEAD CHAIN EYES WITH ORANGE/AMBER EPOXY

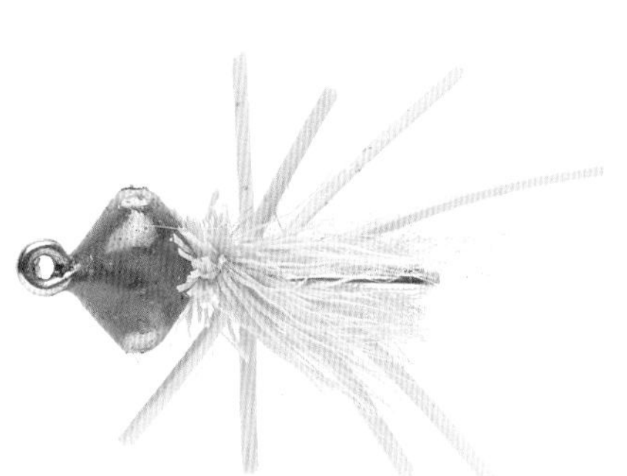

Snook Deceiver

IF LEFTY KREH SAYS THIS IS ONE OF HIS FAVOURITE SNOOK FLIES then you need to tie some. It's always interesting how some colours have a particular attraction for certain species. The killing colour often depends on the water conditions or the prevailing light levels. This deceiver variant is a barramundi favourite when they are in a coloured water. Lots of mobility, a strong visual presence and you are well on the way to success. Fish it deep and around structure for best results. Try using the current to drift the fly into deeper holes.

WHERE: SALTWATER AND BRACKISH WATER IN TROPICAL OR SUB-TROPICAL AREAS

WHEN: ALL YEAR

WHAT: SNOOK, REDFISH, BARRAMUNDI

HOW: AN ATTRACTOR BAIT FISH PATTERN

HOOK: 1 TO 2/0 STAINLESS O'SHAUGHNESSY
BODY: GOLD MYLAR
WING: SIX YELLOW SADDLE HACKLES AND A GRIZZLE SADDLE ON EITHER SIDE
COLLAR: LONG FIBRES OF RED DYED SQUIRREL WITH RED CRYSTALFLASH OVER
HEAD: PAINTED RED WITH WHITE/BLACK EYE

Troutmaster Damsel

PART OF MY ROLE as a fly designer for Fulling Mill is to represent the company at the annual Troutmaster competition finals in association with *Trout Fisherman* magazine at Grafham Water. This fly was given as a thank you to every entrant in the 2001 event and has since proved itself as a great spring and summer fly on stillwaters. It is that deadly mix of hare's ear, partridge and seal's fur which may not look anything special to us but does wonders for a trout's appetite.

WHERE: STILLWATERS AND RIVERS IN TEMPERATE OR SUB ARCTIC REGIONS

WHEN: YEAR ROUND BUT BEST IN SUMMER

WHAT: TROUT, GRAYLING

HOW: ALL-PURPOSE NYMPH

HOOK: 10 TO 8 CURVED 2X SHANK
TAIL: BROWN PARTRIDGE FIBRES
BODY: HARE'S EAR DUB WITH OVAL GOLD RIB
THORAX: GOLDEN OLIVE SEAL'S FUR WITH HEN PHEASANT OVER
HACKLE: BROWN PARTRIDGE UNDER THORAX CASE
EYES: BLACK MONO

Bait Runner

THIS SUPERB BAIT FISH PATTERN uses the strength and mobility of polar fibre to create a perfect imitation of a little fish with the eyed effect. This is one of the best of the modern flies for saltwater but it has also proved itself for pike, nile perch and even taimen. I am worried about the future for large taimen, as it is being grossly over exploited and sensible efforts will need to be taken to preserve this special fish. Tie this fly in a variety of colours to suggest several different bait fishes.

WHERE: WORLDWIDE IN SALTWATER AND MANY FRESHWATER VENUES

WHEN: ALL YEAR

WHAT: VIRTUALLY ANY PREDATORY FISH

HOW: SMALL FISH IMITATION

HOOK: 3/0 TO 1 STAINLESS O'SHAUGHNESSY
TAIL: MYLAR TUBING WITH GLUED IN AND TRIMMED OLIVE HACKLE
BODY: SILVER BRAID WITH RED FLUORESCENT FLOSS
WING: PAIR OF OLIVE-DYED GRIZZLE SADDLE HACKLES WITH POLAR FIBRES IN RED, PEARL AND OLIVE AND MORE PEARL AND RED AS A HACKLE UNDERNEATH THE HOOK

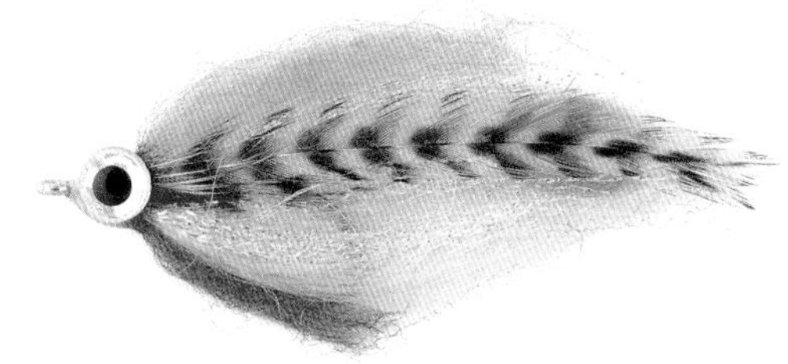

Mini Puff

USED MAINLY FOR BONEFISH, this is the one to reach for when they are at their spookiest. It is especially good for shallow water around midday at high tide when the fish are into the very margins. I would suggest you add another 1.2 m (9 ft) onto the standard 2.7 m (9 ft) leader for these occasions when delicate presentation is the key to success. The great Lefty Kreh reckons this one is indispensable and who is going to argue otherwise! Use the smaller size for small bonefish as too many fly fishers persist with large flies when only small fish are around.

WHERE: FLATS IN THE TROPICS

WHEN: ALL YEAR

WHAT: BONEFISH

HOW: PROBABLY SUGGESTS A SAND SHRIMP

HOOK: 2 TO 8 O'SHAUGHNESSY
WING: TAN CALF TAIL WITH PEARL CRYSTALFLASH AND TWO GRIZZLE COCK HACKLES
HEAD: FLUORESCENT HOT PINK CHENILLE AROUND BEAD CHAIN EYES

Mouse Rat

FLY TYING AT ITS MOST IMITATIVE and guaranteed to bring a smile from any fly fisher who has ever experienced the heart-stopping take of a largemouth bass to this fly or watched an Alaskan leopard rainbow trout suck in a mouse as daintily as its chalk stream cousin takes a mayfly. Make no mistake, bass, trout, pike and many other species love to eat mice, and given half a chance will add this morsel of pure protein to their diet. Not the easiest pattern to fish well, but once you have learned the technique it is thrilling fishing all the way!

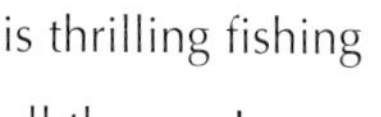

WHERE: WORLDWIDE FROM TUNDRA STREAMS TO WARM-WATER LAKES

WHEN: SPRING BEST FOR TROUT, BUT ALL YEAR FOR BASS AND OTHER FISH

WHAT: TROUT, GRAYLING, LAKE TROUT, PIKE, LARGEMOUTH AND SMALLMOUTH BASS, TAIMEN

HOW: IMITATES A MOUSE – WHAT ELSE!

HOOK: 2 SALMON IRON
TAIL: A PIECE OF LEATHER
BODY: SPUN AND TRIMMED DEER HAIR
EARS: LEATHER
EYES: BLACK BEADS
WHISKERS: BLACK HAIR

Apte Tarpon fly

THE APTE TARPON FLY IS THE FORERUNNER of numerous colour options. When Florida's Stu Apte produced this fly for tarpon he thought that it would suggest the tarpon's favourite food, the Palolo worm and that the wiggle of the long spade hackles would be too

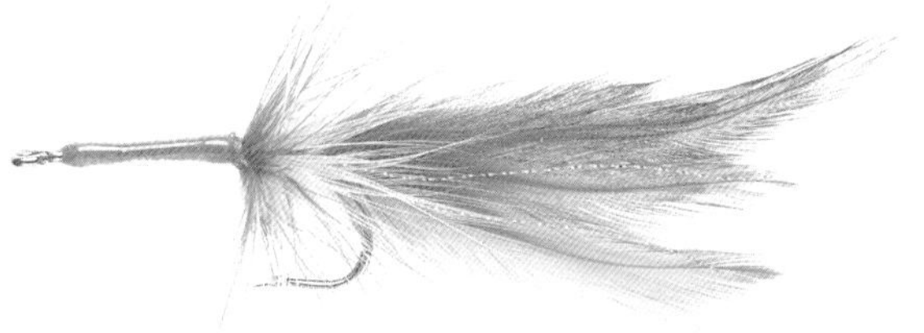

much for a highly predatory fish to resist. My personal tarpon experience is not extensive but I can vouch for the fact that they are an awesome opponent on a fly rod. This style of tying has been adapted to some freshwater lures such as the Nomad (see page 165) but remains the supreme saltwater fly.

WHERE: IN TROPICAL SALTWATER

WHEN: ALL YEAR

WHAT: TARPON BUT ALSO MANY OTHER SALTWATER PREDATORS

HOW: COLOUR AND ACTION SUGGESTS MANY FOOD FORMS

HOOK: 3/0 SALTWATER O'SHAUGHNESSY
TAIL: LONG SADDLE HACKLES, TWO PAIRS, RED AND YELLOW
HACKLE: PALMERED RED AND YELLOW LONG FIBRES SADDLE
BODY: RED TYING THREAD HEAVILY VARNISHED OR EPOXY RESIN COATED

Ugly Bugger

I GUESS YOU COULD BELIEVE THAT THIS IS THE OFFSPRING from a mating between a Montana Nymph (see page 360) and a Nomad (see page 165). Whatever the fish think it is, it really does work on newly introduced stock fish in lakes. There are colour variants galore, but this is the one for summer when damsel nymphs are about.

I caught my second ever 9 kg (20 lbs) rainbow trout on this fly. A super fly to give to a beginner's class when you need success. Also a rather neat pattern for largemouth bass and other predators.

WHERE: STILLWATER IN TEMPERATE AND SUB-TROPICAL REGIONS

WHEN: ALL YEAR

WHAT: TROUT, PIKE, PERCH, LARGEMOUTH BASS

HOW: AN ATTRACTOR

HOOK: 6 TO 10 STANDARD SHANK
TAIL: OLIVE MARABOU
BODY: OLIVE FRITZ THEN FLUORESCENT GREEN CHENILLE WITH A PALMERED OLIVE HACKLE AND BLACK CHENILLE OVER

Missing Link

BRIAN O' KEEFE IS BOTH A FABULOUS PHOTOGRAPHER and a great angler too who spends a lot of time observing fish and fishing. Those who observe nature often come up with superb patterns and this nice mouthful of a fly suggests many food forms and simply looks tasty. An excellent goby pattern for sand flats, it works best with a strip retrieve to

attract fish. Then let it settle and then wait for the fish to pounce! A simple fly for the newcomer to saltwater fly fishing who is itching to get a fish on one of his own tyings

WHERE: TROPICAL SALTWATER AREAS

WHEN: ALL YEAR

WHAT: BONEFISH, PERMIT, REDFISH

HOW: SUGGESTS FOR MANY FOOD ITEMS

DRESSING: HOOK SIZE 2–6 STAINLESS O' SHAUGHNESSY
TAIL: GOLD CRYSTALFLASH WITH BEIGE CRAFT FUR AND FLANKING CREE SADDLES
BODY: TAN SUEDE CHENILLE WITH PALMERED GINGER HACKLE
EYES: BEAD CHAIN

Green Butt Skunk

WHERE: JUST ABOUT ANYWHERE THAT TROUT OCCUR

WHEN: ALL YEAR

WHAT: BROWN, SEA TROUT AND RAINBOW TROUT, STEELHEAD

HOW: AN ATTRACTOR PATTERN

HOOK: 2 TO 10 SALMON IRON
TAIL: RED COCK HACKLE FIBRES
BUTT: FLUORESCENT GREEN CHENILLE OR FLOSS
BODY: BLACK CHENILLE OR FLOSS WITH SILVER OVAL RIB
WING: NATURAL POLAR BEAR HAIR
HACKLE: BLACK COCK SADDLE

THIS IS A BEAUTIFUL FLY which looks good and is a pleasure to tie. An exceptionally good pattern for steelhead and non-migratory rainbow trout as well as their old-world relatives, the brown trout. Fished down and across with a range of line densities in streamy water, or with a gentle retrieve where the current is slack, the Green Butt Skunk is one of the great standby patterns for those frustrating days when the fish are playing hard to get.

Articulated Leech

LEECH PATTERNS ARE used the fly fishing world over, relying heavily on the seductive movement of marabou and rabbit or long-fibred saddle hackles. Possibly nothing moves as well as marabou fibres and just see how it behaves when fished in a current. It is very much a fly for rainbows and brown trout in colder, deeper waters, but it is effective for other species too. Fish it in stillwater with a fast strip but in rivers cast downstream to make full use the current.

WHERE: WORLDWIDE IN RIVERS AND LAKES

WHEN: ALL YEAR

WHAT: TROUT, STEELHEAD, PACIFIC SALMON, LARGEMOUTH BASS, TAIMEN

HOW: A MARVELLOUSLY ATTRACTIVE MOVEMENT TO FIRE UP PREDATORS

HOOK: 3/0 TO 4 MARABOU TAIL AND PALMERED MARABOU. BODY LINK THE SHANK WITH A DACRON LOOP TO THE FRONT HOOK WHICH CAN BE FROM 3/0 TO 4 AND PALMER WITH MARABOU. ADD SOME PURPLE CRYSTALFLASH AND ADD BEAD CHAIN EYES

Breadcrust

THERE ARE MANY TIMES when fishing streams and rivers that you need a general-purpose searching pattern that imitates a host of food items. Such a fly needs to be grub-like and a bland, non-spooking colour. The Breadcrust suits all these criteria. An old pattern that remains a very firm favourite, especially in semi-Arctic regions and in rivers with plenty of fine gravel in among larger stones. Fish it weighted and use a sight indicator in rough water.

WHERE: RIVERS WORLDWIDE IN TEMPERATE AND SEMI-ARCTIC REGIONS

WHEN: ALL YEAR

WHAT: TROUT, GRAYLING, CHAR, CUTTHROAT

HOW: AN ALL-PURPOSE NYMPH

HOOK: 8 TO 14 STANDARD SHANK
BODY: RUSTY ORANGE RABBIT DUBBING RIBBED WITH A STRIPPED HACKLE STALK
HACKLE: GRIZZLE HEN

Grannom

THE GRANNOM IS AN early season sedge which occupies the trout like no other fly. The problem with the grannom is that it can be absent for a whole a season altogether but then occur in huge numbers the following year. Chalk stream anglers speak of the grannom hatch in almost reverential tones and it clearly is an experience to be enjoyed.

WHERE: LIMESTONE RIVERS IN THE UK AND EUROPE

WHEN: LATE SPRING TO EARLY SUMMER

WHAT: TROUT, GRAYLING

HOW: ADULT GRANNOM IMITATION

HOOK: 14 LIGHTWEIGHT STANDARD SHANK
TAG: BRIGHT GREEN FLOSS
BODY: DUBBED RABBIT UNDERFUR
WING: GROUSE OR HEN
HACKLE: RED GAME COCK

Abel Anchovy

WHERE: WORLDWIDE IN ANY SALTWATER LOCATION

WHEN: ALL YEAR

WHAT: MOST SALTWATER PREDATORS

HOW: ADMIRABLY SUGGESTS A RANGE OF BAIT FISH

HOOK: 4/0 TO 2 SALTWATER O'SHAUGHNESSY
BODY: SILVER OR PEARL FLAT DIAMOND BRAID
COLLAR: A SPREAD OF WHITE BUCKTAIL OR POLAR HAIR
WING: BUCKTAIL OR POLAR HAIR. LAYERS OF BLUE ON GREEN ON WHITE THEN SILVER OR PEARL FLASHABOU WITH PEACOCK HERL OVER
HACKLE: TIED BEARD STYLE OF RED CRYSTAL HAIR
HEAD: LARGE DOLL'S EYES COVERED WITH NAIL VARNISH

THIS FLY HAS A NUMBER OF VARIATIONS which makes it work for many different saltwater applications. Its main feature is the large eye, a feature prominent on most bait fishes. Steve Abel, a fine fisherman with numerous IGFA (International Game Fish Association) records to his name, also makes the most wonderful fly reels. Any fly that carries his name is certain to be extremely good. Although a saltwater fly, I have also caught lake trout and pike on this pattern.

Fonzie Fly

MY DAUGHTER FIONA (FONZIE) made this fly when she was just eight years old, and I first used it in Alaska when I could see – but not catch – a monster chinook. This king salmon took the Fonzie Fly on my first cast and measured a striking 130 cm (51 inches). Since then the Fonzie Fly has become an accepted pattern and has taken many king salmon, chum, coho and steelhead. Fiona has even caught her own 13.6 kg (30 lb) king salmon with the fly she designed.

WHERE: ALASKAN RIVERS AND DOWN THROUGH BRITISH COLUMBIA TO OREGON, AS WELL AS THE GREAT LAKES AND RIVER SYSTEMS IN NEW YORK STATE

WHEN: JUNE AND JULY IN ALASKA BUT VARIABLE TO THE RUN ELSEWHERE

WHAT: KING SALMON (CHINOOK), CHUM, COHO, STEELHEAD

HOW: AN ATTRACTOR RELYING ON HOT COLOURS

HOOK: 2 SALMON IRON
TAIL: LARGE BUNCH OF HOT PINK MARABOU
BODY: PURPLE FLASHABOU FIBRES
UNDERWING: PURPLE FLASHABOU FIBRES
WING: BRIGHT BLUE MARABOU

Black Nosed Dace

THE LATE ART FLICK INVENTED THIS SUPER FRY imitation which is effective from the far northern climes of Alaska to the warm stillwaters of Europe, through Asia and Australia and even in the rivers and stillwaters of South America. Tied in different sizes, it works on all manner of freshwater species. There are very few fish that don't eat fry at some time in their life. Best fished in short strips, this long-time favourite can easily be adapted to saltwater tying and is equally effective for striped bass!

WHERE: WORLDWIDE IN RIVERS AND STILLWATER

WHEN: ALL YEAR BUT PARTICULARLY WHEN FRY ARE ABUNDANT

WHAT: ALL PREDATORY FISH

HOW: SUGGESTS A BABY FISH

HOOK: 6 TO 10 4X LONG SHANK
TAIL: RED WOOL
BODY: FLAT SILVER TINSEL WITH OVAL SILVER RIB
WING: THREE LAYERS – WHITE BUCKTAIL, BLACK BEAR THEN BROWN BUCKTAIL

Hairy Mary

SALMON FLIES ARE OFTEN NAMED AFTER LADIES, which makes this one a little worrying, but whatever its origin, this simple hairwing is an excellent fly for summer Atlantic salmon and grilse. Use it with faith on the eastern seaboard of the USA or in Iceland, Ireland, Scotland, Norway and Russia. Some areas still have good runs of Atlantic salmon. It wasn't long ago that I had little hope for the future of this noble fish, but with catch-and-release ethics gaining moderate acceptance within the UK, I now believe there is a chance its numbers may recover.

WHERE: NORTHERN HEMISPHERE IN CLASSIC ATLANTIC SALMON RIVERS

WHEN: GENERALLY BEST UNDER MODERATE- TO LOW-FLOW CONDITIONS

WHAT: ATLANTIC SALMON, SEA TROUT, STEELHEAD

HOW: A TYPICAL HAIRWING ATTRACTOR-STYLE SALMON FLY

HOOK: 6 TO 12 SALMON IRON OR DOUBLE
TAIL: GOLDEN PHEASANT CREST WITH AN OVAL GOLD TINSEL TAG
BODY: BLACK FLOSS WITH OVAL GOLD TINSEL RIB
HACKLE: BRIGHT BLUE COCK HACKLE FIBRES
WING: BROWN BUCKTAIL

Improved Shadow

I MODIFIED PETER DEANES' ORIGINAL FLY to make a better fly for stillwater mayfly hatches and then found it was also good on rivers in the latter stages of the hatch when the fish are becoming choosy after seeing too many natural mayflies. Adding orange to a fly can be so important for trout. This pattern is definitely best if it is a bit mangled and can barely float. Then it suggests a failed fly which has drowned. Many fish will feed on the larger mayfly, and I do well with this one for carp. It also took my best river chub from the River Test.

WHERE: MOSTLY IN THE NORTHERN HEMISPHERE IN RIVERS AND LAKES THAT HAVE HATCHES OF THE LARGER MAYFLY

WHEN: BEST IN MID SUMMER

WHAT: TROUT, GRAYLING, SMALLMOUTH BASS, CARP

HOW: SUGGESTS A CRIPPLED MAYFLY AT HATCHING STAGE

HOOK: 10 OR 12 2X SHANK
TAIL: COCK PHEASANT CENTRE TAIL FIBRES
BODY: THREE PALMERED SOFT-FIBRED COCK BADGER HACKLES THEN A HOT ORANGE COCK HACKLE AND THEN ANOTHER BADGER HACKLE. USE HOT ORANGE TYING THREAD FOR BEST EFFECT

Terry's Para Emerger

TERRY GRIFFITHS LOVES THE PARACHUTE dressing and made this little gem to suggest the hatching stage of the chironomid pupa. A magic way to fish this is to target an individual riser on stillwater as it cruises up a wind lane and to then drop this fly into its cruise path and wait. A quiet slurp and the fly is gone. The white wing of calf tail makes it easy to see this fly even in poor light. The black version is best for early season, while olive and tan are other essential colours.

WHERE: STILLWATER AND SOME RIVERS IN TEMPERATE REGIONS

WHEN: SPRING TO AUTUMN

WHAT: TROUT

HOW: SUGGESTS THE HATCHING STAGE OF THE CHIRONOMID

HOOK: 14 CURVED SHANK
BODY: BLACK FEATHER FIBRE WITH FINE PEARL TINSEL RIB
THORAX: RUST OR ORANGE POLYPROPYLENE
WING POST: WHITE CALF BODY HAIR
HACKLE: GRIZZLE COCK

Klinkhamer

WHERE: WORLDWIDE IN RIVERS AND TO SOME EXTENT IN STILLWATER

WHEN: ANY TIME WHEN THERE IS A HATCH

WHAT: TROUT, GRAYLING, CHAR, SMALLMOUTH BASS, BLUEGILL

HOW: NON-SPECIFIC IMITATION BUT EXACT PRESENTATION IS NEEDED

HOOK: 8 TO 14 2X SHANK FINE WIRE
BODY: DUBBED SYNTHETIC RIBBED WITH FINE SILVER WIRE OR THREAD
THORAX: PEACOCK HERL OF WHITE POLY YARN
HACKLE: COCK HACKLE OF COLOUR APPROPRIATE TO MATCH BODY

IT TOOK THE INGENUITY OF HANS VAN KLINKEN of Holland to work out a way of exactly suggesting the emergent stage of aquatic insects at a time when the emerger type of fly was becoming popular. This fly, evolved initially for grayling, has transformed dry fly fishing.

The parachute hackle is not new, but by bending the hook shank to make the entire body of the fly become subsurface it immediately turns the fly into the perfect emerger. Surprisingly large as dry flies go, it should be carried in a variety of colours.

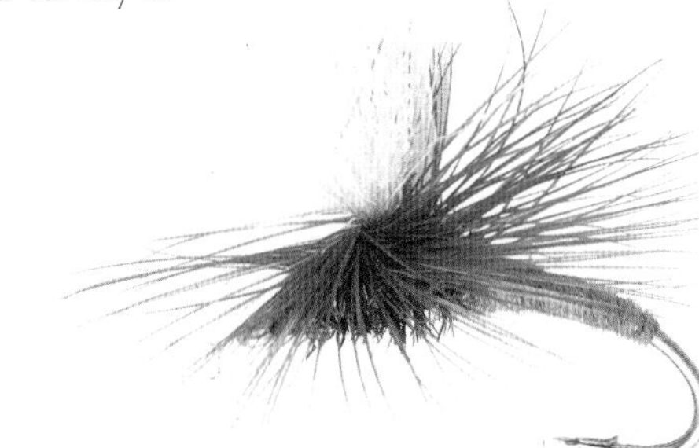

Adam's Irresistible

THERE IS SOMETHING ABOUT A DRY FLY with a fat body that really turns on a fish, and although the original Adams (see page 144) is deadly, this version makes it an entirely different pattern. It floats like a cork, and as such is very useful for rough water or fisheries where you might catch a lot of fish and do not want to be constantly drying out a fly or changing to a fresh one. It makes a very good beetle pattern and in high summer is superb when cast alongside banks or under bushes or when allowed to drift out with the breeze on large stillwaters.

WHERE: WORLDWIDE IN ALL SORTS OF RIVERS AND OFTEN IN STILLWATER

WHEN: BEST IN SPRING AND SUMMER

WHAT: TROUT, GRAYLING, CHAR, SMALLMOUTH BASS, BLUEGILL

HOW: GREAT GENERAL IMPRESSIONIST DRY, BUT ALSO A GOOD BEETLE IMITATION

HOOK: 10 TO 16 STANDARD SHANK
TAIL: BLACK MOOSE BODY HAIR
BODY: NATURAL DEER CLIPPED TIGHT
WING: GRIZZLE COCK HACKLE TIPS
HACKLE: MIXED RED GAME COCK AND GRIZZLE COCK

Dawson's Olive

AN INTERESTING COMBINATION OF COLOURS which triggers a reaction in trout when damsel and dragon flies are around. Very good in weeded and slightly coloured water when fished with a slow-sinking line and a steady retrieve. It works well for bass, and is typical of many marabou-based lures which are often improved by mixing the wing and tail colours. In this case, the little touch of blue seems to appeal to fish that feed on damsels.

WHERE: STILLWATER IN TEMPERATE AND SUB-TROPICAL REGIONS

WHEN: ALL YEAR, BUT BEST IN WARMER WATER

WHAT: TROUT, LARGEMOUTH AND SMALLMOUTH BASS, BLUEGILL

HOW: AN ATTRACTOR LURE BASED ON SIZE AND MOVEMENT

HOOK: 8 TO 12 2X SHANK
TAIL: YELLOW MARABOU
BODY: OLIVE CHENILLE RIBBED WITH OVAL GOLD TINSEL
WING: OLIVE MARABOU
HACKLE: DYED BLUE GUINEA FOWL TIED FALSE
HEAD: GOLD BEAD

Anorexic Hare's ear

FLY FISHING MUST ALWAYS be a bit of a puzzle, and I believe we have to accept that fish choose to ignore the hook and the nylon and instead see only the possibility of something edible. A scrap of hare's ear with an insignificant rib hardly warrants a decent hook, but this style of tying will often fool the largest of fishes. Fish this to wised-up brown trout in ultra-clear water. It is also a very good competition fly for hard-pressed fish.

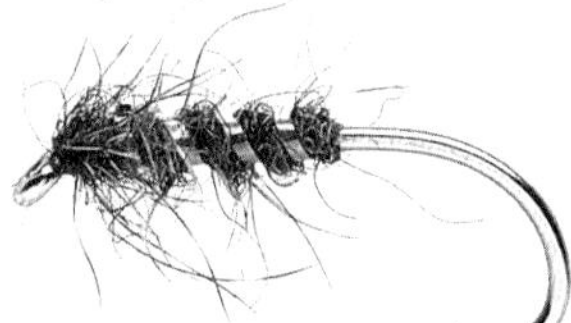

WHERE: WORLDWIDE IN CLEAR STILLWATER AND SLOW SECTIONS OF RIVERS

WHEN: LATE SPRING AND SUMMER WHEN WATER CLARITY AND VISIBILITY IS BEST

WHAT: BROWN AND RAINBOW TROUT

HOW: SUGGESTS SMALL FOOD FORMS

HOOK: 10 TO 14 STANDARD SHANK
BODY: TIED ONLY AT THE THIRD OF SHANK NEAR THE EYE. USE A DUBBING SPINNER CATCH IN A FLUFF OF HARE'S EAR AND RIB WITH THE FINEST COPPER WIRE

Daddy

THE DADDY-LONG-LEGS OR CRANE-FLY is a common terrestrial which is a weak flier and frequently gets blown onto the water. Trout love them and will very readily eat them, even taking the artificial fly when there are no natural daddy-long-legs around.

WHERE: STILLWATER AND RIVERS IN TEMPERATE REGIONS

WHEN: LATE SPRING TO AUTUMN, BUT LATE SUMMER IS BEST

WHAT: TROUT, SMALLMOUTH AND LARGEMOUTH BASS

HOW: EXCELLENT IMITATION OF ADULT DADDY-LONG-LEGS (CRANE-FLY)

HOOK: 10 OR 12 2X SHANK
BODY: TAN RAFFINE
WING: CREE COCK HACKLE POINTS
LEGS: DOUBLE-KNOTTED COCK PHEASANT CENTRE TAIL FIBRES
HACKLE: CREE COCK

This is a standard style that is excellent when the natural insect is on the water. Fished static or allowed to move with the breeze, this fly will often catch a larger than average fish. I know it seems illogical, but fish this fly just below the surface of the water with a very slow retrieve and the takes will be extremely good indeed.

Cactus Cluster

THIS IS AN UNUSUAL ADAPTATION OF A MODERN MATERIAL (Fritz) to suggest an equally unusual behavioural pattern of chironomid adults when they ball together and skitter around on the surface. Usually chironomids hatch and fly away from water very quickly before mating, and this may be some sort of group mating ritual. I have seen it on Lake Eucumbene in Australia and occasionally on other high-altitude lakes, but this cluster pattern also works on most stillwaters, especially in a calm.

WHERE: STILLWATER WORLDWIDE IN TEMPERATE REGIONS; BUT BEST AT HIGHER ALTITUDES

WHEN: LATE SPRING TO MID-SUMMER

WHAT: TROUT

HOW: RESEMBLES A CLUSTER OF ADULT CHIRONOMIDS

HOOK: 10 TO 12 STANDARD SHANK
BODY: ORANGE FRITZ WITH A GINGER COCK HACKLE PALMERED THROUGH.
NOTE: VARIANTS ARE GREEN, RED AND BLACK

Bivisible

THIS FLY IS VERY EASY TO TIE and has almost unlimited variations providing you keep to the white hackle at the front. It floats well if treated and creates the illusion of size with virtually no weight or bulk. Very good for difficult light conditions and broken water and makes an excellent dapping fly. Dapping is an art mostly practised in Ireland and Scotland, but is also so good for searching large expanses of stillwater and attracting fish to the surface that it deserves recognition worldwide.

WHERE: WORLDWIDE IN RIVERS AND STILLWATER

WHEN: ALL YEAR BUT BEST FROM SPRING TO AUTUMN

WHAT: TROUT, GRAYLING, SEA TROUT, ATLANTIC SALMON

HOW: NON-SPECIFIC BUT STIMULATING SURFACE PATTERN

HOOK: 8 TO 14 STANDARD SHANK
TAIL: RED GAME HACKLE FIBRES
BODY: PALMERED RED GAME COCK HACKLE (USE TWO OR MORE FOR LARGER HOOKS)
HACKLE: WHITE COCK HACKLE. VARIANTS ARE BLACK, GREY AND DUN

Czech Nymph

THE ENORMOUS POPULARITY OF THIS NYMPH came about after the Czechoslovakian team used it in the World Fly Championships to show the rest of the world how to fish for grayling and trout in rivers using their close-quarter nymphing techniques. Now used to take both trout and grayling in rivers wherever they swim the world over.

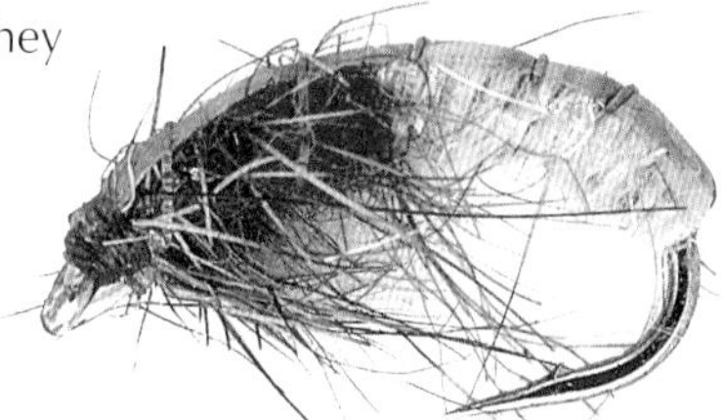

WHERE: WORLDWIDE IN FREESTONE RIVERS IN TEMPERATE AND SUB-ARCTIC REGIONS

WHEN: ALL YEAR

WHAT: GRAYLING, TROUT, WHITEFISH

HOW: SUGGESTS A STONEFLY NYMPH

HOOK: 8 TO 14 CURVED SHANK
BODY: CREAM COLOUR WOOL WITH FLAT PEARL TINSEL RIB
THORAX: ORANGE SEAL'S FUR AND HARE BODY FUR
BACK: PALE YELLOW LATEX STRIP

Light Cahill

ANOTHER EXCELLENT PATTERN to suggest the pale watery and many other light-coloured ephemerids, it can also be tied in a dark format using a brown body and red game hackle. The use of wood duck flank feathers for the wing enhances the fly's killing powers. This American pattern works really well in Australia, New Zealand, South Africa and Argentina.

WHERE: WORLDWIDE IN RIVERS

WHEN: ALL YEAR BUT BEST FROM SPRING TO MID-SUMMER

WHAT: TROUT AND GRAYLING

HOW: SUGGESTS MANY PALE EPHEMERIDS

HOOK: 12 TO 18 STANDARD SHANK FINE WIRE
TAIL: CREAM COCK HACKLE FIBRES
BODY: CREAM SEAL'S FUR
HACKLE: CREAM OR LIGHT GINGER COCK
WING: WOOD DUCK CAROLINA OR MANDARIN DUCK FLANK FIBRES

Mohawk

THIS IS A RELIABLE PATTERN FOR PIKE and is excellent for other species with lots of teeth. Tying the bucktail in lots of little sections gives a very solid profile and a light, easy-to-cast fly. Use it on a floating line to fish in and over weeds especially if you also fit a weed guard, or fish it with a slow sinking line to make it rise and fall during the retrieve. You can make up your own colour combinations depending on which species you are chasing, but if all fails, try orange and black.

WHERE: WORLDWIDE IN FRESH- AND SALTWATER

WHEN: ALL YEAR

WHAT: PIKE, WALLEYE, LAKE TROUT, TIGER FISH, PEACOCK BASS, NILE PERCH, DORADO

HOW: GENERAL ATTRACTOR LURE

HOOK: 4/0 FINE WIRE PIKE HOOK
BODY: FLUORESCENT RED TYING THREAD
WING: SMALL SECTIONS OF BLACK BUCKTAIL AND A FEW FIBRES OF PEARL CRYSTALFLASH AND THEN A COUPLE OF SECTIONS OF RED BUCKTAIL

Swimming Damsel

THIS IS A CLEVER USE OF A BENT HOOK SHANK to suggest the undulating motion of a swimming nymph. This fly works well for trout feeding on damsel nymphs. Sometimes we just have to accept that we don't really know why a fly works, but if it does then why change it? Whatever the reason, damsels are the prime food item for fish in lakes, ponds and slow-flowing parts of rivers, so you must have imitations.

WHERE: WORLDWIDE IN STILLWATER AND SLOW-FLOWING RIVERS IN TEMPERATE REGIONS

WHEN: ALL YEAR BUT BEST IN SUMMER

WHAT: TROUT, SMALLMOUTH AND LARGEMOUTH BASS, BLUEGILL, CARP

HOW: SUGGESTS A MOVING DAMSEL FLY NYMPH

HOOK: 8 TO 12 2X SHANK
TAIL: LIGHT OLIVE HEN HACKLE FIBRES
BODY: FINE OLIVE WOOL RIBBED WITH COPPER WIRE
WING CASE: OLIVE RAFFINE
THORAX: FINE OLIVE WOOL
EYES: BLACK BEADS ON BLACK MONO
LEGS: DYED OLIVE GRIZZLE COCK HACKLE FIBRES

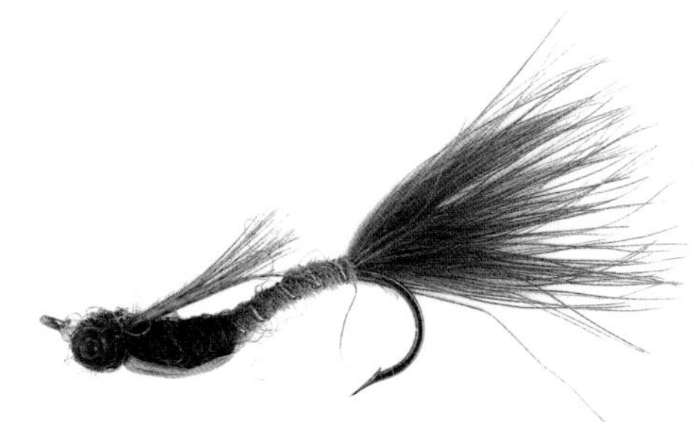

Viva

MANY BLACK FLIES incorporate a touch of fluorescent green in their tying to provide a lure that trout just cannot resist. Very effective for newly-stocked fish, it is usually best fished under low light conditions and is often a first-choice pattern when fishing the small, managed fisheries that are so common in the UK, Europe and which are becoming popular in the US. Usually best fished with an intermediate density line and a quickish retrieve.

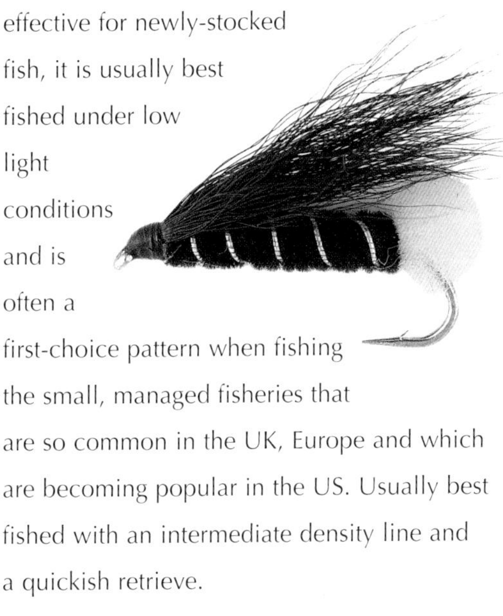

WHERE: WORLDWIDE IN STOCKED STILLWATER

WHEN: ALL YEAR

WHAT: RAINBOW AND BROWN TROUT AND MOST SALMONIDS

HOW: A RELIABLE LURE IN ALL STILL WATERS

HOOK: 6 TO 14 STANDARD OR NYMPH 2X SHANK
TAIL: FLUORESCENT GREEN NYLON WOOL
BODY: BLACK CHENILLE WITH SILVER TINSEL RIB
WING: BLACK DYED SQUIRREL TAIL FIBRES OR BLACK MARABOU
HACKLE (OPTIONAL): BLACK HEN TIED AS BEARD

Olive Gulper Special

THIS NEAT LITTLE FLY resembles other patterns, but I include it because of the importance of having an olive-bodied version. Many mayflies have bodies in varying shades of olive, as do many chironomids and terrestrials, and you can successfully use this pattern to represent a whole range of insects. Useful for tricky fish because the tying style allows the fly to settle very carefully on the water which avoids spooking a cautious fish. Tying flies with a parachute hackle is a most useful technique to master.

WHERE: WORLDWIDE IN RIVERS IN TEMPERATE REGIONS

WHEN: LATE SPRING TO AUTUMN

WHAT: TROUT, GRAYLING, CUTTHROAT

HOW: EXCELLENT RESEMBLANCE TO A SMALL OLIVE MAYFLY AND MANY OTHER INSECTS

HOOK: 14 TO 20 STANDARD SHANK
TAIL: GRIZZLE COCK HACKLE FIBRES
BODY: OLIVE RABBIT UNDERFUR
WING: WHITE POLYPROPYLENE YARN
HACKLE: GRIZZLE COCK HACKLE DYED LIGHT OLIVE

Grey Goose

THIS SIMPLE NYMPH WAS THE BRAINCHILD OF Frank Sawyer, the celebrated river keeper on the River Avon, in the UK. All I have done is to vary it slightly and make it a better stillwater pattern. In its original format, without the hackle, it is an excellent river pattern. Grey is a bland colour that does not spook fish and can be shown time and again to the same fish. I find this one often works best when retrieved very quickly to provoke an aggressive chase and take to fish in feeding stillwater.

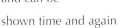

WHERE: WORLDWIDE IN RIVERS AND STILLWATER

WHEN: ALL YEAR BUT SPRING AND SUMMER ARE BEST

WHAT: TROUT, GRAYLING AND MANY OTHER FRESHWATER SPECIES

HOW: A GENERAL-PURPOSE SUGGESTIVE NYMPH PATTERN

HOOK: 10 TO 16 STANDARD SHANK
TAIL: FIBRES OF GREY FEATHER (I USE A PEACOCK UNDERTAIL FEATHER)
ABDOMEN THORAX AND WING CASE: FIBRES OF GREY FEATHER
RIB: VERY FINE COPPER WIRE
HACKLE: ONE TURN OF SHORT-FIBRED GREY HEN HACKLE

Shuck fly

OCCASIONALLY YOU MAY CATCH A TROUT that is clearly feeding from the surface, but when its stomach contents are examined it contains nothing but a whitish slime. What the cunning trout is actually eating is the pupal shuck, the skin left behind after a chironomid hatches. When a big hatch is happening on stillwater, you can sometimes see a slick formed on the downwind shore from thousands of shucks. This specialist fly is a creation of Chris Ogbourne, who captained the English Flyfishing team during their best years. It is ideal for really difficult days and is a great fly in a flat calm.

WHERE: STILLWATER IN TEMPERATE REGIONS

WHEN: SUMMER

WHAT: TROUT

HOW: COPIES THE PUPAL SHUCK OF A CHIRONOMID

HOOK: 12 TO 14 STANDARD SHANK FINE WIRE
TAIL: A FEW WISPS OF CREAM POLAR HAIR
SHUCK: CUT FROM VERY THIN ETHAFOAM AND TIED WITH ORANGE THREAD

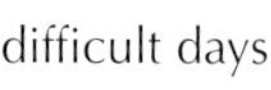
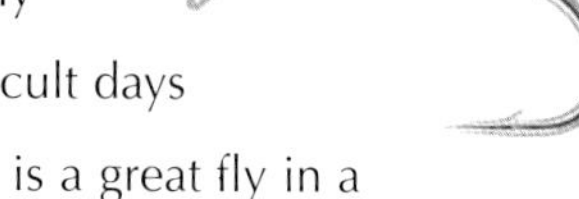

Ace of Spades

DATING FROM THE 1960s and conceived by David Collyer, this is a much-improved black lure incorporating a matuka-style that provides a denser profile. It is probably best used as a cold-weather lure for stillwater trout, either fished very slowly or with a fast, erratic strip. It can also be very effective when fished as a point fly with a

small nymph on a dropper a metre (3 ft) away, when the trout takes the nymph which it believes is being chased by the lure.

WHERE: WORLDWIDE IN ANY STILLWATER WHERE PREDATORY FISH OCCUR

WHEN: USUALLY BEST DURING SPRING AND AUTUMN

WHAT: BROWN AND RAINBOW TROUT, LANDLOCKED CHAR, SALMON AND BLACK BASS

HOW: A BASIC BLACK LURE FOR ATTRACTING ATTENTION

HOOK: 6X TO 10 4X LURE HOOK
BODY: BLACK CHENILLE WITH OVAL SILVER TINSEL RIB
WING: PAIR OF BLACK HEN HACKLES TIED DOWN MATUKA-STYLE WITH THE RIB
OVERWING: BRONZE MALLARD STRIPS
HACKLE: GUINEA FOWL TIED FALSE

PVC Nymph

JOHN GODDARD OFTEN CALLS INTO MY FLY SHOP and customers are stunned to see this living legend picking through the materials as he researches yet another pattern. John came up with the PVC nymph many years ago, and it is still a first-choice pattern for stillwater trout feeding on the nymph of olive ephemerids. It is also excellent for well-weeded limestone rivers when cast upstream into weed fronds and allowed to drift back into a trout's lie.

WHERE: WORLDWIDE IN STILLWATER AND ALSO LIMESTONE RIVERS

WHEN: USUALLY BEST FROM SPRING TO EARLY SUMMER

WHAT: TROUT, GRAYLING, SMALL AND LARGEMOUTH BASS, BLUEGILL

HOW: PERFECTLY SUGGESTS THE NYMPH OF POND AND LAKE OLIVE MAYFLY AND MANY EPHEMERIDS

HOOK: 12 TO 16 STANDARD SHANK
TAIL: OLIVE CONDOR HERL TIPS (USE DYED SUBSTITUTE)
BODY: COPPER WIRE WITH OLIVE CONDOR HERL OVER AND COVERED WITH A LAYER OF CLEAR PVC
THORAX: OLIVE CONDOR HERL WITH WING CASE OF PHEASANT TAIL FIBRES

Coch-y-Bonddu

COCH-Y-BONDDU is the Welsh name for a small beetle, which always induces a feeding frenzy in trout. The beetles are usually found in wild areas which have poor vegetation, so this is a pattern for high country waters. Many stillwaters rely on falls of terrestrial insects to supplement the rather meagre rations their nutritionally depleted environment can supply, and beetles are a prime source of such food. Early summer is when beetles take wing, and this is the best time to use this little fly.

WHERE: WORLDWIDE BUT USUALLY IN POOR-QUALITY ENVIRONMENTS

WHEN: EARLY SUMMER

WHAT: TROUT, LAKE TROUT, GRAYLING, CHAR

HOW: SUGGESTS MANY SMALL BEETLES

HOOK: 10 TO 14 STANDARD SHANK
BODY: A TAG OF FLAT GOLD TINSEL AND THEN PEACOCK HERL TIED FAT
HACKLE: DARK FURNACE

Pete's Red Brown

I DEVELOPED THIS PATTERN FOR BROWN TROUT which feed on the brightly-coloured male stickleback in spring and I have since found it to be a very good general-purpose nymph for most stillwaters. Resident trout develop a real taste for sticklebacks and will actively hunt them in shallow water where they breed. Fish this pattern very slowly and erratically and expect occasional violent takes. I first tied it with flat copper tinsel for the body, but now use copper Fritz for a better effect.

WHERE: WORLDWIDE IN STILLWATER, BUT ESPECIALLY IN THE NORTHERN HEMISPHERE

WHEN: ALL YEAR, BUT SPRING IS BEST

WHAT: BROWN AND RAINBOW TROUT BUT ALSO VERY GOOD FOR PANFISH AND SMALLMOUTH BASS

HOW: INTENDED TO SUGGEST A STICKLEBACK BUT IS ALSO A GOOD IMPRESSIONIST PATTERN

HOOK: 8 TO 12 2X NYMPH
TAIL: PEACOCK HERL CLIPPED SHORT
BACK: PEACOCK HERL
BODY: FINE COPPER FRITZ WITH LIGHT BROWN OSTRICH HERL RIB
COLLAR: NEON MAGENTA CHENILLE
HEAD: PEACOCK HERL

Jim's Goldeneye

I LOVE THIS PATTERN from the clever mind of Jim Orthwein, probably because it caught me a 70-cm (27-inch) bonefish on a day when I felt I had really earned that fish. This fly has several IGFA line class records to its credit, and I strongly suggest you have a couple in your box for the day when you have the chance to cast at a big bonefish. It isn't the easiest fly to tie, and because the hook is a freshwater 4X long shank, which needs to be bent after the fly is tied, you should varnish a few hooks before tying to give them a degree of salt-proofing.

WHERE: TROPICAL SALTWATER FLATS

WHEN: ALL YEAR

WHAT: BONEFISH, PERMIT

HOW: SUGGESTS A MANTIS SHRIMP

HOOK: 4 4X SHANK
TAIL: NUGGET OF GOLD FISHAIR DOUBLED OVER AND TO ONE SIDE OF THE BODY
BODY: CLEAR SWANNUNDAZE OVER GOLD MYLAR TUBING WITH A BROWN SADDLE HACKLE PALMERED AND CLIPPED WITH THE FISHAIR TWISTED AND TIED OVER THE BACK.
HEAD: GOLD BEAD CHAIN AND THEN THE FISHAIR AND MYLAR TRIMMED OFF AND 4 PECCARY BRISTLES ADDED
NOTE: APPLY PLENTY OF VARNISH TO HEAD AND BACK.

Grenadier

MODERN CHIRONOMID IMITATIONS make much of the orange wing buds or cheeks in their tyings and there is no doubt that this is a key factor to their success but older patterns incorporating orange were also hugely successful. I have always loved using this fly on lakes when there is a bit of a ripple and I can fish it close to the surface. Trout just roll on it with utter confidence and there must be a simple trigger in this pretty little fly which is enough to convince them that this is the genuine article. Use it on the top or middle dropper in a traditional three fly cast from a drifting boat and it's a winner.

WHERE: STILLWATERS AND SLOW RIVERS IN TEMPERATE REGIONS

WHEN: SPRING THROUGH TO FALL

WHAT: TROUT

HOW: ADULT CHIRONOMID IMITATION

HOOK: SIZE 16 TO 10 STANDARD SHANK
BODY: DUBBED ORANGE SEAL'S FUR WITH GOLD WIRE RIB
HACKLE: HEN GREENWELL

Amber Nymph

CADDIS (SEDGE) FLIES can make a major contribution to a fish's diet. In some waters fish feed heavily on the larval form; others feed on the pupal form, and often the adult stage is also eaten, too.

This lovely pattern was an early attempt to imitate the pupal stage and is a top choice for stillwater if you suspect caddis are being fed on, but aren't sure of the species. I have found it to be work extremely well in Canada for the redfin form of the lake trout, which undoubtedly is very fond of caddis. Fish it in the dropper position with a larval imitation on point, but when the hatch happens fish two together.

WHERE: WORLDWIDE IN TEMPERATE AND ARCTIC REGIONS IN STILLWATER

WHEN: BEST FROM LATE SPRING TO AUTUMN

WHAT: TROUT, GRAYLING, WHITEFISH, CHAR, LAKE TROUT, SMALLMOUTH AND LARGEMOUTH BASS, BLUEGILL

HOW: A GENERAL-PURPOSE IMITATION OF A CADDIS (SEDGE) PUPA

HOOK: 8 TO 12 STANDARD SHANK
BODY: AMBER SEAL'S FUR
THORAX: BROWN SEAL'S FUR
WING: CASE BROWN FEATHER FIBRE
HACKLE: GINGER OR HONEY HEN FIBRES TIED FALSE

Black Bear Hair

A VERY SIMPLE FLY USING A STRIP OF BLACK BEAR FUR. It's tough, moves well when wet, has the basic attraction of black, is easy to tie, gives a very solid profile and appeals to most predators without causing alarm. If you are in some far-flung place and really stumped for flies it's usually easy enough to find some sort of hair and make up this style of fly. You can even use fuse wire to bind it to a hook. Simple, but effective and that's as good a motto as you could wish for with any fly.

WHERE: WORLDWIDE RIVER OR SEA

WHEN: YEAR ROUND

WHAT: JUST ABOUT ANY PREDATORY SPECIES

HOW: A FOOD ITEM
DRESSING: HOOK 2 TO 10 4X TO 6X SHANK

BODY: BLACK DUBBING, CHENILLE
HACKLE: HEN GREENWELL
WING: STRIP BLACK BEAR
RIB: OVAL TINSEL

Floating Smelt

SMELT ARE THE NUMBER ONE BAIT FISH in many parts of the watery world, whether it be salt or fresh. However, you need to know how predators work to understand this one's uses. Lots of fish rush into bait fish shoals,

creating mayhem trying to stun the little fishes. They then cruise slowly back to mop up the cripples. Stunned bait fish frequently rise to the surface, and hence this floating smelt needs to be cast into areas of feeding activity and allowed to sit quietly until sucked in.

WHERE: LARGER FRESHWATER LAKES AND SALTWATER ESTUARIES IN NEW ZEALAND AND SUBARCTIC

WHEN: ALL YEAR

WHAT: TROUT, LAKE TROUT, PIKE, WALLEYE, LANDLOCKED STRIPED AND STRIPED BASS, BLUEFISH, SEA TROUT, REDFISH, AND MANY OTHER SALTWATER PREDATORS

HOW: COPIES A WOUNDED OR DEAD SMELT

HOOK: 2 TO 6 4X SHANK
TAIL: GREY MARABOU
BODY: LAYER OF ETHAFOAM COVERED WITH FINE PEARL MYLAR TUBE WHICH IS THEN PAINTED WITH OLIVE ON THE BACK AND A RED GILL STRIPE AND A YELLOW AND BLACK EYE EFFECT

Pink Pollywog

WHERE: RIVERS IN ALASKA, BRITISH COLUMBIA, WASHINGTON, OREGON AND THE GREAT LAKES

WHAT: PRIMARILY COHO, CHUM, BUT ALSO HUMPBACK SALMON IN SMALL VERSIONS

WHEN: SUMMER AND EARLY AUTUMN WHEN THE FISH ARE RUNNING, BUT BEST IN WARM WATER

HOW: A SURFACE-ACTIVE ATTRACTOR RELYING HEAVILY ON THE SALMON'S LOVE OF PINK

HOOK: 1/0 TO 4 LONG SHANK STANDARD SALMON
TAIL: GENEROUS BUT NOT TOO LONG BUNCH OF HOT PINK MARABOU
BODY: TIGHTLY SPUN HOT PINK DEER HAIR SNIPPED TO SHAPE
WING: TIED FORWARD OF PINK DEER OR BUCKTAIL

THIS DELIGHTFULLY-NAMED PATTERN was developed on the Alagnak river in Alaska as a chum salmon dry fly and very quickly became a favourite for coho (silver) salmon. Both these aggressive salmon love pink flies and will readily attack a waking surface pattern if tied in hot pink. Chum will often prefer an almost dead drift, especially when fresh off the tide, while silver salmon like something to chase and prefer it to wake. If you like to fish the dry fish then this one will really get your pulse racing as these exciting salmon take off the top. Never underestimate a chum – it's one of the toughest salmon and causes more broken gear than any other salmon.

CDC Hare's Ear

WHERE WOULD MODERN FLY TYING BE without the preen gland feathers from waterbirds? This simple pattern is my first choice for rivers or lakes where trout are feeding on the emergent stage of very small chironomids or midges. It sits in the surface film, where its wing is easy to see, it floats really well and it suggests all manner of insects. I carry a little pot with a mix of CDC from hook sizes 18 to 12 and change the fly as soon as I have caught a couple of fish in order to let it dry properly. Fish with fine leaders and a rod rated 5 or less and it will encourage trout or grayling to take a look – and by then you are halfway there.

WHERE: WORLDWIDE IN RIVERS AND LAKES

WHEN: ALMOST ANY TIME, BUT BEST IN THE WARMER MONTHS AND PARTICULARLY IN WEAK LIGHT

WHAT: TROUT, GRAYLING, CHAR

HOW: VAGUELY SUGGESTS AN EMERGING INSECT BUT IS DEFINITELY EDIBLE

HOOK: 18 TO 12 STANDARD SHANK FINE WIRE
BODY: DUBBED HARE'S MASK; BEST WITH A DUBBING SPINNER
WING: ONE OR TWO GREY CDC FEATHERS (DUCK'S PREEN GLAND FEATHER)

Girdle Bug

SOME FLY PATTERNS defy logic but are amazingly successful. The Girdle Bug is a prime example, and it has to be those rubber legs that attract and mesmerize a fish into believing it has found food. If I can ever catch the king of fishes, the noble Atlantic salmon, with this fly then they have to be the cause. I suspect that the fishes pick up the wriggling rubber legs through the seasons in their lateral line.

WHERE: WORLDWIDE IN RIVERS, LAKES AND EVEN SALTWATER

WHEN: ALL YEAR

WHAT: ALL SPECIES

HOW: AN ATTRACTOR PATTERN

HOOK: 6 TO 12 2X TO 4X SHANK
BODY: BLACK CHENILLE
TAIL AND LEGS: BLACK, WHITE OR RED RUBBER

Marabou Muddler

CLIPPED DEERHAIR HEADS create all manner of underwater turbulence and attraction for predators. If you add the wonderful mobility of marabou plumes with a bit of flash and colour you really do have the universal lure. Other than plankton feeders, weed eaters and tiny insect eaters, I really can't think of a single fish that won't at some time have a go at a Marabou Muddler. Fish it in the surface, deep and slow in stillwater, bumbled through the rocks in a river or worked in the surf. It works anywhere and can mean all things to all fish.

WHERE: WORLDWIDE

WHEN: ALL YEAR

WHAT: JUST ABOUT ANY SPECIES OF FISH

HOW: CAN SUGGEST A NUMBER OF AQUATIC INSECTS

HOOK: 6 TO 10 4X SHANK
TAIL: RED FEATHER FIBRES
BODY: SILVER, FLAT DIAMOND BRAID
WING: BLACK MARABOU TOPPED WITH PEACOCK HERL
HEAD AND COLLAR: DEERHAIR OPTIONS ARE YELLOW, BROWN, OLIVE, WHITE AND ORANGE

Shipman's Buzzer

IT'S AN ACCOLADE TO HAVE YOUR NAME forever associated with a fly you invented and the UK's Dave Shipman scored big time with this one. When chironomids are hatching and trout are selectively feeding on the emergent stage this fly works wonders cast directly into the path of a cruising fish. It will also pull in fish when fished blind in a big wave and is primarily a stillwater pattern intended to be fished in the surface film. Use colour variants for different times of the year and species hatches. Competition fishers often use three on the same leader!

WHERE: WORLDWIDE ON STILLWATERS IN TEMPERATE REGIONS

WHEN: SPRING THROUGH TO LATE SUMMER

WHAT: TROUT

HOW: SUGGESTS THE EMERGENT STAGE OF CHIRONOMIDS

DRESSING: HOOK SIZE 14 TO 10 STANDARD SHANK
TAIL AND HEAD: TUFT WHITE POLYPROPYLENE YARN OR ANTRON
BODY: SPARSELY DUBBED SEALS FUR (USE A DUBBING SPINNER) AND RIBBED WITH A FEW TURNS OF FLAT PEARL TINSEL

Green Highlander

IS IT THE NAME OR IS IT THE REALLY PRETTY DRESSING that makes this fly so popular for summer Atlantic salmon? I don't know, but it is very effective when the water begins to warm up and the fish are more inclined to rise up for a fly. Invented on the River Spey in Scotland in 1880, like many other traditional salmon patterns this fly can be tied fully dressed, as a hair wing, or as a tube. There is a distinct style to classic salmon flies which is more to do with the aesthetics of fly tying that it is with fishing, but nevertheless these patterns are remarkably effective.

WHERE: SALMON RIVERS WORLDWIDE IN TEMPERATE REGIONS

WHEN: MIDSUMMER TO EARLY AUTUMN

WHAT: SALMON

HOW: GENERAL ATTRACTOR

HOOK: 10 TO 4 SALMON IRON OR DOUBLE SALMON IRON
TAG: OVAL GOLD TINSEL
TAIL: GOLDEN PHEASANT CREST
BUTT: BLACK OSTRICH OR FLOSS
BODY: HALF YELLOW FLOSS, HALF GREEN SEAL'S FUR
HACKLE: TIED FALSE MIXED YELLOW AND GREEN COCK FIBRES
WING: BASE GOLDEN PHEASANT TIPPET WITH MIX OF RED AND BLACK SQUIRREL OR BUCKTAIL OVER

Red Setter

WHERE: WORLDWIDE IN LAKES AND RIVERS IN TEMPERATE REGIONS

WHEN: BEST IN THE AUTUMN AS THE SPAWNING RUN HAPPENS

WHAT: TROUT, SALMON

HOW: SUGGESTS FISH EGGS

HOOK: 6 TO 10 2X SHANK
TAIL: FOX SQUIRREL TAIL FIBRES
BODY: HOT-ORANGE CHENILLE
HACKLE: LONG-FIBRED GINGER SADDLE (ONE AT THE CENTRE, ONE AT THE HEAD)

ORIGINALLY USED AS AN EGG IMITATION, this New Zealand pattern is recognized around the world as a very good general-purpose stillwater fly. Many countries see nothing wrong with fishing for salmonids on their spawning migrations, and at such times the fish really devour the eggs. In New Zealand, the best river fishing is when the trout migrate from the lakes, and the same thing happens in the USA. This is frowned on in the UK where strict close seasons protect spawning trout and salmon.

Zulu

HAVE YOU EVER NOTICED how so many of the old-fashioned flies that work so well for wild brown trout have a mix of red, black and silver in the dressing? That combination must really mean something to a trout, and the Zulu is a prime example – although of course it will also take a variety of fish. It is best when fished in water where food is scarce and the fish must be opportunist feeders. Tied slim, it's a great point fly on a wet fly cast, while tied bushy it makes a wonderful top dropper, especially on rough and overcast days with a good wind.

WHERE: WORLDWIDE IN STILLWATER AND FREESTONE STREAMS

WHEN: ALL THROUGH THE SEASON BUT OFTEN BEST IN INCLEMENT WEATHER

WHAT: TROUT, GRAYLING, SEA TROUT

HOW: A GENERAL-PURPOSE ATTRACTOR PATTERN

HOOK: 8 TO 14 STANDARD SHANK
TAIL: RED WOOL
BODY: BLACK FLOSS OR WOOL RIBBED WITH OVAL SILVER TINSEL
HACKLE: BLACK HEN OR COCK AND SOMETIMES PALMERED

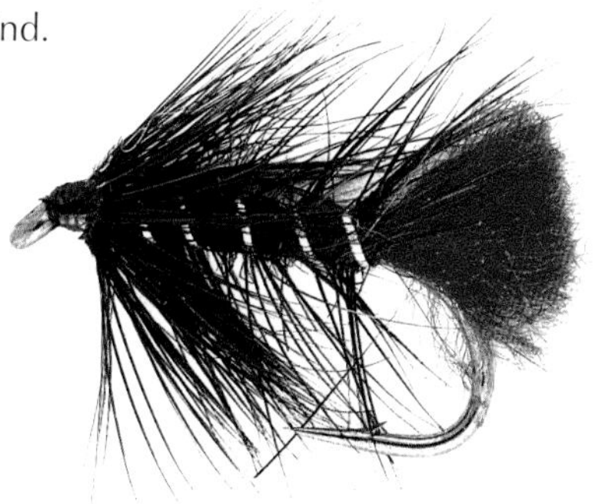

Dredger

WHERE: RIVERS IN TEMPERATE AND SUBARCTIC REGIONS

WHEN: UNDER EXTREME WEATHER CONDITIONS

WHAT: MIGRATORY SALMONIDS

HOOK: 4 TO 6 4X SHANK. FISH THIS FLY HOOK POINT UP.
TAIL: FLUORESCENT ORANGE AND BLACK MARABOU WITH ORANGE, BLACK AND PEARL CRYSTAL FLASH
BODY: FLUORESCENT ORANGE GLO-BRITE FLOSS WITH PALMERED BLACK SADDLE HACKLE RIBBED WITH GOLD WIRE
HEAD: BLACK DUMBBELL EYES PAINTED WHITE, FLUORESCENT ORANGE AND BLACK. FLUORESCENT GREEN AND PURPLE ARE ALTERNATIVES

THERE WILL ALWAYS BE TIMES when fishing for migratory salmonids when the water conditions will make things difficult. For example, you may experience extreme cold, very heavy flows or high turbidity. You could just go home and wait until things improve or develop techniques which while they may only earn a single fish, can be worth ten taken under ideal conditions. The Dredger works best when fished hard on the bottom.

Cinnamon Sedge

AN INVALUABLE STANDARD SEDGE (caddis) pattern that represents many pale-coloured sedge as well as the important cinnamon sedge. Hatching in mid-summer, this lovely insect will often crawl onto your body and I can't believe there is a single fly fisher who will not pause to admire it. This pattern can be used with confidence wherever caddis occur, particularly as dusk settles. Many anglers head for home too early in summer and miss the magical last hour when a seemingly empty river comes to life.

WHERE: WORLDWIDE IN RIVERS AND STILLWATER IN TEMPERATE REGIONS AND SUBARCTIC

WHEN: MID-SUMMER

WHAT: TROUT, GRAYLING, SMALLMOUTH BASS

HOW: A SPECIFIC AND ALL-PURPOSE SEDGE (CADDIS) IMITATION

HOOK: 12 TO 10 2X STANDARD SHANK
BODY: CINNAMON TURKEY HERL
WING: CINNAMON HEN OR TURKEY
HACKLE: LIGHT GINGER COCK

Henryville Special

THIS IS ONE OF A GREAT MANY SIMILAR-LOOKING CADDIS (SEDGE) PATTERNS although this one, by Hiram Brobst, is the standard to judge others by. It's a beautiful fly to tie, and serves to match the hatch for many caddis adults. It floats high, matches the profile of the natural insect, has a good colour and can be skittered without sinking. Although there are many thousands of caddis species worldwide, you will find that unless your fish are super-fussy, this fly will get you by almost anywhere.

WHERE: WORLDWIDE IN RIVERS AND STILLWATER IN TEMPERATE REGIONS

WHEN: SUMMER TO AUTUMN

WHAT: TROUT, GRAYLING, SMALLMOUTH BASS, BLUEGILL

HOW: SUGGESTS AN ADULT CADDIS (SEDGE) FLY

HOOK: 10 TO 18 STANDARD SHANK OR 2X SHANK
BODY: OLIVE FUR (RABBIT OR SIMILAR) WITH PALMERED GRIZZLE COCK
WING: A FEW FIBRES OF LEMON WOOD DUCK AND THEN GREY MALLARD OVER-TIED ROOF STYLE
HACKLE: LIGHT RED GAME COCK WOUND FULL

Gold Bead Mayfly

I STILL CAN'T DECIDE WHETHER THE GOLD BEAD actually attracts or just adds weight – maybe it's a bit of both – but when you need to fish deep in a stream this all-purpose mayfly nymph will catch extremely well. Trout love this fly, and you can really trick them if you use the rod tip to lift the fly up in the current in front of a stationery fish. Upstream nymph fishing is a real art, and when used in conjunction with a sight indicator it reveals how often a fly is taken by a fish that you know nothing about.

WHERE: WORLDWIDE IN STREAMS AND STILLWATER IN TEMPERATE REGIONS

WHEN: ALL YEAR

WHAT: TROUT, GRAYLING, CUTTHROAT, SMALLMOUTH BASS

HOW: MAYFLY NYMPH IMITATION

HOOK: 12 TO 16 STANDARD SHANK
TAIL: LEMON WOOD DUCK FIBRES
BODY: BROWN ANTRON RIBBED WITH FINE COPPER WIRE
THORAX: GOLD BEAD WITH PHEASANT TAIL FIBRES OVER
HACKLE: A FEW FIBRES OF GREY PARTRIDGE ON EITHER SIDE OF THE BEAD

Jassid

THIS GOOD BEETLE IMITATION has a number of variants worldwide, of which a significantly important one for the central Tasmanian lakes has a bright red polypropylene body. However, the original works very well for many beetle species worldwide, and anyone fishing high-altitude lakes or tundra regions would be well advised to have a stock of such patterns to hand. I particularly like the Jassid because it uses the unique feather from the Jungle Cock, which I breed.

WHERE: WORLDWIDE IN LAKES AND SOME RIVERS IN TEMPERATE ZONES ESPECIALLY IN HIGH COUNTRY

WHEN: USUALLY MID-SUMMER IN THE MID-AFTERNOON

WHAT: TROUT

HOW: SUGGESTS SEVERAL BEETLE SPECIES

HOOK: 16 TO 22 STANDARD SHANK FINE WIRE
BODY: BLACK TYING THREAD (OR BRIGHT RED POLYPROPYLENE)
HACKLE: PALMERED GINGER COCK THEN CLIPPED TOP AND BOTTOM
WING: TIED FLAT, A SINGLE JUNGLE COCK EYE FEATHER

Platinum Blonde

JOE BROOKS IS A LEGEND AMONG FLY FISHERS as he both explored new venues and developed new techniques and flies. The blonde series of patterns are simple but deadly and you can't ask for more than that from any fly pattern. Originally tied with bucktail (as this one is) they translate well to modern fibres such as polar bear hair. Fish these in saltwater for most predators. They are very good for striped bass, blue fish, redfish, sea trout and various jack (trevally), and are great fun to fish around docks and structures.

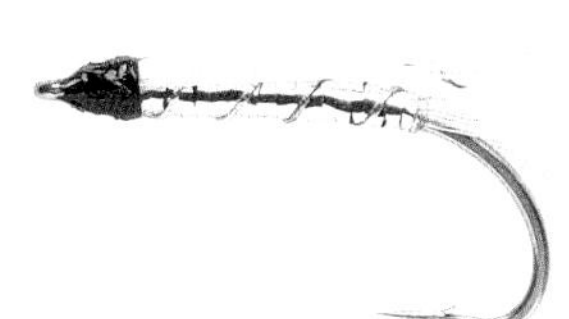

WHERE: WORLDWIDE IN SALTWATER, ALTHOUGH TYPICALLY IN WARMER WATER VENUES

WHEN: ALL YEAR DEPENDING ON THE SPECIES PRESENT

WHAT: ALMOST ALL SALTWATER PREDATORS AND GOOD TOO FOR PACIFIC SALMON SPECIES

HOW: SUGGESTS BAIT FISH

HOOK: 2 TO 3/0 STAINLESS O'SHAUGHNESSY
TAIL: WHITE BUCKTAIL
BODY: FLAT SILVER TINSEL WITH AN OVAL SILVER RIB
WING: WHITE BUCKTAIL

Claret Bumble

THE BUMBLE SERIES WERE INVENTED FOR IRELAND'S LOUGHS by Kingsmill Moore and have more than proved their worth as a lake fly fished either on the point as a general wet fly, or on the top dropper position as a bob fly. Later in the year they take sea trout very well in the great Irish lough. Interestingly, they have been found to work very well for sea trout in the Falklands rivers and now also in Tierra del Fuego. Claret has always been a great colour for brown trout and these Southern hemisphere browns all came from original UK stock which adapted to a new environment and it is no surprise that they too have a liking for claret. Don't fish with light leaders as takes to Bumbles are very positive.

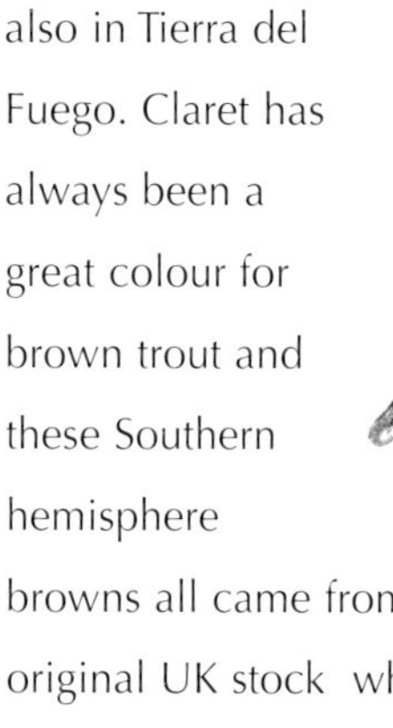

WHERE: LARGER STILLWATERS AND SOME RIVER SITUATIONS IN TEMPERATE REGIONS

WHEN: SPRING THROUGH TO FALL

WHAT: PRIMARILY BROWN TROUT AND SEA TROUT

HOW: MAYBE IT SUGGESTS A LARGE STRUGGLING INSECT

HOOK: 8 TO 12 STANDARD SHANK
TAIL: GOLDEN PHEASANT TIPPETS
BODY: VARYING SHADES OF CLARET SEALS FUR PALMERED THROUGH WITH A BLACK AND A CLARET COCK HACKLE THEN WITH FINE GOLD WIRE
HACKLE: STRIPPED BLUE JAY

Peacock Nymph

THIS PATTERN USES PEACOCK PLUMAGE but is unusual as it uses the blue part of the peacock eye. As a consequence you won't get many tied from each feather. Getting the proportions right is absolutely vital with this pattern. Its a marvellous little ephemerid imitation for both rivers and stillwaters. This pattern originated in a fly shop that used to be close to London's Heathrow. The tying is a study in neatness and there is no doubting the effectiveness of the blue sheen. It excels on hard-fished waters. Tie some if you fish limestone or freestone streams and they will serve you well.

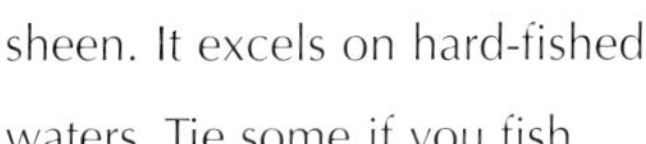

WHERE: RIVERS AND STILLWATERS IN TEMPERATE REGIONS

WHEN: YEAR ROUND BUT BEST SPRING TO FALL

WHAT: TROUT, GRAYLING

HOW: EPHEMERID NYMPH IMITATION WITH COLOUR APPEAL

HOOK: 16 TO 12 STANDARD SHANK
TAIL: COCK PHEASANT CENTRE TAIL FIBRES
BODY: QUILL FROM BLUE CENTRE OF PEACOCK EYE
THORAX: PHEASANT TAIL FIBRES OVER THE REST OF THE BLUE QUILL

Sar-Mul-Mac Mullet

THE BRAINCHILD OF DON BANTON, this fly will cater for most prey fish situations in saltwater, and being suitably large, will be acceptable to many species with big mouths. I don't know how any bait fish ever manage to reach maturity as you only have to hang around a harbour or bridges to see the carnage that goes on. Use this one for tarpon around the bridges and rips in the Florida Keys, but hang on to your rod as the take can be awesome.

WHERE: WORLDWIDE IN SALTWATER

WHEN: ALL YEAR

WHAT: MOST PREDATORS, ESPECIALLY TARPON, BARRAMUNDI

HOW: AN EXCELLENT BAIT FISH PATTERN

HOOK: 3/0 STAINLESS O'SHAUGHNESSY
TAIL: WHITE BUCKTAIL
WING: SIX WHITE SADDLE HACKLES, WHITE BUCKTAIL, SILVER FLASHABOU, GREY MARABOU AND TWO GRIZZLE HACKLES
CHEEKS: TEAL FLANK
HEAD: RED AND WHITE CHENILLE WITH GREY OVER AND LARGE AMBER BEAD EYES

Reef Demon

ALSO KNOWN AS WHOLLY MACKEREL, this is a fabulous creation from Tom Kintz. Although difficult to cast with a 12-weight, I used it successfully at night for tarpon around the pillars of Florida's Seven Mile Bridge. Intended for larger, almost oceanic species, this is a marvellous fly for dolphin fish, trevally and other big saltwater predators. It seems a shame to use such a lovely fly that will get torn to bits!

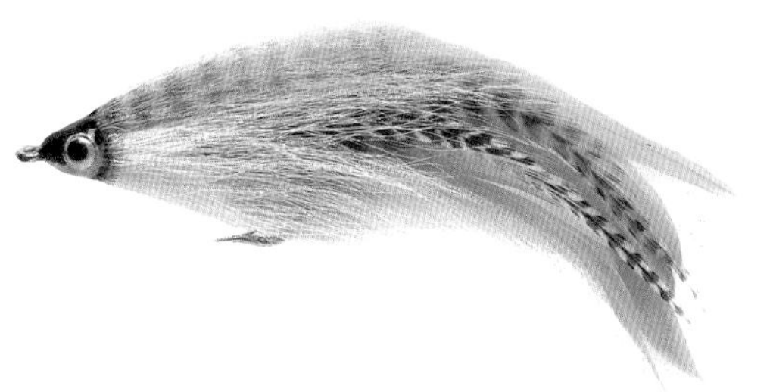

WHERE: WORLDWIDE IN SALTWATER, BUT BEST IN WARMER WATERS

WHEN: ALL YEAR

WHAT: THE LARGER PREDATORS SUCH AS TREVALLY, TARPON, DOLPHIN FISH

HOW: EXCELLENT IMITATION OF MACKEREL

HOOK: 4/0 O'SHAUGHNESSY
TAIL: HACKLES IN PAIRS OF CHARTREUSE, BLUE, GRIZZLE AND PEARL FLASHABOU
BODY: PEARL MYLAR BRAID
COLLAR: WHITE BUCKTAIL AND PEARL FLASHABOU
TOPPING: CHARTREUSE BUCKTAIL WITH PANTONE MARKINGS
HEAD: EPOXY WITH BLACK SILVER EYES

Activator

BEADS ARE USED IN FLY DRESSING for many purposes, but to my knowledge it was Barry Salter who first got the idea of using a variety of coloured beads simply superglued onto a curved hook. He originated many combinations that work for trout in rivers and stillwaters, and to prove that all fish will take them, he has even float fished them for coarse fish like carp (I witnessed him take seven fish species, including Chinook Salmon, from an Alaskan river). Use this fly for trout in the springtime with a very slow retrieve about 2 metres (6 ft) down in lakes – the takes are very positive.

WHERE: WORLDWIDE IN RIVERS AND STILLWATER

WHEN: ANY TIME OF YEAR BUT CERTAIN COLOUR COMBINATIONS WORK BETTER AT PARTICULAR TIMES

WHAT: BEST FOR TROUT BUT WILL WORK FOR VIRTUALLY ANY FRESHWATER SPECIES

HOW: MIGHT BE TAKEN FOR CADDIS (SEDGE) GRUB OR CHIRONOMID PUPA, OR MAYBE IT JUST LOOKS EDIBLE

HOOK: 8 TO 12 CURVED SHANK SEDGE HOOK
BODY: COLOURED GLASS BEADS SUPERGLUED ONTO HOOK IN DIFFERENT COLOUR COMBINATIONS

Showgirl

A TRUE ALASKAN PATTERN devised to attract the aggressive Pacific salmon as it enters freshwater. Chinook, coho and chum are the target species and can be very feisty in their first couple of days in a river. It's as though they know what is to come and are already excited, so when something pink and fluffy swims by they just have to grab it. Fished on very fast-sinking tip lines close to the bottom, the dead drift is best, although coho do like the fly high in the water with a fast strip.

WHERE: RIVERS IN ALASKA, BRITISH COLUMBIA AND THE GREAT LAKES

WHEN: JUNE TO OCTOBER

WHAT: CHINOOK, CHUM, COHO

HOW: AN ATTRACTOR PATTERN

HOOK: 2 OR 1/0 SALMON IRON
WING: HOT-PINK MARABOU PLUMES WITH PURPLE SCHLAPPEN FEATHERS AND FIBRES OF PURPLE AND PEARL CRYSTALFLASH AND FLASHABOU

Partridge and Orange

PERHAPS SUGGESTING THE NYMPH OF A STONEFLY that has been washed from its home, this classic fly for freestone streams is best when fished on a two- or three-fly cast, tied sparse and worked downstream and across. The tasty orange body and straggling insect-type legs make it a much-loved pattern for wet fly fishers, but it also has its uses when tied short on larger hooks for stillwater rainbow trout. The legendary Richard Walker took a one-time UK rainbow trout record of over 8 kg (18 lb 4 oz) on a Partridge and Orange fly.

WHERE: WORLDWIDE IN FREESTONE STREAMS

WHEN: ALL YEAR

WHAT: TROUT, GRAYLING

HOW: GENERAL-PURPOSE WET FLY, WHICH PERHAPS SUGGESTS A STONEFLY NYMPH

HOOK: 10 TO 16 STANDARD SHANK
BODY: ORANGE FLOSS OR SILK TIED THIN
HACKLE: SINGLE TURN OF BROWN PARTRIDGE

Blood Donor

I AM INCLUDING IN THIS BOOK several flies that are imitations of the bloodworm (chironomid larvae) because they are so important for stillwater fly fishers. I devised this one in 1999. It is very good fished 'on the drop' when any subsequent twitch of the line will make one end of the fly move. This is just what a trout expects to see of a free-swimming bloodworm and takes are very positive. Try it cast upstream among weed tresses on limestone rivers and allow it to drift back.

WHERE: WORLDWIDE IN STILLWATER AND IN MANY RIVER LOCATIONS

WHEN: ALL YEAR

WHAT: PRINCIPALLY TROUT BUT ALL FRESHWATER SPECIES EAT THIS FLY

HOW: IMITATES THE LARVAL STAGE OF THE CHIRONOMID

HOOK: 10 OR 12 STANDARD SHANK OR CURVED BUZZER HOOK
BODY: A RED PLASTIC BEAD WITH TWISTED RED FLEXI FLOSS ABOUT 1.25 CM (¾ INCH) LONG THREADED THROUGH EACH SIDE AND SUPERGLUED INTO POSITION

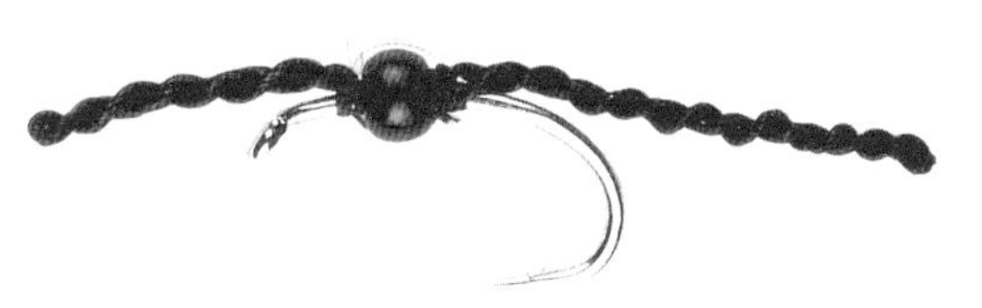

Clouser Minnow

I WONDER IF BOB CLOUSER ever dreamed that his pattern would become so successful for predatory fish in salt- and freshwater. The style of tying provides good movement and action with a pronounced eye effect. The heavy eyes keep it fishing with the hook pointing upwards so that you can cast into snaggy areas with little risk of fouling. Chartreuse and white is a favourite colour combination. The list of species taken on this one fly is now well over 100. A truly great fly and an absolute must for a saltwater fly box.

WHERE: WORLDWIDE IN FRESH- AND SALTWATER

WHEN: ALL YEAR

WHAT: OVER 100 SPECIES OF FISH

HOW: THE UNIVERSAL ATTRACTOR FOR PREDATORS

HOOK: 3/0 TO 6 O'SHAUGHNESSY. FISH THIS FLY HOOK POINT UP
WINGS: CHARTREUSE FISH HAIR WITH PEARL CRYSTALFLASH
EYES: LEAD PAINTED RED WITH BLACK PUPIL
THROAT: WHITE FISH HAIR

Alder Larva

IN EARLY SPRING you will sometimes see what appears to be a large, dark caddis (sedge) fly with heavily veined wings crawling around on bank-side vegetation. No sedge fly this but an alder fly, which although living as a nymph in the water, will crawl to the margins to hatch, returning to the water to lay its eggs. Trout rarely take the adult but avidly feed on the larva. You can successfully offer this fly in the margins of a stillwater bed yet to be choked with weed growth. Takes can be very exciting indeed.

WHERE: STILLWATER IN THE UK AND EUROPE

WHEN: SPRING

WHAT: TROUT

HOW: SUGGESTS THE LARVA OF THE ALDER FLY

HOOK: 8 OR 10 2X SHANK
TAIL: TWO COCK BADGER HACKLE POINTS
BODY: CLARET SEAL'S FUR RIBBED WITH OVAL GOLD TINSEL
THORAX: OFF-WHITE WOOL
HACKLE: BROWN PARTRIDGE

Black and Peacock Spider

THIS SIMPLE FLY really does look like an edible, juicy bug with its fat, glistening body and straggly hackles! It's a very popular pattern to begin with when learning fly tying because it requires only the basic techniques and makes a deadly pattern very quickly.

WHERE: WORLDWIDE IN STILLWATER OR RIVERS

WHEN: ANY TIME OF THE YEAR

WHAT: TROUT, GRAYLING, SEA TROUT

HOW: MAYBE SUGGESTS A BEETLE OR SNAIL (LOOKS LIKE SOME KIND OF BUG)

HOOK: 8 TO 16 STANDARD SHANK
BODY: PEACOCK HERL TIED FAT
HACKLE: BLACK HEN

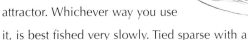

Use it wherever trout occur in either stillwater or a stream. Fish near the surface to suggest a beetle; deep down to look like a snail, or just use as an all-round attractor. Whichever way you use it, is best fished very slowly. Tied sparse with a long-fibred hen hackle it is a great fly around weed beds in high summer in stillwater.

Filoplume Leech

THERE ARE LOTS OF FLY PATTERNS where you can never be sure just what a fish thinks the fly might be when it takes it, but I am pretty certain that this one is taken for a dragonfly larva. It is certainly ugly enough and that's what it takes to imitate one of these squat brutes. In Australia, they are called mudeyes and are very important on stillwater fisheries in that vast country. I shall never forget fishing Lake Eucumbene in New South Wales, Australia, when my friend Richard Tilzey suggested fishing with mudeyes and I had no idea what they were. I bought a dozen only to realize they were dragonfly larvae. More recognition of this fly form is needed elsewhere in the world because the trout loves it.

WHERE: WORLDWIDE IN STILLWATER IN TEMPERATE REGIONS

WHEN: ALL YEAR BUT BEST IN WARMER MONTHS

WHAT: TROUT, SMALLMOUTH AND LARGEMOUTH BASS, BLUEGILL, CARP

HOW: IMPRESSION OF A DRAGONFLY LARVA

HOOK: 4 TO 10 4X SHANK
TAIL: BROWN MARABOU FROM COCK PHEASANT
BODY: BROWN FILOPLUME FEATHERS FROM COCK PHEASANT

Russian River Coho

AN EXCEEDINGLY POPULAR FLY FOR FISHING in Alaska when the unfortunate sockeye salmon run in their thousands. Probably the best meat of all the salmon species, there is no harm in cropping their immense runs, but don't kid yourself that they actually 'take' the fly. Of course the occasional one does, but in the main it is an effective system for simply hooking the fish in the mouth, which this 'fly' makes acceptable. It is a different story when the coho make their runs as they are an aggressive fish and will eagerly grab this fly.

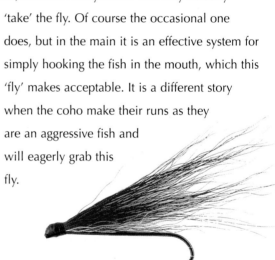

WHERE: ALASKA AND BRITISH COLUMBIA

WHEN: JULY AND AUGUST

WHAT: SOCKEYE AND COHO SALMON (RED AND SILVER)

HOW: FOR SOCKEYE IT'S A HOOKING SYSTEM; FOR COHO AN ATTRACTOR

HOOK: 2 6X LONG SHANK
WING: RED OVER WHITE BUCKTAIL AND MANY OTHER COLOUR COMBINATIONS

Apte Too Plus

THE BRAINCHILD OF STU APTE, this is a fly with colour and movement designed for fishing in and around mangroves, estuaries, rock, coral and weed. It is fitted with Mason hard nylon loop to keep the tail from tangling around the hook bend. This pattern, in many colour variations, is a lovely one to fish on 9 to 10-weight rods for smaller tarpon and all other inshore fishes that feed on bait fish. The faster you retrieve, the more the rabbit strip tail will wiggle and the more it drives a predator to strike. Remember to make your fly behave like a terrified bait fish.

WHERE: SALTWATER IN TROPICAL AND SEMI-TROPICAL AREAS

WHEN: ALL YEAR

WHAT: TARPON, REDFISH, SNOOK AND BARRAMUNDI AMONG MANY OTHERS

HOW: GENERAL-PURPOSE BAIT FISH

HOOK: 1/0 STAINLESS O'SHAUGHNESSY
TAIL: PALE YELLOW RABBIT STRIP AND PEARL CRYSTALFLASH
BODY: TYING THREAD
COLLAR: GREY FOX SQUIRREL TAIL
HEAD: EPOXY RESIN WITH PAINTED BLACK AND YELLOW EYE

Brown Bomber

THE FABULOUS RIVERS OF THE KOLA PENINSULA and their immense runs of Atlantic salmon have shown just how good the fishing must have been in Scotland at the beginning of the twentieth century. The Brown Bomber is one of the new breed of surface active flies which really works in these rivers. This pattern evolved from steelhead fishing in the USA and no tier is better than Canada's Warren Duncan at spinning and clipping the deer hair to a perfect profile, and at high speed. Bombers are best when the water has warmed to early summer temperatures and when used over reasonably fresh fish in water up to four feet deep.

WHERE: CANADA, ICELAND, KOLA PENINSULA, USA, SCOTLAND, TIERRA DEL FUEGO

WHEN: LATE SPRING TO HIGH SUMMER

WHAT: ATLANTIC SALMON, STEELHEAD, SEA TROUT

HOW: SURFACE ACTIVE ATTRACTOR

HOOK: SIZE 1/0–4
TAIL: BROWN CALF TAIL
BODY: TIGHTLY SPUN AND CLIPPED DEER HAIR
HACKLE: PALMERED, LONG-FIBRED BROWN COCK
WING: BROWN CALF TAIL TIED FORWARD

Black Midge

JUST AS A BLACK GNAT (see page 242) will solve many problems for you, so will this even smaller tying which works on fish that are taking only tiny nibbles of food. We frequently fall into the trap of using flies that imitate the larger members of various insect groups when in fact most of what a trout or grayling eats is very small indeed. Check the stomach contents of a fish and you will be amazed at how many little bugs are in there. Of course, your tackle must balance the little flies.

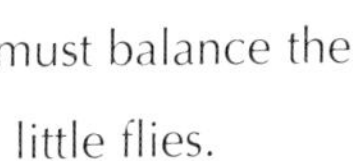

WHERE: WORLDWIDE IN RIVERS AND STILLWATER

WHEN: ALL YEAR

WHAT: TROUT, GRAYLING, CUTTHROAT

HOW: COPIES MANY SMALL DARK INSECTS

HOOK: 20 TO 26 STANDARD SHANK FINE WIRE
TAIL: BLACK COCK HACKLE FIBRES
BODY: BLACK POLYPROPYLENE DUBBING
HACKLE: BLACK COCK

Harewater Pup

THE LEGENDARY AMERICAN ANGLER DAVE WHITLOCK evolved this family of ugly bugs which, in a range of colours, will serve very well for many predatory fish situations. Initially designed for largemouth bass, they are now firm favourites for pike, dorado, peacock bass and taimen. The tough rabbit and deerhair combination makes a durable fly with great movement and creates underwater disturbance for predators to home in on. You can also use dyed material if you are allergic to the natural rabbit and deerhair. Tie in weedguards with 9 kg (20lb) hard nylon Mason.

WHERE: LAKES AND RIVERS IN TEMPERATE AND SUB-TROPICAL REGIONS

WHEN: ALL YEAR BUT BEST IN WARMER MONTHS

WHAT: LARGEMOUTH AND PEACOCK BASS, PIKE, DORADO

HOW: GENERAL ATTRACTOR

HOOK: 4 TO 3/0 SALMON IRON
TAIL AND BACK: BLACK RABBIT TIED DOWN MATUKA-STYLE WITH COPPER WIRE
BODY: BLACK RABBIT
COLLAR: BLACK DEERHAIR
THROAT: RED CRYSTALFLASH
HEAD: BLACK DEERHAIR WITH RED AND BLACK EYES

Adult Demoiselle

IN HIGH SUMMER when weed beds project from the water surface you will often see clouds of blue damsels hovering just over the water or perched on the weed tips. This all too tempting mouthful can really excite both trout and bass such that they will leap clear of the water to try and knock the fly down. Hopefully the fish then has an easy meal from the stunned fly trapped in the surface tension. Tricky to copy but this fly will often catch the odd fish for you on an otherwise almost impossible day. Resist the temptation to strike if a fish leaps at your fly, wait until you see the leader move.

WHERE: STILLWATERS AND SLOWER RIVERS IN TEMPERATE REGIONS

WHEN: HIGH SUMMER

WHAT: TROUT, SMALL AND LARGEMOUTH BASS, BLUEGILLS

HOW: MIMICS THE ADULT DEMOISELLE WHICH ONLY BRIEFLY ALIGHTS ON THE SURFACE AND IS AN OCCASIONAL TARGET FOOD ITEM

HOOK: SIZE 12 OR 10 STANDARD SHANK LIGHT WIRE
TAIL, BODY AND THORAX: BLUE DYED DEERHAIR
HACKLE: POST OF WHITE ANTRON WITH WHITE COCK HACKLE WOUND PARACHUTE

Collie Dog

SALMON WILL OFTEN NIP AT A FLY WITHOUT TAKING hold of it properly, and using a long tail is just asking for trouble. So why this pattern, which is nothing but a tail, is so amazingly effective is a mystery.

WHERE: SALMON AND SEA TROUT RIVERS IN TEMPERATE REGIONS

WHEN: ALL YEAR

WHAT: ATLANTIC SALMON, SEA TROUT, STEELHEAD

HOW: IT HAS TO BE DOWN TO THE WIGGLE, WHICH EXCITES THE FISH

TUBE: PLASTIC OR ALUMINIUM FROM 2.5–5 CM (1–2 INCHES)
WINGS: BLACK GOAT OR MONKEY HAIR, VERY LONG AND MAYBE A COUPLE OF STRANDS OF PEARL CRYSTAL HAIR

The wriggling long hair really gets salmon going, and fished across a pool or worked through slow water, a Collie Dog will excite a salmon like no other fly. It can also be skated across the tail of a pool for sea trout and I am sure would work well for summer steelhead.

Real Daddy

FLY FISHERS WILL INSTANTLY RECOGNIZE THIS PATTERN as an imitation of the daddy-long-legs or crane-fly. Trout in particular love this close copy of the natural insect and seem to take it well out of season. This fly, using ethafoam for the body, is a wonderful floater and is particularly deadly on stillwater for the larger, grown-on fish. One of my favourite flies.

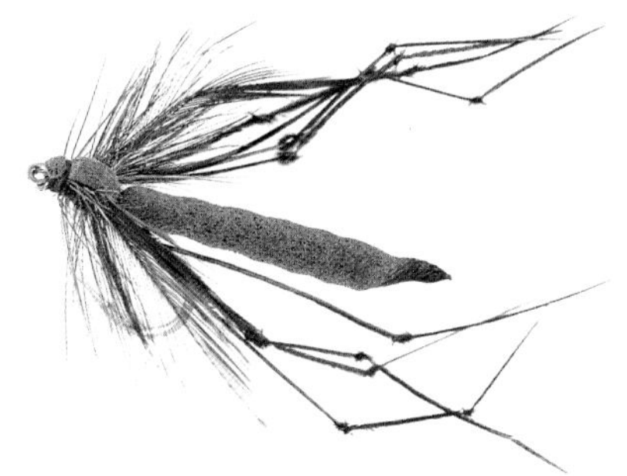

WHERE: WORLDWIDE (INSECTS LIKE THIS OCCUR JUST ABOUT EVERYWHERE)

WHEN: LATE SUMMER FOR THE BEST HATCHES

WHAT: TROUT, SEA TROUT, CARP, SMALLMOUTH AND LARGEMOUTH BASS

HOW: EXACT IMITATION OF AN ADULT DADDY-LONG-LEGS (CRANE-FLY)

HOOK: 10 TO 12 STANDARD SHANK
BODY: SHAPED ETHAFOAM TIED ON IN EXTENDED BODY STYLE
WINGS: TIPS OF CREE COCK HACKLE TIED SPENT
LEGS: SIX TO EIGHT DOUBLE-KNOTTED COCK PHEASANT CENTRE TAIL FIBRES
HACKLE: RED GAME OR CREE COCK

Emergent Sparkle Pupa

WHERE: WORLDWIDE IN TEMPERATE AND SEMI-ARCTIC REGIONS IN RIVERS AND STILLWATER

WHEN: LATE SPRING TO AUTUMN

WHAT: TROUT, GRAYLING, CHAR, CUTTHROAT

HOW: IMITATES THE ACTUAL HATCHING STAGE OF THE CADDIS (SEDGE)

HOOK: 12 TO 18 STANDARD SHANK
TAIL: GREEN ANTRON YARN WITH A LITTLE CREAM
UNDERBODY: GREEN ANTRON AND CREAM FUR MIXED AND DUBBED
OVERBODY: GREEN ANTRON YARN
WING: DARK GREY DEERHAIR
HEAD: BROWN RABBIT DUBBED

MY FATHER BOUGHT ME 'THE CADDIS AND THE ANGLER' by Gary La Fontaine when it was first published, and that book taught me more about the caddis (sedge) family than I had gathered from all other sources. It was a sad loss to fly fishing when Gary passed away, but he left behind a great legacy of patterns. This is a real gem for river fishing and is invaluable for those times when trout choose to feed only on the actual hatching stage of the caddis. It is not easy to recognize when this is happening, but when you can't catch anything using an adult or a pupa imitation, this is the fly to reach for.

Egg-Sucking Sculpin

THIS LITTLE BEAUTY is credited to Kirk Fitzer of Vancouver in Washington, who has been my friend and Alaskan guide for the last 13 years. Kirk saw sculpins eating salmon eggs and came up with this pattern for the river rainbows that by late July have seen just about everything and have been caught a few times already. Rainbow trout love to chase and eat sculpin, and to find a sculpin with an egg is a particular delicacy. Fish this fly around cover and structure trying to bounce it along the bottom – a split shot about 60 cm (2 ft) away makes for better presentation.

WHERE: PRINCIPALLY ARCTIC AND SUB-ARCTIC RIVERS WHERE SALMON SPAWN

WHEN: JULY TO SEPTEMBER IS BEST

WHAT: RAINBOW TROUT, LARGE GRAYLING

HOW: SUGGESTS A SCULPIN (BULLHEAD) WITH AN EGG

HOOK: 4 TO 8 4X SHANK
TAIL: STRIP OF TAN RABBIT
BODY: CREAM OLIVE WOOL WITH RABBIT OVER AND TIED DOWN WITH SILVER OVAL
HEAD AND COLLAR: DEERHAIR
HEAD: GLO BUG YARN PEACHY KING

Adams

UNBELIEVABLY USEFUL ON ANY RIVER SYSTEM for trout, grayling or char – in fact just about any fish that feeds off the surface on mayflies or midges. A truly universal pattern which must suggest many different food items to a fish. Best cast upstream to achieve a dead drift and can stand repeated presentation unless a fish is spooked. Try going up or down by two sizes if you can't get a take. Many early summer fly fishers on limestone streams never use anything else. A wonderful pattern too on freestone waters where food is scarcer and the fish more opportunistic.

WHERE: WORLDWIDE IN STREAMS AND RIVERS

WHEN: ALL YEAR BUT BEST IN SPRING AND SUMMER

WHAT: TROUT, GRAYLING, CHAR, SMALLMOUTH BASS

HOW: SUGGESTS MANY SMALL EPHEMERIDS AND MIDGES

HOOK: 10 TO 18 STANDARD SHANK FINE WIRE
TAIL: MIX OF GRIZZLE AND RED GAME COCK HACKLE FIBRES
BODY: FINELY DUBBED MUSKRAT UNDERFUR
WING: GRIZZLE COCK HACKLE TIPS
HACKLE: MIXED GRIZZLE AND RED GAME COCK
MIXED RED GAME COCK AND GRIZZLE COCK

Dunkeld

IF IN SCOTLAND look into the River Tay from the town bridge in Dunkeld and try to visualize just how wonderful the fishing once was before the Atlantic salmon became so persecuted. There, too, you can think of this lovely fly which embodies such charm in its dressing that it is hard to believe fish could refuse it when it flits through the water on a bright and sparkly day. This is a much-loved fly for attracting wild brown trout, and yet is equally effective on both reared rainbow trout and many other species.

WHERE: IN NEARLY ALL FRESHWATER, STILLWATER AND RIVERS

WHEN: THROUGHOUT THE SEASON BUT BETTER IN WARM WATER ON BRIGHT DAYS

WHAT: BROWN, RAINBOW, CUTTHROAT AND SEA TROUT, SALMON, CHAR

HOW: ESSENTIALLY AN ATTRACTOR PATTERN ON STANDARD WET FLY STYLING

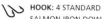

HOOK: 4 STANDARD SALMON IRON DOWN TO 16 STANDARD SHANK FOR TROUT
TAIL: GOLDEN PHEASANT CREST
BODY: FLAT GOLD TINSEL WITH GOLD WIRE RIB
WING: BRONZE MALLARD OR HAIRWING SUBSTITUTE ON LARGER HOOKS
HACKLE: HOT-ORANGE COCK TIED FALSE EITHER FULL OR PALMERED

Black Pennell

ALTHOUGH AN OLD-FASHIONED FLY, this remains as deadly as when it was first tied. Use it for any stillwater location in the early part of the season. It excels when fished during a hatch of black chironomids (buzzers). Very good in a dropper position, this simple fly has helped me win many competitions. Used in streams it is a great all-rounder and will also frequently tempt sea trout and salmon. You can add a bit of extra fizz in coloured water by putting a little Glo-brite orange floss in with the tail.

WHERE: WORLDWIDE IN STILLWATER OR FREESTONE STREAMS

WHEN: ESPECIALLY GOOD IN SPRING AS THE WATER WARMS UP

WHAT: TROUT, GRAYLING, SEA TROUT, SALMON

HOW:MOST LIKELY SUGGESTS A HATCHING CHIRONOMID

HOOK: 8 TO 16 STANDARD SHANK
TAIL: GOLDEN PHEASANT TIPPETS
BODY: BLACK FLOSS RIBBED WITH OVAL OR FINE FLAT SILVER TINSEL
HACKLE: BLACK HEN OR COCK TIED SPARSE BUT LONG

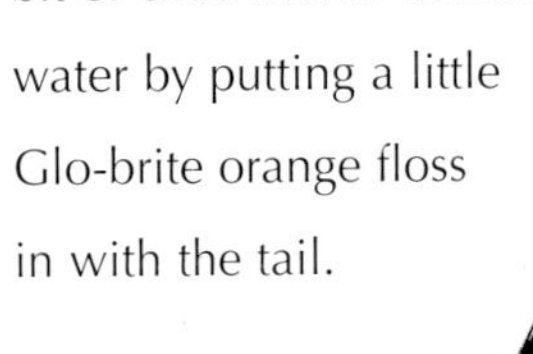

Glow Bead Black and Peacock Spider

YOU CAN MAKE ANY FLY into a glo version using either plastic beads or plastic strip which can be light-activated to glow with an eerie green phosphorescence. Glowing is a natural phenomenon, particularly in the oceans, and there is no doubt that fish are attracted to this light. I first used a fly like this for stillwater brown trout some 30 years ago in the very last stages of summer evenings and it also works for me on very difficult, mature fish on hard-fished waters. The little beads have now made things much easier than using plastic strips.

WHERE: WORLDWIDE IN RIVERS AND STILLWATER

WHEN: POOR LIGHT CONDITIONS

WHAT: TROUT BUT MANY OTHER SPECIES TOO

HOW: ADDS A NEW DIMENSION TO A BASIC PATTERN

HOOK: 8 STANDARD SHANK
BODY: PEACOCK HERL AND WOUND AS A FULL COLLAR LUMINOUS HEAD

Bonefish Special

THIS IS A FAVOURITE OF CHICO FERNANDEZ, who has produced many great saltwater patterns. An effective fly for bonefish in areas where they are heavily fished for. Although patterns are clearly important, the key factor with bonefish is to have a perfect presentation and unless you are fortunate enough to fish the flats frequently I suggest you practise your casting. It seems an expensive shame to use the first few days of a trip learning the techniques when practicing beforehand would help so much.

WHERE: SHALLOW TROPICAL SALTWATER

WHEN: ALL YEAR

WHAT: BONEFISH AND MANY OTHER SALTWATER SPECIES

HOW: COULD BE A CRAB OR A SHRIMP

HOOK: 4 TO 6 SALTWATER O'SHAUGHNESSY
TAIL: ORANGE MARABOU
BODY: FLAT GOLD TINSEL WITH CLEAR NYLON OVER WHITE BUCKTAIL WITH GRIZZLE HACKLE TIPS OVER

Mallard and Claret

CLARET RARELY FIGURES IN MODERN TYINGS yet is heavily represented in many 'traditional' wet flies. This is one of the very best of the traditional flies, and is a must for early season work on stillwater or rivers, especially if there is a chill in the air and a bit of colour in the water. The bronze mallard wing feather is a beautiful feather and tied in well it shows you have mastered the art of wet fly winging. Actually, the fly is better tied with a rolled wing for fishing, but looks better in the box when tied properly. I use this fly when the large, early black chironomid is hatching.

WHERE: RIVERS AND STILLWATER IN TEMPERATE AND SUBARCTIC REGIONS

WHEN: ALL YEAR BUT BEST EARLY IN THE SEASON

WHAT: TROUT

HOW: A GENERAL-PURPOSE WET FLY

HOOK: 8 TO 14 STANDARD SHANK
TAIL: GOLDEN PHEASANT TIPPETS
BODY: CLARET SEAL'S FUR RIBBED WITH OVAL GOLD TINSEL
HACKLE: CLARET HEN
WING: BRONZE MALLARD

Bubble Sedge

CADDIS (SEDGE FLY) IMITATIONS are so important for fly fishers that this one warrants inclusion for its sheer inventiveness, as well as being an extremely effective pattern too. The hatching stage of caddis larvae seems to make them particularly attractive and vulnerable to trout and that's why a good imitation will cover many situations.

WHERE: RIVERS AND LAKES IN TEMPERATE AND SUBARCTIC REGIONS

WHEN: SUMMER THROUGH EARLY FALL

WHAT: TROUT, GRAYLING, SMALLMOUTH BASS, BLUEGILL

HOW: SUGGESTS HATCHING CADDIS (SEDGE)

DRESSING: HOOK 14 TO 8 2X SHANK
BODY: OLIVE ANTRON
HACKLE: GINGER HEN
SHUCK TAN RAFFENE
HEAD: DUBBED ANTRON WOOL
FEELERS PARTRIDGE HACKLE FIBRES

Deschutes Caddis

A TYPICAL SILHOUETTE FOR MANY ADULT CADDIS (SEDGE) PATTERNS, this fly incorporates deerhair for additional floatation where the river flow is swifter and more riffled. The Deschutes River in Oregon has a surprisingly heavy flow, where less buoyant patterns are easily drowned. Rainbow trout on this river are famed as a specific strain known as 'redsides', and will rise well to dry caddis patterns. Many similar situations can be found throughout the world. I have even been told this pattern works well in Kashmir.

WHERE: WORLDWIDE IN RIVERS AND LAKES IN TEMPERATE REGIONS

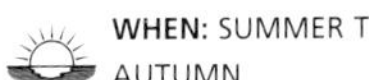

WHEN: SUMMER TO AUTUMN

WHAT: TROUT, GRAYLING, SMALLMOUTH BASS, BLUEGILL

HOW: SUGGESTS AN ADULT CADDIS (SEDGE) FLY

HOOK: 8 TO 12 STANDARD SHANK
TAIL: DEER BODY HAIR TIED VERY SHORT
BODY: YELLOW DYED RABBIT UNDERFUR
WING: DEER BODY HAIR
HACKLE: RED GAME COCK

Flashtail Whistler

INVENTED BY DAN BLANTON, the Whistler series of flies are undeniably effective for many inshore species and they really do whistle when being cast. The bead chain eyes not only give the eyed effect, but are a simple way of adding weight to the head to achieve a diving action. This colour combination is best for estuaries where the water is murky. Speculative casting around structure and mangroves from a drifting boat is an excellent way to search for fish, and this is a great cast-and-search fly.

WHERE: WORLDWIDE IN SALTWATER, BUT BEST IN WARMER AREAS

WHEN: ALL YEAR

WHAT: ALL INSHORE PREDATORS BUT ESPECIALLY BARRAMUNDI, REDFISH, SNOOK, SEA TROUT

HOW: A GENERAL-PURPOSE ATTRACTOR

HOOK: 1/0 TO 3/0 STAINLESS O'SHAUGHNESSY
TAIL: YELLOW BUCKTAIL WITH SILVER FLASHABOU PLUS MULTI-COLOUR CRYSTALFLASH AND TWO GRIZZLE COCK HACKLES
BODY: RED CHENILLE WITH LONG-FIBRED RED COCK HACKLE
EYES: BEAD CHAIN

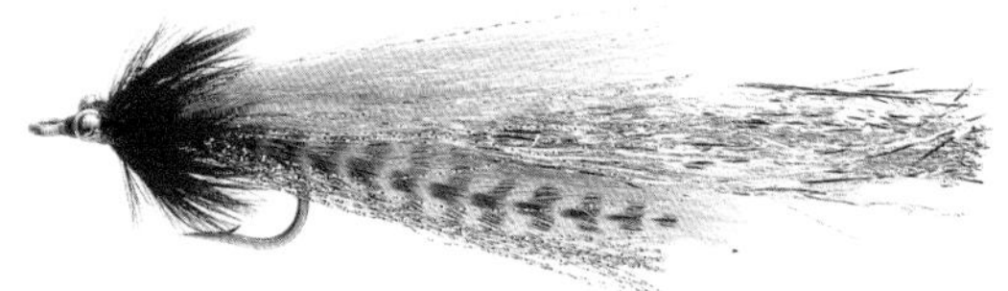

CDC Spinner Red Quill

WOULD ALFRED LUNN, whose definitive work is still the bible for chalkstream anglers, be pleased to see this modern version of his famous Lunn's Particular (see page 299)? I think he would, because he was a great observer of insect hatches and would have embraced the use of CDC feathers had they been in use in his day. One thing is certain, this pattern will have been cast onto his hallowed waters of the River Test at Houghton in southern England.

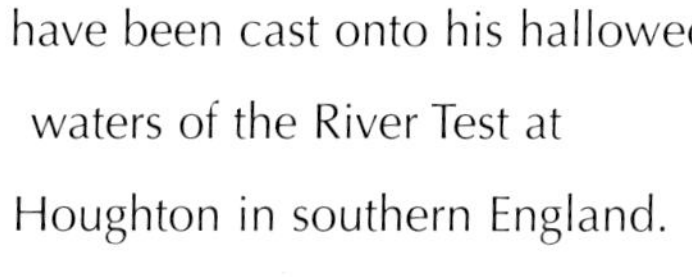

WHERE: LIMESTONE RIVERS IN TEMPERATE REGIONS

WHEN: SUMMER

WHAT: TROUT, GRAYLING, CUTTHROAT

HOW: IMITATES THE SPENT STAGE OF A SMALL MAYFLY

HOOK: 16 TO 18 STANDARD SHANK FINE WIRE
TAIL: DUN BETTS TAILING FIBRES
BODY: STRIPPED RED GAME COCK HACKLE
WINGS: NATURAL AND WHITE CDC TIED SPENT

Dog Nobbler

THIS ALL-PURPOSE LURE makes full use of the pulsating effect of marabou, the Woolly Worm body tying and the diving effect of the weighted head. It is deadly for newly stocked trout but works on all species anywhere. The style of retrieve and density of line used can vastly alter the action and appeal of this lure, and although there are endless colour variations and combinations, plain black and plain white take some beating. An excellent confidence booster for newcomers to fly fishing.

WHERE: WORLDWIDE IN LAKES, RIVERS AND SALTWATER

WHEN: ALL YEAR

WHAT: ALL SPECIES

HOW: THE ACTION, COLOUR AND MOVEMENT TRIGGERS THE RESPONSE

HOOK: 2 4X LONG SHANK THROUGH TO 10 STANDARD SHANK
TAIL: LARGE BUNCH OF MARABOU FIBRES
BODY: CHENILLE RIBBED WITH A PALMERED COCK HACKLE AND OVAL TINSEL
HEAD: A SPLIT SHOT GLUED ON THEN PAINTED WITH AN EYE EFFECT

All Purpose Medium

THERE ARE MANY FLIES which can truly serve a multitude of purposes but this one was designed from the outset to have broad band appeal without being specific. Trout which aren't too fussy can be fooled into thinking that this fly could be any one of a number of insects. Everybody hopes to be out on the water during a dream hatch but we often have to take what nature gives and this is a fly for just such days.

WHERE: TEMPERATE AND SUBARCTIC RIVERS AND STILLWATERS

WHEN: YEAR ROUND BUT BEST IN WARMER MONTHS

WHAT: TROUT, GRAYLING

HOW: ALL-PURPOSE NYMPH

HOOK: 8 TO 14 STANDARD SHANK
TAIL: PHEASANT TAIL FIBRES
BODY: DUBBED HARE'S EAR MIXED WITH SEAL'S FUR
THORAX: SAME AS BODY AND WITH PHEASANT TAIL FIBRE WING CASE
HACKLE: CLIPPED PARTRIDGE

Pearl Zonker

WHERE: WORLDWIDE IN ALL FRESH- AND SALTWATER RIVERS AND LAKES

WHEN: ALL YEAR

WHAT: ALL PREDATORY SPECIES OF FISH

HOW: USES THE MOBILITY OF RABBIT FUR TO CREATE THE ILLUSION OF LIFE AND FOOD

HOOK: 2 TO 10 AND 6X LONG SHANK AND STANDARD SHANK
BODY: PEARL MYLAR TUBE TIED IN AT THE BEND WITH RED THREAD
WING: STRIP OF RABBIT FUR CUT LENGTHWISE TIED IN AT THE BEND AND AT THE HEAD
HACKLE: RED ON ORANGE COCK HACKLE FIBRES

ZONKERS USE THE WONDERFUL mobility of rabbit fur to great effect as a means of inducing predatory fish to feed. The shimmying action of wet rabbit in a current or when retrieved in stillwater, has an almost magnetic effect on fish and they just can't help but investigate. If tied with a body other than mylar tubing, I lash the rabbit fur to the hook shank with a ribbing matuka-style for greater strength. This original fly makes a very good lure for bass, both largemouth and smallmouth, plus striped bass and European sea bass.

Ally's Shrimp

THIS ONE FLY PROBABLY ACCOUNTS for more salmon caught in Scotland than any other. This is principally because the salmon is fished by so many people, but also because this pattern really is effective. Quite why Atlantic salmon so willingly take an orange fly remains a puzzle. If they refuse the orange fly try a yellow or purple version.

WHERE: SALMON RIVERS WORLDWIDE IN TEMPERATE AND SUBARCTIC REGIONS

WHEN: ALL YEAR BUT USUALLY SPRING TO AUTUMN

WHAT: ATLANTIC SALMON, SEA TROUT, CHAR AND MOST PACIFIC SALMON SPECIES

HOW: SHRIMP IMITATION

HOOK: 4 TO 12 EITHER SINGLE, DOUBLE OR TREBLE SALMON
TAIL: BUNCH OF ORANGE BUCKTAIL AT LEAST AS LONG AS BODY
BODY: IN TWO SECTIONS – REAR IS RED FLOSS, FRONT IS BLACK FLOSS RIBBED WITH OVAL SILVER TINSEL
WING: NATURAL GREY SQUIRREL WITH OVERWING OF GOLDEN PHEASANT TIPPETS
HACKLE: BEARD OF GREY SQUIRREL THEN FULLY WOUND LONG, HOT ORANGE COCK

Fibre Caddis

FLY FISHING MAGAZINES often include letters asking why the trout they catch have lots of little stones or twigs in their bellies. The answer, and it's so obvious when you know, is that trout eat caddis (sedge) larvae complete with the stones and twigs used to make their homes. The stomach dissolves the food and leaves the building materials behind.

This pattern is a great way to imitate the natural caddis, just make sure you fish it on the bottom and very slowly. Vary the colour to match the species.

WHERE: FREESTONE STREAMS IN TEMPERATE AND SUBARCTIC REGIONS

WHEN: ALL YEAR

WHAT: TROUT, CHAR, GRAYLING, CUTTHROAT

HOW: IMITATES CADDIS (SEDGE) LARVAE

HOOK: 14 TO 6 2X SHANK
BODY: TWO OR THREE SOFT HACKLES PALMERED AND TRIMMED
THORAX: TOUCH OF HOT GREEN, ORANGE OR PALE YELLOW FLOSS
HACKLE: SHORT-FIBRED BROWN PARTRIDGE

Goldfish

I KNOW THIS ISN'T ANYTHING SPECIAL as a tying but almost all predators would eat a goldfish even if they saw one. This is probably because change triggers their aggressive tendencies. Where I live and manage a trout fishery, we have a pair of kingfishers nesting each year. One spring, I watched an adult return to the nest with a goldfish and chuckled at its audacity. Two nights later I saw the kingfisher raiding my goldfish pond. No wonder my pond stocks were diminishing!

WHERE: FRESH OR SALTWATER WORLDWIDE

WHEN: YEAR ROUND

WHAT: MOST PREDATORS

HOW: ATTRACTOR LURE

HOOK: 6 TO 2/0 STANDARD SHANK
TAIL: ORANGE AND PEARL CRYSTAL HAIR
BODY: ORANGE FRITZ WITH PALMERED WHITE COCK SADDLE HACKLE
WING: ORANGE MARABOU WITH ORANGE BUCKTAIL OVER
HEAD: ORANGE THREAD WITH EYE AND EPOXY

Max Canyon

THE FIRST TIME I VISITED PORTLAND, Oregon, USA, I met Doug Stewart, who invented this fly and used his creation to catch my first Deschutes steelhead. That was in 1986 and I'm so pleased that in latter years the mighty Deschutes River is making a comeback.

Doug created a superb fly here along classical steelhead tradition. Its subtle mix of colours provokes these ghostlike fish into making a positive strike. Good for sea-run brown trout, Atlantic salmon, char and many other salmonids.

WHERE: RIVERS OF THE PACIFIC NORTHWEST, ALASKA, KAMCHATKA, THE GREAT LAKES AND CHILE

WHEN: ALL YEAR DEPENDING ON THE RUN

WHAT: STEELHEAD

HOW: AN ALL-ROUND ATTRACTOR, BUT NOT GARISH

HOOK: 2 TO 8 SALMON IRON
TAG: FLAT SILVER TINSEL
TAIL: MIXED ORANGE AND WHITE COCK HACKLE FIBRES
BODY: REAR THIRD IS ORANGE WOOL, REST IS BLACK WOOL, ALL WITH OVAL GOLD RIB
HACKLE: BLACK HEN
WING: ORANGE CALF TAIL WITH WHITE CALF OR POLAR BEAR HAIR OVER
CHEEKS: JUNGLE COCK

Greenwell's Glory

NO BOOK ON FLY PATTERNS WOULD BE COMPLETE without this classic. A fantastic fly during any hatch of smaller upwing flies with an olive bias, it is a pattern that needs careful attention to detail to be tied well. A Greenwell cape is actually a light furnace. A badger cape dyed fiery brown is a good substitute for this subtle colour.

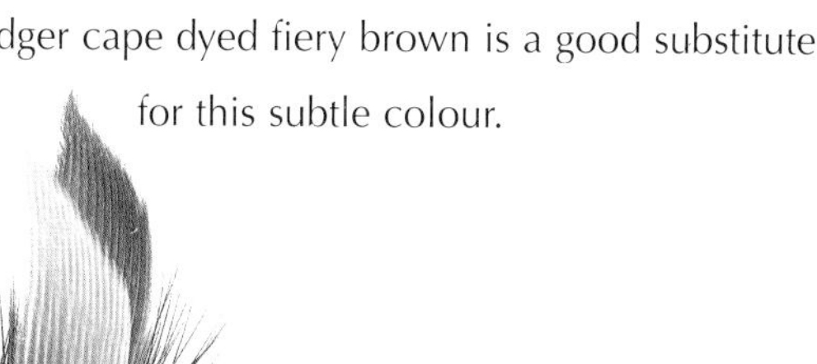

WHERE: RIVERS THROUGHOUT THE WORLD AND STILLWATER WHERE OLIVE EPHEMERIDS HATCH

WHEN: BEST IN SPRING AND SUMMER

WHAT: TROUT, GRAYLING

HOW: EXCELLENT IMITATION OF A WIDE VARIETY OF OLIVE EPHEMERIDS

HOOK: 12 TO 16 STANDARD SHANK LIGHT WIRE
TAIL (OPTIONAL): LIGHT FURNACE COCK HACKLE FIBRES
BODY: PRIMROSE TYING THREAD DARKENED WITH WAX AND THEN RIBBED WITH FINE GOLD WIRE
HACKLE: LIGHT FURNACE COCK
WINGS: ENGLISH BLACKBIRD BUT STARLING WITH OLIVE DYE IS FINE

Carp Biscuit

THIS FLY IS INTENDED TO SUGGEST A PIECE OF BAIT used as an inducement to get carp feeding on the surface. By far the best time is when the water warms. Cast the fly to individual fish or just leave it in the general area of feeding where you have thrown pieces of dog biscuit. Carp on fly gear are brilliant fun and a worthy quarry.

WHERE: WORLDWIDE IN TEMPERATE AND TROPICAL REGIONS

WHEN: SUMMER TO AUTUMN

WHAT: CARP

HOW: RESEMBLES A PIECE OF DOG BISCUIT

HOOK: 8X OR 10 2X SHANK
BODY: SPUN AND CLIPPED DEERHAIR IN VARIOUS SHADES OF BROWN

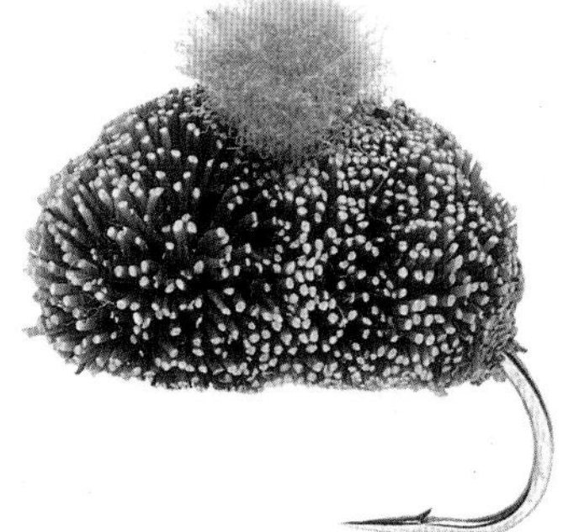

Night Fly

THIS SPECIAL FLY FOR STRIPED BASS is best used around structures with overhead light – such as piers, rocky headlands and harbours where predators can see their target against the lighter surface. Only in recent years has it also been found that tarpon will take a fly well at night around the bridges of Route 1 through the Florida Keys. Most predatory fish are very active at night – and this darker style of fly usually works much better than a bright one. Striped bass are a modern-day success story for fly fishers since conservation measures increased their numbers many fold.

WHERE: EASTERN SEABOARD OF THE USA AND SOME INLAND FRESHWATER SITES

WHEN: BEST IN SUMMER AND EARLY AUTUMN

WHAT: STRIPED BASS, AND OTHER PREDATORS

HOW: SUGGESTS A SMALL BAIT FISH

HOOK: 2/0 TO 4 SALTWATER O'SHAUGHNESSY
WING: YELLOW THEN GREEN BUCKTAIL WITH THREE PAIRS YELLOW DYED GRIZZLE SADDLES THEN OVERLAID WITH NATURAL BUCKTAIL AND LAYERS OF DARK GREEN BUCKTAIL AND BLACK. FINISH OFF WITH A GOLD AND BLACK PAINTED EYE

Ostrich Scud

CRUSTACEA ARE AN IMMENSELY IMPORTANT element in the diet of most fish. In freshwater, the gammarus or scud, is sometimes found in staggering numbers and fish will grow very quickly on a diet of these little shrimps.

WHERE: WORLDWIDE IN STILLWATER AND RIVERS IN TEMPERATE AND ARCTIC REGIONS

WHEN: ALL YEAR

WHAT: TROUT, GRAYLING, SMALLMOUTH BASS, BLUEGILL, CARP

HOW: CLOSE COPY OF A SCUD

HOOK: 10 TO 18 CURVED SHANK
BODY: OLIVE OSTRICH HERL
SHELLBACK: CLEAR PVC RIBBED WITH CLEAR NYLON

This simple tying replicates the shape and colour of scuds and is a marvellous pattern to fish in and around weed beds in summer. A fun way to fish an Ostrich Scud is to leave one on the bottom of a lake in shallow water and wait for a cruising trout to intercept it.

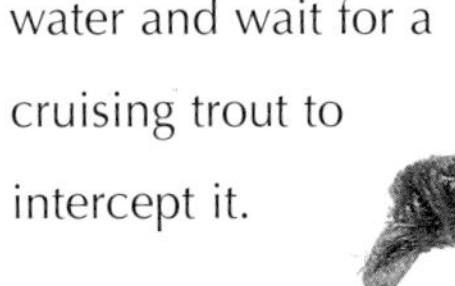

Nomad

THIS OUT-AND-OUT ATTRACTOR is deadly on stocked waters for both rainbow and brown trout. It is the fly of the Nomad Fly Fishers in the UK and began as the delightfully named 'Idiot Proof Nymph' with the Scottish branch of the club. When tied tarpon style it acquired its new name and an almost mystical following. This is a Cat's Whisker variant – almost any colour can be made to work although there are days when the fish will only have eyes for just the one colour. It is best fished with the clear intermediate sinking lines.

WHERE: MAINLY STOCKED STILLWATER IN TEMPERATE REGIONS

WHEN: ALL YEAR

WHAT: TROUT, PIKE, PERCH

HOW: AN ATTRACTOR

HOOK: 8X TO 12 2X SHANK
TAIL: WHITE MARABOU
BODY: PEARL FRITZ, GOLD BEAD AND FLUORESCENT GREEN TYING THREAD

Grey Ghost

WHERE: STILLWATERS IN TEMPERATE/SUB ARCTIC REGIONS

WHEN: YEAR ROUND

WHAT: ANY PREDATORY SPECIES

HOW: SUGGESTS BAIT FISH

HOOK: SIZE 2 6X SHANK SOMETIMES EVEN BIGGER
BODY: ORANGE FLOSS RIBBED WITH FLAT SILVER TINSEL
WING: FOUR GREY COCK SADDLE HACKLES OVER WHITE BUCKTAIL
HACKLE: WHITE BUCKTAIL, PEACOCK SWORD AND GOLDEN PHEASANT CREST
CHEEKS: SILVER PHEASANT BODY FEATHER WITH JUNGLE COCK

THIS IS AN OUT-AND-OUT STREAMER FLY designed to be trailed behind a boat and not cast. The very long wind structure will invariably snag up around the hook bend if this fly is cast conventionally. Trolling/trailing a fly is far more effective than many would care to admit and this is as good a pattern as you could ever wish to have to suggest a small fish. Stuck for food or desperate for success? Trail a fly on a lake and you are likely to succeed. Amazing how the old flies are often the best.

Polar Shrimp

DEFINITELY ONE OF THE GREAT ALASKAN PATTERNS. Orange suggests not only the fresh eggs of the sockeye salmon which are food to a multitude of species, but also the flesh of salmon itself, which is a very popular food item in northern rivers. I believe this fly acts as a trigger to many of these fish and, although the fish may not be sure what they are taking it for, they do so very confidently. Any river system that has spawning runs of Pacific salmon will respond well to this pattern.

WHERE: ALASKA, BRITISH COLUMBIA, KAMCHATKA, WASHINGTON, OREGON AND THE GREAT LAKES

WHEN: SUMMER TO AUTUMN

WHAT: RAINBOW TROUT, GRAYLING, CHAR, COHO, HUMPBACK, STEELHEAD

HOW: A TRIGGER FLY SUGGESTING EGGS OR FLESH

HOOK: 2 TO 6 SALMON IRON
TAIL: RED COCK HACKLE FIBRES
BODY: FLUORESCENT ORANGE CHENILLE
WING: NATURAL POLAR BEAR HAIR
HACKLE: HOT ORANGE COCK

Blue White Deceiver

DECEIVERS ARE THE UNIVERSAL BAIT FISH FLY. You can use any colour combination to mimic any small fish and be confident that your fly will work. When I am fishing clear saltwater and near to the surface I have always liked blue-backed white patterns because they resemble the little mackerel common in southwest England where I grew up. A tremendous pattern for any of the mackerel/tunny family and also for striped and European bass. Fish with short, fast strips and always be ready for the fast attack as you go to recast.

WHERE: WORLDWIDE IN SALTWATER

WHEN: ALL YEAR

WHAT: ALL PREDATORS BUT PARTICULARLY BASS AND MACKEREL

HOW: RESEMBLES BABY MACKEREL

HOOK: 2 TO 3/0 STAINLESS O'SHAUGHNESSY
TAIL: WHITE COCK SADDLE HACKLES AND PEARL; CRYSTALFLASH
COLLAR: WHITE BUCKTAIL
WING: BLUE BUCKTAIL, BLUE GRIZZLE SADDLE HACKLES, PEARL CRYSTALFLASH AND PEACOCK HERL
HEAD: BLACK WITH EYES PAINTED BLACK AND YELLOW

Skating Caddis

A VERY CLEVER PATTERN that mimics the way adult caddis (sedge) skitter across the water surface after hatching. Davy Wotton came up with this tying. To fish this fly properly takes a particular skill with a long rod and light line to impart the necessary action to the fly.

WHERE: WORLDWIDE IN RIVERS AND STILLWATER IN TEMPERATE AND SUB-ARCTIC REGIONS

WHEN: SPRING TO AUTUMN

WHAT: TROUT, GRAYLING, LAKE TROUT, CHAR

HOW: ADULT SEDGE IMITATION

HOOK: 12 2X SHANK
BODY: INSECT GREEN GLISTER
WINGS: ELK HAIR IN TWO BUNCHES
THORAX: INSECT GREEN POLYPROPYLENE WITH OLIVE FEATHER FIBRE BACK
LEGS: BROWN PARTRIDGE

Hatching Sedge Pupa

WHERE: WORLDWIDE IN TEMPERATE REGIONS IN RIVERS AND STILLWATER

WHEN: ANY TIME OF YEAR BUT COOLER MONTHS ARE BEST

WHAT: TROUT INCLUDING CUTTHROAT AND SEA TROUT

HOW: EMERGING SEDGE IMITATION

HOOK: 8 TO 12 STANDARD SHANK
TAIL: RED IBIS SUBSTITUTE AND A FEW FIBRES OF PEACOCK SWORD
BODY: FLAT SILVER TINSEL WITH SILVER OVAL OR WIRE RIB
HACKLE: BLACK HEN
WING: PEACOCK SWORD WITH SLIP OF RED IBIS SUBSTITUTE ON EACH SIDE

THIS IS AN EXCELLENT REPRESENTATION OF AN EMERGING SEDGE (CADDIS) and works equally well in rivers or lakes. Allow to slowly sink then draw to the surface in a long sweep, or twitch along just under the surface. You can expect trout to take very firmly so don't fish with too light a leader. Orange, olive or cream are the most useful options. Look for the localized areas where the natural sedge are hatching. Used as part of a 3-fly cast for trout in large stillwaters, this pattern is surprisingly effective.

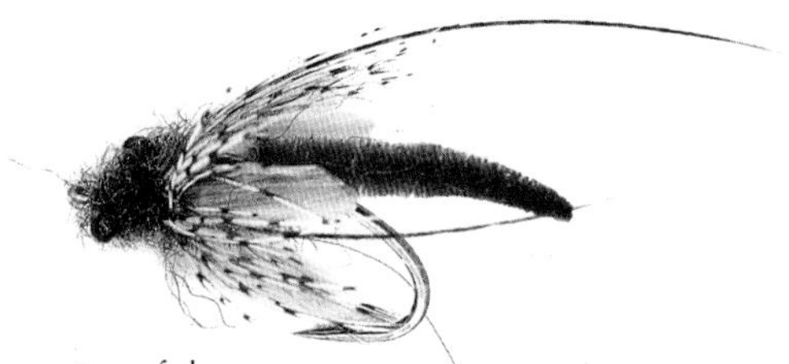

Black Deceiver

ANY PATTERN CAN HAVE AN ALL-BLACK OPTION, and although not specifically imitating one thing in particular, it will score well at certain times or under certain conditions. This particular deceiver is ideal for golden dorado in South America, but as these hard-fighting fish will give your flies a tough time make sure you have a good supply. For this particular fish it is also worth tying them on stinger hooks to get a better hold in their tough mouths.

WHERE: WORLDWIDE IN RIVERS OR SALTWATER

WHEN: ALL YEAR

WHAT: ANY PREDATORY SPECIES, BUT GOLDEN DORADO IN PARTICULAR

HOW: GENERAL ATTRACTOR LURE

HOOK: 4 TO 3/0 O'SHAUGHNESSY
TAIL: SIX BLACK COCK SADDLE HACKLES AND STRANDS OF COPPER CRYSTALFLASH
WING: BLACK BUCKTAIL ABOVE AND BELOW HOOK
THROAT: RED CRYSTAL HAIR
HEAD: BLACK WITH WHITE EYE

Woolly Bugger

MANY FLY FISHERS USE NOTHING ELSE FOR TROUT and, although there is no such thing as a 'fail-me-never', this fly comes very close to being infallible throughout the world.

The giant sea run brown trout of Tierra Del Fuego have provided sport which no one could ever have imagined possible following their introduction decades ago as brown trout. The programme of catch-and-release has increased their average weight and allowed some individuals to exceed 13 kg (30 lbs). This one fly, in its many colour combinations, suggests a wide variety of food items and works on all waters for all species.

WHERE: WORLDWIDE

WHEN: ALL SEASONS

WHAT: ALL SPECIES

HOW: NON SPECIFIC BUT SUGGESTS LIFE AND IS THEREFORE EDIBLE

HOOK: SIZE 2–10
TAIL: BLACK MARABOU WITH A FEW STRANDS PEARL CRYSTAL FLASH
BODY: BLACK CHENILLE WITH A PALMERED BLACK HACKLE AND SILVER WIRE RIB

Invicta

ONE OF THE MOST DIFFICULT OF THE STANDARD WET FLIES to tie well, the Invicta incorporates many fly tying techniques, and all within a remarkably short amount of hook shank. It can suggest a hatching caddis (sedge) pupa, a struggling insect trapped in the surface film, or tied with a silver body, it suggests a small fish. Trout love it and in larger sizes it is really good for sea trout. It also makes a good top dropper for summer grilse (a small salmon) and I have even caught lake trout on it when they feed on caddis.

WHERE: WORLDWIDE IN STILLWATER AND RIVERS

WHEN: ALL YEAR BUT BEST IN LATE SUMMER TO AUTUMN

WHAT: TROUT, SEA TROUT, LAKE TROUT, SMALLMOUTH BASS

HOW: SUGGESTS INSECTS AND LITTLE FISHES IN GENERAL, BUT PARTICULARLY RESEMBLES CADDIS (SEDGE)

HOOK: 6 TO 14 STANDARD SHANK
TAIL: GOLDEN PHEASANT CREST
BODY: YELLOW OR AMBER SEAL'S FUR PALMERED THROUGH WITH A RED GAME COCK HACKLE AND THEN RIBBED WITH GOLD WIRE
HACKLE: BLUE JAY FIBRES TIED FALSE
WING: PAIRED HEN PHEASANT TAIL SLIPS

Green Eyes

I HAVE NEVER HAD THE PLEASURE OF MEETING ALASKA'S HANK PENNINGTON, who invented this fly, but he needs to fish those who try to get their guests to foul sockeye salmon in the mouth. This fly they take fair and square in the mouth. I once used this fly in a slow pool full of sockeye salmon and could see fish slip up out of the school to take it as it dead drifted over them despite my opinionated guide declaring that each capture was just a fluke. If you aren't sure why this works, try cleaning a fresh run sockeye and you will see that the stomach often has a bright green slime in it. Enough said!

WHERE: ALASKA, BRITISH COLUMBIA AND KAMCHATKA

WHEN: JULY ONWARDS DEPENDING ON THE RUN

WHAT: SOCKEYE SALMON

HOW: MUST LOOK LIKE PLANKTON, WHICH SOCKEYE SALMON EAT

HOOK: RED GAMAKATSU 1 TO 6
WING: APPLE GREEN OR GLO-BRITE GREEN WOOL

Cuba Bonefish

CUBA BECAME A GREAT NEW SALTWATER ARENA when it opened up to tourists although it remains a difficult venue for USA anglers to get to. As with all new locations, they seem to quickly evolve new fly patterns, most of which are soon forgotten. This fly is very popular at many bonefish camps and has proved to be a very worthwhile pattern for use just about

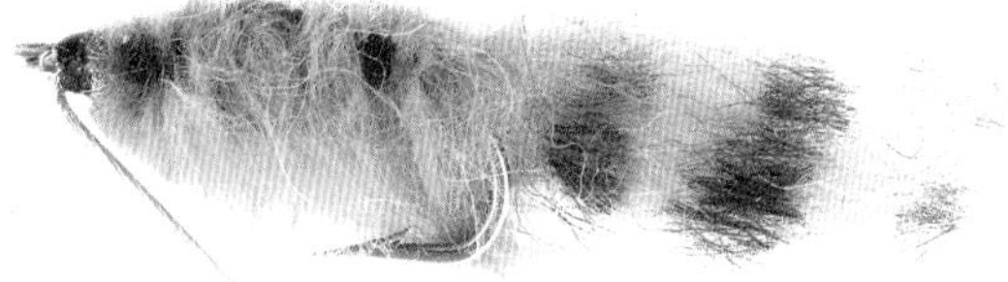

anywhere on the flats. Probably taken for either a goby or a mantis shrimp it relies on that soft buff colour which works so well over sand and marl. Tied with or without the heavy eyes, it is a great fly to take with you as part of your first bonefish selection.

WHERE: FLATS IN TROPICAL REGIONS

WHEN: YEAR ROUND

WHAT: BONEFISH

HOW: SMALL FISH IMITATION

HOOK: 2 TO 6 SALTWATER O SHAUGHNESSY
TAIL: TAN CRAFT FUR WITH BLACK FELT TIP MARKER BARS

Duck's Dun

FISHING THE DRY FLY is always reckoned to be the cream of fly fishing, and whenever the ephemerids hatch on rivers or lakes there is no better sight than to watch their sail-like wings appear on the water's surface. Charles Jardine, the UK fly fishing supremo, put his fertile mind to solving the difficulties of tempting stillwater trout to take the adult pond and lake olives, and devised the Duck's Dun, a fly equally effective on rivers and still waters.

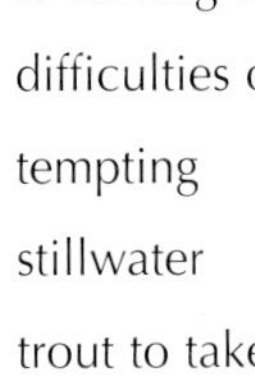

WHERE: WORLDWIDE IN RIVERS AND STILLWATER

WHEN: SPRING AND SUMMER

WHAT: TROUT, GRAYLING, CHAR, SMALLMOUTH BASS

HOW: IMITATES THE ADULT STAGE OF POND AND LAKE OLIVES

HOOK: 14 TO 16 STANDARD SHANK FINE WIRE
TAIL: A FEW FIBRES OF GRIZZLE HEN
BODY: LIGHT YELLOW OLIVE SYNTHETIC DUBBING ON FINE PRIMROSE THREAD
WING: TWO CDC FEATHERS BACK-TO-BACK AND UPRIGHT
HACKLE: DARK BLUE DUN SPREAD THROUGH THORAX AND CLIPPED UNDERNEATH TO 'V' SHAPE

Clint's Lemming

THIS FLY IS THE RESULT OF MANY YEARS of observation as an Alaskan guide and endless experimentation at the vice by American fly tier Clint Duncan, looking to imitate a tundra vole or lemming. Lemmings will always try to swim against the current with the head up and the rear end underwater. Work this pattern around any structure and the smartest rainbow trout will be fooled, as will the biggest bass in the lake. Wiggle the rod tip to make the swimming action and enjoy matching the hatch!

WHERE: WORLDWIDE FROM TUNDRA STREAMS TO WARM-WATER LAKES

WHEN: SPRING BEST FOR TROUT BUT ANY TIME FOR OTHER SPECIES

WHAT: TROUT, TAIMEN, LAKE TROUT, PIKE, LARGEMOUTH AND LANDLOCKED STRIPED BASS

HOW: IMITATES A SWIMMING LEMMING IN TWO PARTS.

HOOK: 4 TO 2/0 SALMON IRON
TAIL: STRIP OF MUSKRAT SKIN
BODY: MUSKRAT SKIN WOUND AROUND HOOK SHANK. LINK WITH A NYLON LOOP TO A HOOK SHANK WITH THE SPIN DEER HAIR AND THEN TRIM TIGHT UNDERNEATH BUT WIDE AND STRAGGLY ON TOP AND TO THE SIDE

Black and Orange Tube

TUBE FLIES ARE A MEANS OF USING A LONG-BODIED PATTERN for salmon and trout without the need for a large, heavy single hook.

WHERE: WORLDWIDE IN RIVERS AND LAKES, BUT USUALLY IN TEMPERATE REGIONS

WHEN: ALL YEAR

WHAT: ATLANTIC SALMON, SEA AND LAKE TROUT, STEELHEAD, BROWN AND RAINBOW TROUT

HOW: SUGGESTS ALL MANNER OF FOOD OR SIMPLY ACTS AS AN INDUCEMENT TO ATTACK

HOOK: TUBE OF PLASTIC, ALUMINIUM OR BRASS FROM 1.25 CM (½ INCH) TO 7.5 CM (3 INCHES)
BODY: BLACK FLOSS RIBBED WITH OVAL SILVER TINSEL
WING: TIED IN BUNCHES AROUND THE TUBE OF BLACK AND ORANGE GOAT OR BUCKTAIL

Tubes use relatively small trebles and the tube itself may be made from plastic, aluminium or brass to achieve different presentations depending on the water level and temperature. Many lake and reservoir trout anglers troll tube flies to take the larger, grown-on specimens.

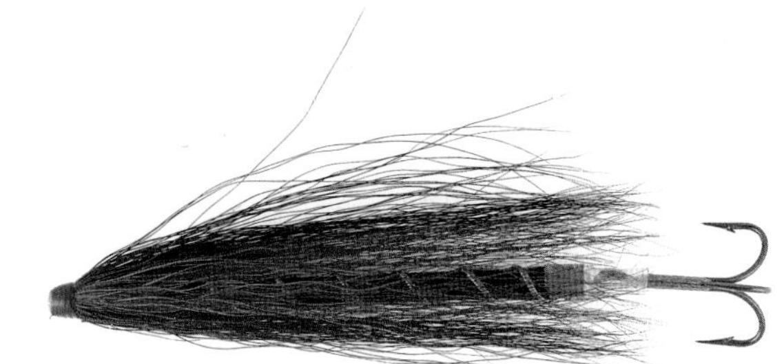

Fritz Rabbit

EQUALLY AT HOME AS A FRESH- OR SALTWATER LURE, this can only be an attractor that provokes aggression as I can't believe that anything would take it to be a food item. Whatever the reason, this ugly pattern certainly works and can

definitely have its day under a wide range of conditions. Olive or black rabbit versions work too, and this is a particularly deadly lure for newly-stocked rainbow trout.

WHERE: WORLDWIDE IN FRESH- OR SALTWATER

WHEN: ALL YEAR

WHAT: MOST PREDATORY SPECIES

HOW: GENERAL ATTRACTOR

HOOK: 8 4X SHANK OR STAINLESS O'SHAUGHNESSY
TAIL AND BACK: WHITE RABBIT STRIP WITH LUMINESCENT GREEN BEAD
BODY: CHARTREUSE FRITZ WITH OVAL SILVER RIB
EYES: LEAD DUMBBELL

Sea Bunny

A VARIANT TO MANY STANDARD TARPON TYINGS. By using rabbit fur, the fly has much more life and movement when retrieved. Many predators home in on patterns with lots of wiggle. Tarpon will take the Sea Bunny in preference to feather versions at times of extreme clarity, but this fly is also good for other species in slightly coloured water.

WHERE: SALTWATER, USUALLY TROPICAL AND SUB-TROPICAL

WHEN: ALL YEAR

WHAT: TARPON, REDFISH, SNOOK, SEA TROUT, BLUEFISH, STRIPED BASS

HOW: AN ALL-PURPOSE ATTRACTOR RELYING ON SINUOUS MOVEMENT

HOOK: 3/0 O'SHAUGHNESSY
TAIL: BLACK RABBIT STRIP WITH RED CRYSTAL HAIR AND RED RABBIT
BODY: RED TYING THREAD WITH PAINTED EYE AND COATED WITH EPOXY

Lead Bug

THIS IS ONE OF THE EARLIEST OF THE 'STALKING' FLIES designed for small, clearwater fisheries with large stocked trout. I developed it at Avington fishery in Hampshire, UK, with the intention that it should have minimalist dressing, be fast-sinking and should suggest an ephemerid nymph. The colour, shape and lead wire segmentation do just that, and the fly is cast to sighted fish. The fish must then either investigate or refuse to look at it again. If it chases, you should keep retrieving until the fish grabs the fly. Exciting stuff!

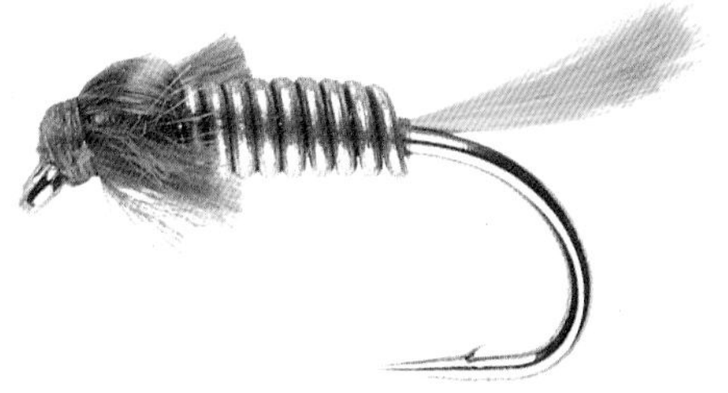

WHERE: STOCKED STILLWATER FISHERIES WHERE THE WATER IS VERY CLEAR, USUALLY IN THE UK, BUT ALSO IN EUROPE AND THE USA

WHEN: BEST WHEN THE SUN IS IN A HIGH POSITION AS IT GIVES GOOD VISIBILITY

WHAT: STOCKED TROUT: BROWN, RAINBOW AND BROOK

HOW: A MINIMALIST SUGGESTIVE PATTERN FOR STALKING

HOOK: 8 TO 12 STANDARD SHANK
TAIL: SHORT TUFT OF OLIVE FLOSS
BODY: LEAD WIRE
THORAX BACK AND LEGS: OLIVE FLOSS

Hoglouse

THIS CRUSTACEAN FIGURES HIGHLY in stomach samples from trout taken in deeper water from lakes. Surprising then that this very important food has so few effective imitations. This dressing is extremely good and there is absolutely no doubt that reservoir and lake trout recognise it for exactly what it is. The hoglouse looks a bit like a shrimp but swims level, not on its side, and can be surprisingly quick over short distances. This is a brilliant dropper pattern to use when fishing a Booby deep down in the colder months with a very fast sinking line.

WHERE: STILLWATER IN TEMPERATE AND SUB-ARCTIC REGIONS

WHEN: ALL YEAR

WHAT: TROUT, LAKE TROUT AND MANY OTHER SPECIES

HOW: HOGLOUSE IMITATION

HOOK: 8 TO 10 STANDARD SHANK
TAIL AND FEELERS: EITHER PARTRIDGE OR SPECKLED BROWN HEN
BODY: DUBBED HARES EAR WITH A WHOLE PARTRIDGE HACKLE TIED ON TOP OF SHANK AND WING CASES OVER OF DARK PARTRIDGE TAIL FIBRES

Goat's Toe

ARTIFICIAL FLIES HAVE THE MOST WEIRD AND WONDERFUL NAMES, making it a puzzling world for the newcomer to fly fishing. After a while it does slowly make sense as long as you accept patterns like this as oddballs. This fly is good for wild waters where food is scarce but where trout either live or where migrants pass through. It uses the stunning blue feather from the neck of the peacock, that most exotic of pheasants, which provides fly tiers with such a wealth of material.

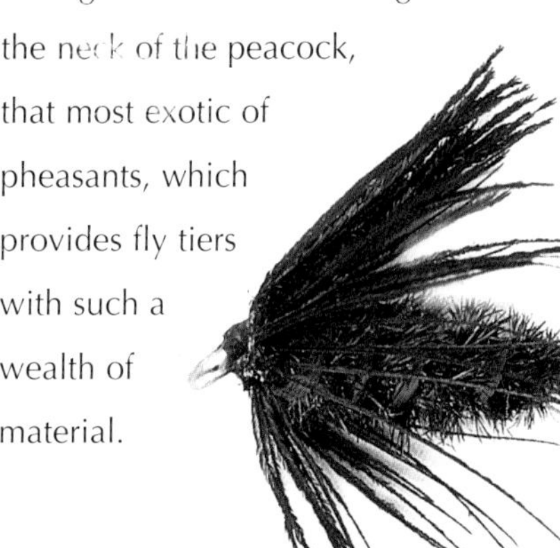

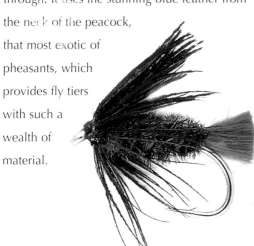

WHERE: WORLDWIDE BUT USUALLY IN MORE EXTREME AREAS WHERE CONDITIONS ARE HARSH

WHEN: SPRING TO AUTUMN

WHAT: MIGRATORY AND RESIDENT TROUT AND SALMON

HOW: A BASIC SUGGESTIVE PATTERN

HOOK: 10 TO 6 STANDARD SHANK
TAIL: BRIGHT RED WOOL
BODY: PEACOCK HERL RIBBED WITH SCARLET FLOSS
HACKLE: BLUE PEACOCK NECK FEATHER (LONG IN FIBRE)

Shallow H_2O fly

NOTICE THAT ONCE AGAIN THIS SALTWATER FLY is a marriage chartreuse and white. Another Lefty Kreh special, this is a magic combination for saltwater. Intended for bonefish in the shallowest of places where they are ultra-cautious and need a soft-landing fly, this pattern requires accurate casting of at least 24 metres (80 feet). I prefer to use a longer-than-normal leader to aid careful presentation and to keep the fly line away from the fish.

WHERE: TROPICAL SALTWATER FLATS

WHEN: ALL YEAR

WHAT: BONEFISH

HOW: A COLOURED PATTERN THAT LOOKS LIKE A SHRIMP

HOOK: 4 STAINLESS O'SHAUGHNESSY. FISH THIS FLY HOOK POINT UP
BODY: ONE-THIRD WHITE CHENILLE, TWO-THIRDS CHARTREUSE
WING: GENEROUS AMOUNT OF CHARTREUSE BUCKTAIL

Martinez

MANY GENERAL-PURPOSE NYMPH PATTERNS work for one angler and not another. It must be down to either pure faith, which I think transmits itself down the line, or the way the fly is fished. This pattern is one that I have seen used to great effect by the great Gary Brooker of 60s pop group Procol Harum who fishes my syndicate trout lakes. A wonderfully buggy fly that uses a partridge hackle, a feather that just says 'insect legs' to me and fishes too.

WHERE: WORLDWIDE ON RIVERS AND STILLWATER

WHEN: ALL YEAR BUT SPRING AND EARLY SUMMER ARE BEST

WHAT: TROUT, GRAYLING, CHAR

HOW: A BROAD-SPECTRUM NYMPH WITH DEFINITE FISH APPEAL

HOOK: 8 TO 12 STANDARD SHANK OR 2X NYMPH
TAIL: A FEW FIBRES OF GUINEA FOWL FEATHER
BODY: BLACK RABBIT UNDERFUR DUBBED AND RIBBED WITH SILVER WIRE
THORAX: BLACK RABBIT UNDERFUR WITH A GREEN RAFFINE WING CASE OVER
HACKLE: TWO TURNS GREY PARTRIDGE

Janssen's Minnow

THIS IS A VERY SPECIAL TYING STYLE which creates a close copy of small bait fishes. It really is a brilliant concept, but for me it's one of those flies that either works a dream or not at all. I know it's going to be good when little fish follow the fly because then when the attack comes my fly will be the straggler of the shoal that doesn't escape! I know lots of other anglers who do really well in very different circumstances with Janssen's minnows.

WHERE: WORLDWIDE IN SALT- AND FRESHWATER

WHEN: ALL YEAR

WHAT: JUST ABOUT ANY SPECIES OF FISH

HOW: BRILLIANT CLOSE COPY OF A BABY FISH

HOOK: 2X TO 8, 2X TO 4X SHANK
TAIL: OLIVE MARABOU FIBRES
BODY: SILVER MYLAR PIPING OVER SHAPED LEAD TAPE
MARKINGS: PAINT AND THEN CLEAR EPOXY OVER

Cooper's Yellow Damsel

THIS VERSION OF THE MONTANA NYMPH (see page 360) was devised in the early 1970s as a summer pattern when damsel fly are hatching, but has since been proven to work most of the year. Why trout take an orange fly when the natural is a pale green I don't know – but they do. Fish with a floating line, 30 cm (12 inch) long, sweeping pulls. An algal tinge to the water really helps this fly. I particularly like this fly because it helped me win the European Open (in 1991) at Dreux in France.

WHERE: WORLDWIDE IN STILLWATER, ESPECIALLY WHEN STOCKED

WHEN: ALL YEAR BUT BEST IN SUMMER

WHAT: RAINBOW AND BROWN TROUT

HOW: A NON-SPECIFIC PATTERN BUT PROVEN TO WORK WHEN DAMSELS ARE HATCHING

HOOK: 8 TO 12 2X NYMPH HOOK
TAIL: BUNCH OF GINGER COCK HACKLE FIBRES
BODY: NAPLES YELLOW CHENILLE
THORAX: ARC CHROME DFM CHENILLE WITH A GINGER COCK HACKLE PALMERED THROUGH AND CHENILLE OVER THE TOP

Brassie

COPPER IS A COLOUR that comes up time and time again in highly successful nymph patterns, most often as a rib but more rarely as the major ingredient. The dull gleam perhaps suggests a spark of life and is enough to trigger a reaction. In the case of the Brassie, I believe that the wire body provides the segmented effect which is another important trigger. This is primarily a river fly but can also be very good as a pattern to cast to sighted fish in stillwater when they are lying deep. Let it rest and then lift as the fish comes past.

WHERE: RIVERS ANYWHERE AND SOME STILLWATER

WHEN: ALL YEAR

WHAT: TROUT, GRAYLING, CHAR, CUTTHROAT

HOW: A GENERAL-PURPOSE NYMPH

HOOK: 10 TO 18 STANDARD SHANK
BODY: COPPER WIRE
THORAX: MUSKRAT FUR WITH GUARD HAIRS

Sea Habit Herring

THE SEA HABIT HAS SPAWNED several killing flies, including this cracking fly – the Sea Habbit Herring. All are the brainchildren of legendary American saltwater ace Trey Combs. His understanding of predatory and migratory fish is outstanding, as is his compassion for the environment they live in. This, in its various colour formats, is up with Lefty's Deceiver (see page 54) as an all-time great saltwater fly and should be used whenever predators are hitting schools of bait fish.

WHERE: WORLDWIDE IN SALTWATER

WHEN: ALL YEAR

WHAT: ALL PREDATORS

HOW: A BAIT FISH PATTERN

HOOK: 2/0 O'SHAUGHNESSY
TAIL: PEARL FLASHABOU
WING: A COMPLEX MIX OF PEARL FLASHABOU, WHITE FISHHAIR LIME GREEN PEARL BLUE PEACOCK AND SILVER CRYSTALFLASH, LIME AND ROYAL BLUE FISHHAIR
HEAD: PEARL MYLAR PIPING WITH A STICK-ON BLACK PRISMATIC EYE AND THEN COVERED WITH EPOXY WHICH IS PANTONED BLUE GREEN ON TOP

Once and Away

THIS MAY BE THE ULTIMATE SUSPENDER MIDGE/CHIRONOMID, and it's no surprise that it comes from the fertile mind of Hans Van Klinken. This little wisp of nothing sits perfectly in the surface film – not on it or under it – which is exactly where fish expect to find the natural fly in its hatching stage. Using this fly is emerger fishing at its best, and the natural grey CDC is uncannily easy to see against the surface. Sometimes the take is so quiet and confident that the tuft of CDC just sinks as the fish sucks the fly in. Very good on those warm, sticky days when even the fish seem jaded.

WHERE: WORLDWIDE IN STILLWATER AND SLOW-FLOWING RIVERS

WHEN: ALL YEAR BUT SPRING TO AUTUMN IS BEST

WHAT: TROUT, GRAYLING

HOW: SUGGESTS HATCHING STAGE OF CHIRONOMID

HOOK: 12 TO 16 2X SHANK FINE WIRE
BODY: STRIPPED PEACOCK QUILL FROM THE EYE
THORAX: PEACOCK HERL
BACK AND WING: CDC FEATHER

Alaskabou

I HAVE SEEN A NUMBER OF VERSIONS of this marabou-based pattern intended for Alaskan salmon. Although it is good fished dead drift with a fast sinking line it can often be better if fished in short sharp pulls to really get the marabou pulsating. Fresh king salmon will actively chase this fly and takes can be surprisingly hard for those used to their more delicate touch.

WHERE: ALASKA

WHEN: JUNE ONWARDS

WHAT: KINGS, CHUM, COHO AND PINK SALMON

HOW: BY THE ACTION AND COLOUR

HOOK: 1/0 TO 4 SALMON IRON
TAIL: LARGE TUFT MARABOU FIBRES
BODY: PALMERED MARABOU FEATHERS
WING: A FEW STRANDS OF APPROPRIATE CRYSTAL HAIR
HACKLE: LONG-FIBRED COCK SADDLE

ALSO TRY CHARTREUSE AND WHITE, ORANGE AND WHITE, PURPLE AND BLACK COLOUR MIXER

Palamino Midge

SUEDE CHENILLE IS USED AS AN extended body to make a lifelike hatching chironomid. Based on a short shank hook to reduce weight allowing the fly to sit high in the surface film. Make a straggly thorax, especially with a little Lite-Brite and you have all the criteria to suggest an emerger struggling for life. Perfect for flat, sticky calms, this fly is a killer if cast to surface cruising trout on sticky days when even the fish seem jaded.

WHERE: STILLWATERS AND SLOW RIVERS IN TEMPERATE REGIONS

WHEN: SPRING THROUGH FALL

WHAT: TROUT

HOW: IMITATES A HATCHING CHIRONOMID

HOOK: 16 TO 12 STANDARD SHANK FINE WIRE
BODY: SINGLE PIECE SUEDE CHENILLE
THORAX: LITE BRITE MIXED WITH SEALS FUR

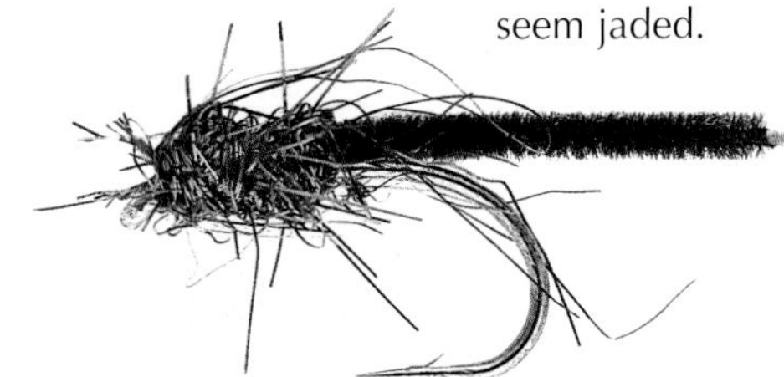

Pink Floozy

I NOW HAVE MORE THAN 14 YEARS' EXPERIENCE of escorting groups to Alaska and every year I get non-fly tiers to try their hand at the vice. As pink is the hot colour for Pacific salmon, the Pink Floozy gets reinvented each summer. In July, the favourite saying by Alaskan guides is 'try anything but pink', because its use will guarantee a chum or humpback salmon. What a wonderful world it would be if we could get Atlantic salmon rivers back to that sort of form.

WHERE: ALASKA, BRITISH COLUMBIA, KAMCHATKA, OREGON, WASHINGTON AND THE GREAT LAKES

WHEN: SUMMER TO AUTUMN

WHAT: PACIFIC SALMON SPECIES

HOW: ATTRACTOR LURE

HOOK: 2 TO 8 SALMON IRON
BODY: PEARL DIAMOND BRAID
WING: PINK MARABOU WITH PINK CRYSTALFLASH
HEAD: HOT PINK TYING THREAD

Glister Damsel

IAN MACKENZIE OF FULLING MILL FLIES IN THE UK came up with this pretty and very effective fly when he needed a promotional pattern using the company colours. Since then there have been a number of colour variants, all of which use the lovely sparkly material known as Glister. There's little doubt that the olive version is a must when the natural damsel nymphs are active in high summer.

WHERE: WORLDWIDE IN STILLWATER IN TEMPERATE REGIONS

WHEN: ALL YEAR

WHAT: TROUT, PERCH, SMALLMOUTH AND LARGEMOUTH BASS, BLUEGILL

HOW: AN EFFECTIVE DAMSEL PATTERN WITH ADDED FIZZ

HOOK: 10 2X SHANK
TAIL: OLIVE MARABOU
BACK: OLIVE MARABOU
BODY: ORANGE GLISTER DIVIDED IN TWO WITH AN OLIVE HEN HACKLE

Red Emerger

BOB CARNILL EVOLVED THIS FLY to represent a hatching buzzer. An extremely good summer fly when fished just under the surface, especially early in the morning on large stillwaters. Red is a important colour for the emergent stage of chironomid imitations. Very often this emphasis of a particular part of an insect makes the fly stand out from the crowd and be selected by the fish. Takes are often very quick and you need to concentrate with an almost static retrieve. Use a long 6-metre (20-ft) leader and floating line.

WHERE: WORLDWIDE IN STILLWATER IN TEMPERATE REGIONS

WHEN: LATE SPRING AND EARLY AUTUMN

WHAT: TROUT, BLUEGILL, SMALLMOUTH BASS

HOW: SUGGESTS AN EMERGING CHIRONOMID

HOOK: 12 TO 14 CURVED SHANK LIGHT WIRE
BODY: FINE RED WOOL RIBBED WITH STRIPPED PEACOCK QUILL
WING: TWO OFF-WHITE COCK HACKLE TIPS
THORAX: RED SEAL'S FUR WITH A LITTLE PINK AND A RED FEATHER FIBRE BACK
HACKLE: LIGHT GINGER COCK

San Juan Worm

I CAN'T STRESS HOW IMPORTANT THE BLOODWORM IS AS A FOOD ITEM, and it is a mystery why so many patterns based on it have evolved for stillwater use and how few have been designed for river use. The San Juan Worm is the principal exception. Use it anywhere, but especially in rivers with sediment deposits and dense weed growth where the bloodworm is likely to live. A modest amount of organic pollution can mean thriving bloodworm beds and make a prime location to fish this fly. Fish it on the dead drift.

WHERE: WORLDWIDE IN RIVERS AND STILLWATER, BUT NOT MUCH IN SUB-ARCTIC

WHEN: ALL YEAR

WHAT: TROUT, CHAR, SMALLMOUTH BASS, BLUEGILL AND MANY OTHER SPECIES

HOW: IMITATES A BLOODWORM

HOOK: 10 CURVED SHANK
BODY: RED CHENILLE WITH ENDS BURNT

Black Ant

THE HUMBLE ANT is one of the world's most successful insects and one part of its life cycle is to take wing for breeding and recolonizing. When this happens, usually in mid- to late summer, the spent adults fall into the water, provoking a rise of fish unlike anything else you may ever experience. Ants, of course, occur in many colours and sizes and this pattern uses high-density foam to make floatation easy for what is otherwise a rather slim pattern.

WHERE: WORLDWIDE IN FRESHWATER

WHEN: USUALLY MIDSUMMER, BUT ALMOST ANY TIME IN TROPICAL COUNTRIES

WHAT: TROUT, GRAYLING, CHAR, BLUEGILL

HOW: A SPECIFIC IMITATION OF AN ANT

HOOK: 12 TO 16 STANDARD SHANK
BODY: A CYLINDER OF BLACK FOAM (COLOUR CAN VARY) TIED HALFWAY ALONG AND IN THE MIDDLE OF THE HOOK
HACKLE: A FEW TURNS OF BLACK COCK HACKLE

Sinfoil's Fry

WHERE: WORLDWIDE IN RIVERS AND LAKES AND ALSO INSHORE SALTWATER

WHEN: ALL YEAR BUT BEST AT PINHEAD FRY STAGE

WHAT: ALL SPECIES OF FISH

HOW: BRILLIANT CLOSE COPY OF FREE-SWIMMING FRY

HOOK: SILVERED 6 TO 12 NYMPH 2X SHANK
BODY: FLAT SILVER, PEARL OR HOLOGRAPHIC TINSEL AND A FEW TURNS OF SCARLET FLOSS ALL OVERLAID WITH A PVC STRIP WETTED WITH CLEAR VARNISH OR EPOXY
WING: A FEW FIBRES OF TEAL FLANK OR BRONZE MALLARD
HEAD: BUILT UP LARGE AND THEN PAINTED BLACK WITH A PROMINENT EYE

TO MY MIND THIS REMAINS ONE OF THE BEST PINHEAD FRY IMITATIONS and it was one of the very first to use PVC to create a translucent body. There are better materials now, but the principal remains the same and if you look at any newly-hatched fry the most noticeable factors are the dominant eye and the see-through body. All species will eat fry, even their own, and you can safely use this pattern anywhere. Also good when trout are feeding on daphnia in the surface in a dead calm. Cast accurately and strip away rapidly for a wonderful take.

Pearl Bead Pheasant Tail Nymph

FISH FEEDING ON NEWLY-HATCHED FRY can either be very easy to catch or puzzlingly difficult. This fly works on the periphery of the feeding activity or where fish are searching out individuals from among stones or weed, rather than being cast in among the main feeding frenzy. It's not even a close imitation but somehow has the necessary

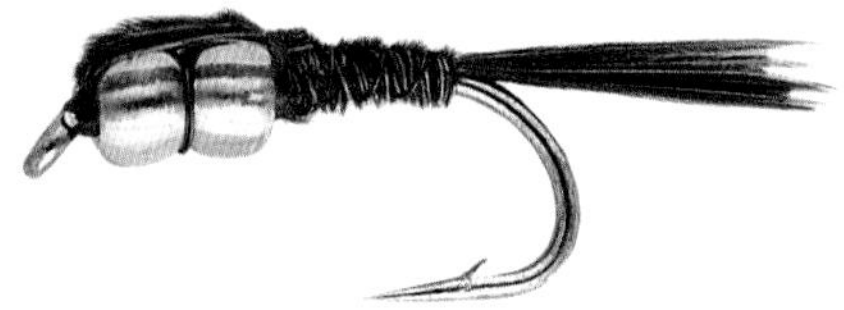

triggers to make a fish accept it, and it works for all species in rivers and stillwater. It is usually best on a floating line and there are times when used with a very long leader (6 m/6½ yards) and long, slow pulls out in the open water of large lakes when it will bring a very large fish, particularly old, resident brown trout.

WHERE: WORLDWIDE IN LAKES AND RIVERS

WHEN: USUALLY SPRING TO LATE SUMMER SOON AFTER EGGS HATCH

WHAT: ALL FRESHWATER SPECIES, BUT PRINCIPALLY TROUT, ARCTIC GRAYLING, CHAR, BASS, CRAPPIES

HOW: SUGGESTS A YOUNG FISH JUST STARTING ITS FIRST FREE-SWIMMING STAGES

HOOK: 10–14 STANDARD SHANK
TAIL: SMALL BUNCH OF COCK PHEASANT CENTRE TAIL FIBRES
ABDOMEN: PHEASANT TAIL FIBRES OVER-RIBBED WITH PEARL THREAD
THORAX: ONE OR TWO TRANSLUCENT PEARL BEADS WITH THE PHEASANT FIBRES PULLED OVER

Madam X

THE HOPPER FROM THE CLOSET! Adding rubber legs to a conventional hopper tying makes a pattern that creates fuss and disturbance on the water surface to convince any suspicious trout that this oddball is alive and really kicking. Although marvellous during hopper time, it is essentially a search-and-destroy operative for rivers and streams in the warmer months when you aren't sure what to use. I have been successful fishing for carp in stillwater with this fly when the carp are cruising reed bed margins and slurping down trapped insects.

WHERE: WORLDWIDE IN TEMPERATE REGIONS IN RIVERS AND SOME STILLWATER

WHEN: LATE SPRING TO AUTUMN

WHAT: TROUT, SMALLMOUTH AND LARGEMOUTH BASS, BLUEGILL, CARP

HOW: AN ULTRA-ACTIVE HOPPER PATTERN

HOOK: 6 TO 10 2X SHANK
TAIL: DEERHAIR
BODY: YELLOW FLOSS
HEAD AND WINGS: DEERHAIR TIED BULLET STYLE
LEGS: WHITE RUBBER TIED 'X' FASHION

Black Nymph

'WHEN IN DOUBT TIE on a small black fly' is sage advice that works the fly fishing world over. This is my all-time favourite for the tough times, and it is just a very simple black nymph tying. Have the necessary faith to fish it slow and deep and on most occasions it will save an otherwise blank day.

WHERE: WORLDWIDE IN ANY FRESHWATER LOCATION

WHEN: ALL YEAR

WHAT: TROUT, GRAYLING AND CHAR IN PARTICULAR, BUT ALSO MOST SPECIES

HOW: CAN BE SUGGESTIVE OF MANY SMALL NYMPHS

HOOK: 10 TO 16 STANDARD SHANK
TAIL: A FEW BLACK HEN HACKLE FIBRES
BODY: A FINE BLACK DUBBING (BLACK RABBIT UNDERFUR IS GOOD) RIBBED WITH SILVER WIRE
HACKLE: BLACK HEN TWO TURNS

Bonefish Critter

A WONDERFUL CRAB PATTERN invented by Tim Borski. I love this one because it not only looks great, is light and easy to cast, but is also nice and soft so fish are slow to eject it. It has also brought me success with bonefish when they are feeding among coral, rock and weed. Bonefish and permit love crabs and these super-smart fish require really good patterns to deceive them as well as good casting skills. It's no coincidence that so many of the best flies for the flats are a tan colour as this matches the sediment and coral sand where the fish find their food.

WHERE: SHALLOW TROPICAL SALTWATER

WHEN: ALL YEAR

WHAT: BONEFISH, PERMIT, REDFISH, SEA TROUT, SMALL TARPON

HOW: AN EXCELLENT CRAB IMITATION

HOOK: 1 TO 4 SALTWATER O'SHAUGHNESSY
TAIL: EYE STALKS OF BURNT MONO
BODY: HOT ORANGE FRITZ THEN LONG FIBRES OF GRIZZLE OR CREE HACKLE FINISHING WITH TAN WOOL PICKED OUT AND TRIMMED
EYES: LEAD DUMBBELLS AND OFTEN WITH A WEED GUARD ADDED

Okey Dokey

ORIGINATING ON A SMALL stillwater in Scotland, this fly is undeniably successful on stocked fisheries when fished under an indicator. Used as a point fly for a three-fly cast, it makes a good anchor pattern and is also proving its worth on rough streams for wild bred fish. Try it when fish are feeding on insects falling into the water from the bankside vegetation.

WHERE: STILLWATERS AND RIVERS IN TEMPERATE REGIONS

WHEN: YEAR ROUND

WHAT: TROUT WITH POTENTIAL FOR MANY OTHER SPECIES

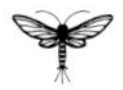

HOW: IT LOOKS LIKE A MUTANT CHIRONOMID BUT IT WORKS

HOOK: 12 TO 8 CURVED SHANK
BODY: GLO – BRITE FLOSS WHITE WITH SILVER WIRE RIB
THORAX: GLO – BRITE ORANGE FLOSS
EPOXY OVER ALL

Clear Wing Spinner

IT'S NOT DIFFICULT TO INCLUDE many of Gary La Fontaine's wonderful inventions simply because they are so very good and solve many tricky situations when fishing clear creeks and limestone streams. Fish in these waters can often be very pressured where there is good public access and need good flies and smart presentations to fool them. This is another 'spent' ephemerid, and because they often collect in tricky back eddies and tiny pockets, you will need to be really sharp with your casting.

WHERE: RIVERS IN TEMPERATE REGIONS WORLDWIDE

WHEN: LATE SPRING TO AUTUMN

WHAT: TROUT, GRAYLING, CUTTHROAT

HOW: IMITATES SPENT STAGE OF A SMALL MAYFLY

HOOK: 14 TO 22 STANDARD SHANK FINE WIRE
TAIL: TWO GRIZZLE COCK HACKLE FIBRES
BODY: BLACK ANTRON
WINGS: CLEAR ANTRON

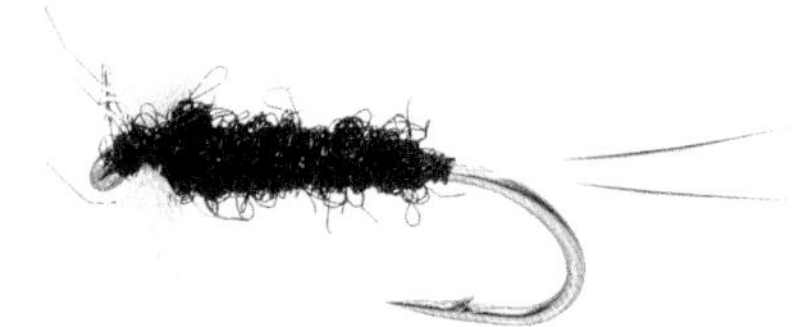

Secret Weapon

HUGH FALKUS WROTE A DEFINITIVE WORK ON SEA TROUT and came up with this pattern for those occasions when this elusive fish only nips the tail of a fly. Putting a sting in the tail will often create a hook-up, which was acceptable in the days when every wild fish was killed. Although Falkus was against catch-and-release, there really is no other option now, and only if the resources can take it should a fish be killed. With this fly, the damage is likely to be too great for successful release.

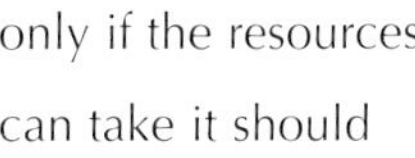

WHERE: SEA TROUT RIVERS IN ICELAND, UK, EUROPE, SOUTH AMERICA AND THE FALKLAND ISLANDS

WHEN: USUALLY FROM SUMMER TO AUTUMN IN LOW-WATER CONDITIONS

WHAT: SEA TROUT

HOW: A GENERAL-PURPOSE FLY, BUT THE TINY TREBLE SOLVES THE PROBLEM OF SHORT TAKES

HOOK: LOW-WATER SALMON 4 TO 8 WITH A LINKED 14 OR 16 TREBLE
BODY: LIGHT BROWN SEAL'S FUR WITH OVAL GOLD TINSEL RIB
HACKLE: RED GAME HEN TIED FALSE
WING: BRONZE MALLARD

Muddler Minnow

INVENTED BY DON GAPEN to suggest a small bullhead species found in streams, the Muddler Minnow took the fishing world by storm. One of those patterns that is wonderful for its original purpose but works equally well in all sorts of situations and when fished in different ways. Try it as a skated sedge, a surface disturber or as a general lure and at all depths and sizes. A fun fly to tie – spinning the deerhair head is a technique which fascinates anyone new to fly tying. Mini Muddlers work for 'loch style' fishing and make a great top dropper fly by drawing up an interested fish which will then often take another fly on the leader. Used as a bullhead imitation, the muddler will frequently fool even an old brown trout, which can be one of the most difficult fish to take on fly.

WHERE: RIVERS AND STILL WATERS

WHEN: ALL YEAR

WHAT: BROWNS AND RAINBOW TROUT

HOW: ATTRACTOR LURE AT ALL DEPTHS

HOOK: SIZE 12–4 2 X AND 3X SHANK
TAIL: OAK TURKEY
BODY: OVAL GOLD TINSEL
WING: OAK TURKEY
HEAD: NATURAL DEERHAIR CLIPPED. LEAVE SOME STRANDS ABOVE AND BELOW THE BODY

Camasunary Killer

ORIGINATING FROM THE ROMANTIC ISLE OF SKYE off western Scotland, this simply-tied fly is a great killer of sea trout. As with most flies containing some blue in the dressing, it works best on fresh fish (fish fresh in from the sea) and is one of the few patterns known to be effective in estuaries where sea trout can often be seen but are tough to catch. I like to believe that this fly would work for Scandinavian sea trout in saltwater, but I have no direct knowledge of it, although friends tell me that in the Falkland Islands it is a useful fly.

WHERE: RIVERS, ESTUARIES AND COASTAL REGIONS WHERE SEA TROUT OCCUR

WHEN: ALL YEAR BUT SPRING TO AUTUMN IS BEST

WHAT: SEA TROUT, ATLANTIC SALMON

HOW: GENERAL PURPOSE WET FLY WITH THE BLUE FACTOR

HOOK: 8 TO 12 STANDARD SHANK
TAIL: ROYAL BLUE WOOL
BODY: ROYAL BLUE AND FLUORESCENT RED WOOL RIBBED WITH OVAL SILVER
HACKLE: BLACK HEN, LONG AND FULL

Colonel's Creeper

THIS ALL PURPOSE NYMPH is attributed to Colonel Unwin who founded Fulling Mill Flies in Kenya.

WHERE: STILLWATERS AND RIVERS IN TEMPERATE AND SUBARCTIC REGIONS

WHEN: ALL YEAR

WHAT: TROUT, GRAYLING, SMALLMOUTH AND LARGE MOUTH BASS, BLUEGILL, CARP

HOW: AN ALL-PURPOSE NYMPH

HOOK: SIZE 8 TO 12 2X SHANK
TAIL: TAIL HARE'S EAR FIBRES
BODY: HARE'S EAR WITH CLEAR POLYRIB

This fly can be a dragon fly larva, a stone fly nymph, a shrimp, a freshwater crab or indeed, whatever the fish wants it to be. I love this version for grayling but the orange or white versions do well for bass. Carp take a fancy to the olive one. Fabulous fly for grubbing around the bottom of stillwaters and tied very large, it would be a great striper fly.

Sooty Olive

FISHING ON THE WILD LOUGHS of western Ireland involves the traditional short lining technique practised from a drifting boat. The Sooty Olive is considered by many to be the 'proper' fly to use and its name is used with almost a quieter tone and with due deference to its fish catching qualities. It works early in the season when the duck fly are on – that's chironomids to the rest of us – and also when the olives begin hatching. It works again later on as a shrimp. Because it is such a local fly to Ireland it can be sometimes be difficult to obtain the right colour materials, but don't compromise or the fly loses its magic!

WHERE: THE LOUGHS OF IRELAND, OTHER WILD STILLWATERS IN THE NORTHERN HEMISPHERE

WHEN: SPRING THROUGH SUMMER

WHAT: TROUT

HOW: SUGGESTS ALL THINGS BUT MOSTLY CHIRONOMIDS AND OLIVES

HOOK: 8 TO 14 STANDARD SHANK
TAIL: GOLDEN PHEASANT TIPPETS
BODY: MIX OF DARK OLIVE AND BROWN SEALS FUR WITH FINE OVAL GOLD RIB
WING: BRONZE MALLARD
HACKLE: SOOTY OLIVE HEN (RED GAME DYED DARK OLIVE)

The Editor

SANDY LEVENTON IS EDITOR OF THE UK'S 'Trout and Salmon' magazine and is a very accomplished fly fisher for Atlantic salmon. He came up with this unusual fly for fresh-run fish and I'm sure it could also be a very good steelhead fly. Translucence is something that salmon fly tiers have not often worked towards, and it was a clever idea to use the fluorescent yellow and green nylon over the silver body. I personally think this fly is a modern version of Arthur Ransome's Elver (see page 282) and it has a great future, especially if Sandy's magazine encourages catch-and-release.

WHERE: RIVERS IN TEMPERATE REGIONS

WHEN: SPRING TO FALL

WHAT: ATLANTIC SALMON AND SEA TROUT

HOW: EXCELLENT FLY FOR FRESH FISH IN CLEAR WATER

HOOK SIZE: 12 TO 6 SALMON IRON SINGLE OR DOUBLE
TAIL: GOLDEN PHEASANT CREST
BODY: PEARL MYLAR RIBBED WITH FLUO YELLOW OR GREEN NYLON
WING: BLACK SQUIRREL OR BUCKTAIL
HACKLE: BLUE COCK FIBRES
CHEEKS: JUNGLE COCK

Yellow Leech

MANY FLIES ARE CALLED LEECH IMITATIONS when they really don't look much like the real thing and certainly don't move like it. Nevertheless, as a generic group of patterns they work pretty well and fool a lot of fish. A colour rarely used in flies is yellow, and if you believe (as I do) that fish see colour, then sometimes giving fish something different can be hugely beneficial to your catch rate. Probably more important in stocked and heavily-fished waters, a Yellow Leech will catch in many situations.

WHERE: WORLDWIDE IN STILLWATER AND RIVERS AND IN COASTAL SALTWATER

WHEN: ALL YEAR BUT BETTER IN COLD WATER

WHAT: TROUT, CHAR, PIKE, LAKE TROUT, WALLEYE, BARRAMUNDI AND MANY SALTWATER SPECIES

HOW: PERHAPS SUGGESTS A LEECH, BUT COLOUR AND MOVEMENT SEEM TO BE THE TRIGGER TO PRODUCE A TAKE

HOOK: 2X TO 10 2X NYMPH OR 4X LURE
TAIL: GENEROUS BUNCH OF YELLOW MARABOU FIBRES
BODY: YELLOW MOHAIR YARN, FIBRES STROKED BACK
HACKLE: LONG-FIBRED YELLOW HEN TIED SLOPING BACK

Trude

THIS ONE I OWE TO TUNDRA TED, a very fine young fly fisher from Minnesota, USA. His grandfather sent me a range of his Trudes and I soon realized that here was a superb general-purpose dry fly and an excellent caddis (sedge) imitation. Of course, I now know that it is a much revered fly in its homeland and is equally effective on rivers and stillwater. There are endless variants but the white wing makes it so easy to see in difficult light, and this variant is my preferred river caddis option.

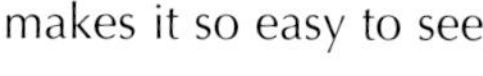

WHERE: WORLDWIDE IN RIVERS AND STILLWATER IN TEMPERATE AND SUB-ARCTIC REGIONS

WHEN: BEST FROM LATE SPRING TO AUTUMN

WHAT: TROUT, GRAYLING, SMALLMOUTH BASS, BLUEGILL

HOW: A GENERAL-PURPOSE DRY FLY BUT ALSO AN EXCELLENT CADDIS (SEDGE) FLY

HOOK: 10 TO 18 STANDARD SHANK
TAIL: GOLDEN PHEASANT TIPPETS
BODY: FLUORESCENT GREEN SYNTHETIC DUBBING
WING: WHITE CALF TAIL
HACKLE: RED GAME COCK

When All Else Fails

AN UNBELIEVABLY SIMPLE PATTERN that relies on the lead wire to suggest a segmented nymph body. The white deer hair simply enables you to see the fly at depth. A 'stalking' pattern, it can be absolutely deadly for stocked trout in clear, stillwater fisheries. Popularized by the late Bill Sibbons of Hampshire, UK, this fly also works very well with grayling or trout in running water where individual fish can be targeted. Not so good fished 'blind', as the takes are so quiet you will not know about them unless you actually see the fish take the fly in its mouth.

WHERE: SMALL, STOCKED, CLEARWATER FISHERIES IN THE UK, EUROPE OR USA, AND ALSO ON RIVERS TO WILD OR STOCKED FISH

WHEN: BEST IN HIGH SUMMER WITH CLEAR WATER WHEN VISIBILITY IS PERFECT

WHAT: RAINBOW, BROWN AND BROOK TROUT, GRAYLING

HOW: SUGGESTS A NYMPH.

HOOK: 10 TO 16 STANDARD SHANK
BODY: LEAD WIRE, SOMETIMES TIED SHORT AND SOMETIMES STAINED OLIVE WITH A PANTONE PEN AND THEN SUPERGLUED OVER
THORAX: FOUR FIBRES OF WHITE DEERHAIR CLIPPED SHORT

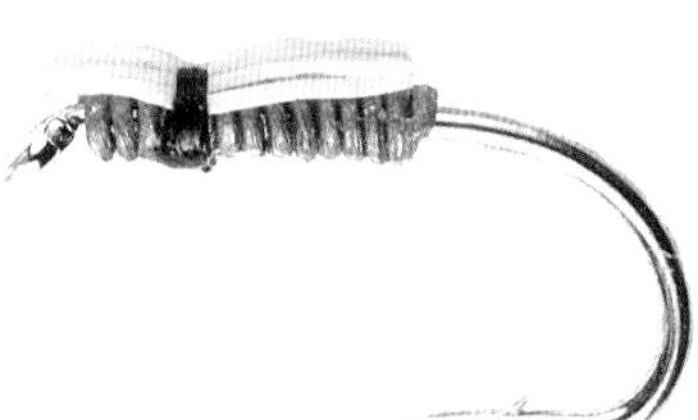

Walker's Mayfly

WHERE: MOST RIVERS OR STILLWATER, BUT BEST WHERE THE LARGER MAYFLY OCCUR

WHEN: ALL YEAR BUT BEST IN LATE SPRING AND SUMMER

WHAT: TROUT, GRAYLING AND MANY OTHER SPECIES OF FISH

HOW: EXCELLENT CLOSE COPY IMITATION OF LARGE EPHEMERID NYMPH

HOOK: 8 TO 12 2X NYMPH SHANK
TAIL: FIBRES OF COCK PHEASANT CENTRE TAIL
BODY: TIED FAT AND WITH OFF-WHITE ANGORA WOOL WITH A RIB OF DARK BROWN FLOSS
BACK: VARNISHED AND SIDES PICKED OUT TO SUGGEST GILLS
THORAX: THE SAME WOOL AS BODY WITH COCK PHEASANT FIBRES FOR THE BACK AND THEN TURNED BACK SO THAT THE ENDS MAKE THE LEGS

THIS MAGNIFICENT CLOSE COPY NYMPH PATTERN was developed by Dick Walker who was the UK's most forward-thinking, all-round angler and typical of someone who came to stillwater fly fishing at a time when the creation of small, stocked ponds was booming in the late 1960s. Walker's Mayfly Nymph is a tremendous nymph for stillwater or rivers, but works just as well where the natural mayfly does not even occur!

Christmas Island Special

WHILE CLEARLY A VARIANT on the Crazy Charlie (see page 431), this Randall Kaufmann special is sufficiently different to be considered separately.

Christmas Island is the ideal place to go to catch your first bonefish as there are lots of average-sized fish and plenty of excellent flats. Even if you are a good trout angler, bonefish are in a different league, so don't set yourself too high an expectation for your first trip – go where sport is just about guaranteed and then work up to the more difficult names.

WHERE: TROPICAL SALTWATER REGIONS

WHEN: ALL YEAR

WHAT: BONEFISH

HOW: A GOOD GENERAL SHRIMP PATTERN

HOOK: 4 TO 8 STAINLESS O'SHAUGHNESSY. FISH THIS FLY HOOK POINT UP
TAIL: PEARL CRYSTALFLASH
BODY: PEARL CRYSTALFLASH
WINGS: PEARL CRYSTALFLASH WITH TAN POLAR FIBRE
EYES: GOLD DUMBBELLS PAINTED WHITE AND FLUORESCENT ORANGE WITH BLACK EYES. OPTIONS ARE ORANGE, PINK AND YELLOW CRYSTAL HAIR

Mickey Finn

WHERE: WORLDWIDE IN LAKES AND SOME RIVERS

WHEN: ALL YEAR BUT BEST IN SPRING AND SUMMER

WHAT: TROUT, LAKE TROUT, CHAR, SALMON, STEELHEAD, CUTTHROAT, PIKE, TIGER FISH

HOW: THE CONTRASTING COLOURS PROVOKE PREDATORY FISH INTO STRIKING

HOOK: 10 2X SHANK THROUGH TO 4 6X SHANK
BODY: SILVER FLAT TINSEL OVER-RIBBED WITH OVAL SILVER
WING: LAYERS OF YELLOW THEN RED THEN YELLOW BUCKTAIL TIED TO LIE CLOSE TO THE HOOK SHANK AND PROJECTING WELL BEYOND THE BEND

THIS SIMPLE OLD-TIMER can still out-fish patterns that are much more modern and complex. Use it where fishing pressure is light, where migratory fish are expected in from the ocean, or just as a colour change from other patterns. I know this fly well for its effectiveness on lake trout in Canada and for the huge char of the Arctic rivers. Tied by Andy Anderson, it's also a favourite of George Bush when he fishes the Tree River from Plummer's Great Bear Lodge. In small sizes it is an excellent summer pattern in lakes for rainbow trout.

Improved Sofa Pillow

ADULT STONEFLIES can be absolutely huge. Fished on the dead drift or skated on rivers and stillwater they can provoke a furious rise if twitched through a light ripple. I have seen huge brown and rainbow trout take these flies under conditions when they really ought to know better, but the lure of that meaty mouthful is just too much for them to resist. Even very large fish eaters will snack on big stoneflies and sometimes even an Atlantic salmon can be tempted to one.

WHERE: WORLDWIDE IN RIVERS AND STILLWATER

WHEN: USUALLY FROM ABOUT MID-SUMMER ONWARDS

WHAT: TROUT, LAKE TROUT, GRAYLING, STEELHEAD, SMALLMOUTH AND LARGEMOUTH BASS, BLUEGILL, CHAR, ATLANTIC SALMON, CARP

HOW: SUGGESTS THE ADULT STONEFLY

HOOK: 6 TO 10 2X LONG SHANK
TAIL: MOOSE BODY OR FOX SQUIRREL TAIL
BODY: ORANGE POLY YARN WITH PALMERED RED GAME COCK HACKLE
WING: FOX SQUIRREL TAIL OR ELK HAIR
HACKLE: RED GAME COCK

Munro Killer

WHERE: NORTHERN HEMISPHERE IN CLASSIC ATLANTIC SALMON RIVERS

WHEN: GOOD THROUGHOUT THE SEASON

WHAT: ATLANTIC SALMON, SEA TROUT, STEELHEAD

HOW: HAIRWING ATTRACTOR-STYLE SALMON FLY

HOOK: 6 TO 12 SALMON IRON AND 6 TO 12 DOUBLE
TAIL: OVAL GOLD TINSEL TAG WITH ORANGE COCK HACKLE FIBRES
BODY: BLACK FLOSS RIBBED WITH OVAL GOLD TINSEL
HACKLE: ORANGE COCK HACKLE FIBRES WITH BLUE DYED GUINEA FOWL
WING: YELLOWISH-BROWN HAIR WITH BLACK HAIR OVER, CAN BE BUCKTAIL OR SQUIRREL

FLIES FOR ATLANTIC SALMON are typically either all-black, black with silver or mostly a marriage of orange and yellow. Within this comes a vastly complex array of patterns which only serve to confuse the issue. Often it comes down to the simple fact that most anglers on a particular river will be using 'the fly of the moment' and therefore most fish will be caught on that fly, which in turn becomes the 'only' fly to use on a particular river. The Munro has no such connections but is a great fly nonetheless.

Killer Bug

THIS NO-NONSENSE GRAYLING BUG was deigned by legendary river keeper Frank Sawyer. Nowadays it is overshadowed by Czech Nymphs and other caddis (sedge) tyings. However, it remains an extremely good pattern even though the original wool is no longer available (although guess who is lucky enough to still have a card of the original Chadwicks 477!). Fortunately there are equally good wools which give the same pinkish hue when wet. The copper wire underbody is an essential part of this pattern's success.

WHERE: RIVERS THROUGHOUT EUROPE

WHEN: ALL YEAR BUT USUALLY LATE SUMMER TO EARLY SPRING

WHAT: GRAYLING

HOW: A BASIC BUG THAT PROBABLY LOOKS LIKE A CADDIS (SEDGE) LARVA

HOOK: 10 TO 14 STANDARD SHANK
BODY: COPPER WIRE OVERLAID WITH LAYER OF FAWN WOOL WITH PINK TINGE

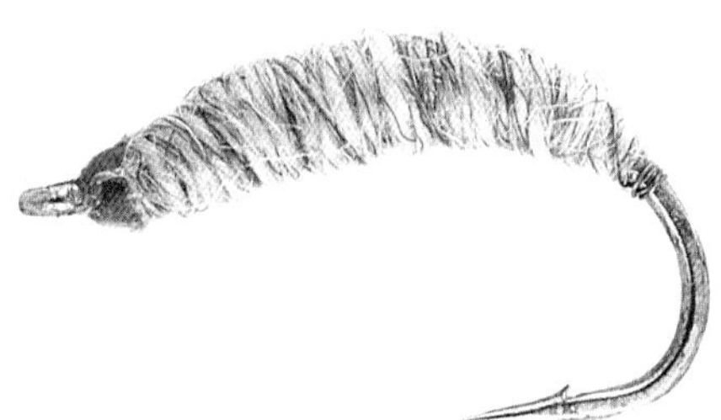

Pearl Stoat Tail

WHERE: WORLDWIDE IN SALMON AND SEA TROUT RIVERS

WHEN: ALL SEASON, BUT OFTEN BEST AT NIGHT AND WHEN LIGHT IS POOR BY DAY

WHAT: ATLANTIC SALMON AND SEA TROUT, ALSO BROWN TROUT IN LAKES AND RIVERS AND STEELHEAD

HOW: A STANDARD BLACK FLY LIFTED WITH A BRIGHT BODY

HOOK: 6 TO 12 STANDARD SALMON IRON OR 6 TO 12 DOUBLE
BODY: PEARL TINSEL RIBBED WITH FINE SILVER WIRE
HACKLE: BLACK COCK HACKLE FIBRES
WING: BLACK SQUIRREL TAIL

THIS IS REALLY JUST AN UPDATE to a long-established fly using the more modern pearl tinsel instead of old-fashioned silver. I'm not sure if it is an improvement, but so much to do with salmon and sea trout fishing is related to confidence and the way you present the fly. Of course, pattern has a lot of bearing on success, but often everyone will be using the same fly and one angler will take the lion's share of the catch. Use this in coloured water or at night when there are shafts of moonlight, to illuminate the body.

Demoiselle

IT MIGHT NOT LOOK MUCH LIKE A DAMSEL NYMPH, but this fly works extremely well when trout are feeding on the natural damsels. Fish it from early summer when the damsels are hatching. Let it sink quite deep in and around weed beds or bottom debris and retrieve a slow sink and draw or occasionally very quickly, remembering that damsel larvae can swim extremely fast over short distances.

WHERE: WORLDWIDE IN LAKES AND PONDS

WHEN: ALL YEAR BUT SPRING AND SUMMER ARE BEST

WHAT: TROUT, SMALLMOUTH AND LARGEMOUTH BASS, BLUEGILL

HOW: SUGGESTS THE LARVAE OF THE DAMSEL NYMPH

HOOK: 8X TO 12 2X NYMPH SHANK
TAIL: BRIGHT GREEN COCK HACKLE FIBRES
BODY: SEAL'S FUR (MIX OF OLIVE, ORANGE, BLUE AND YELLOW) RIBBED WITH OVAL GOLD TINSEL
HACKLE: GREY PARTRIDGE DYED YELLOW

Ted's Stonefly

IT MIGHT LOOK LIKE YET ANOTHER MONTANA VARIANT (see page 360), but this colour combination by Ted Trueblood is not only an effective stonefly imitation but also works very well in spring when caddis (sedge), and alders, are hatching, and again in early and mid summer when large caddis are on the move. Fished high in the water on large stillwaters in mid summer and with a fluorescent orange thorax, it takes rainbow trout feeding on daphnia.

WHERE: WORLDWIDE IN STILLWATER AND RIVERS

WHEN: ALL YEAR BUT DEEP IN SPRING-TIME AND HIGHER IN SUMMER

WHAT: TROUT, LARGE AND SMALLMOUTH BASS

HOW: SUGGESTS STONEFLY, ALDER LARVAE, CADDIS (SEDGE) PUPAE AND GENERALLY LOOKS EDIBLE

HOOK: 12 TO 6 NYMPH HOOK
TAIL: BROWN GOOSE BIOTS
BODY AND WING CASE: BROWN CHENILLE
THORAX: ORANGE CHENILLE WITH BLACK COCK HACKLE PALMERED THROUGH

Willie Gunn

WITHOUT DOUBT this one fly is loved and respected throughout Scotland for its ability to catch early and late-running salmon whether dressed as a single, double, treble, tube or Waddington. If salmon are actually in the river (not necessarily a certainty these days) you will have an excellent chance of finding a fish that will take a Willie Gunn. Although many salmon flies use this colour mix there is definitely something about this fly that puts it above others.

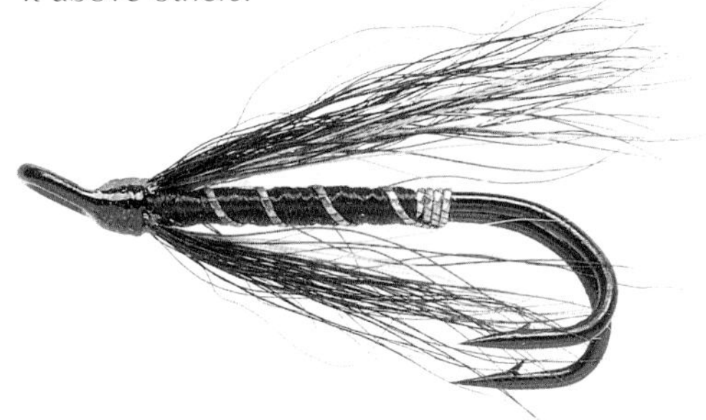

WHERE: ATLANTIC SALMON RIVERS

WHEN: ALL YEAR BUT BEST EARLY AND LATE IN THE SEASON

WHAT: ATLANTIC SALMON, SEA TROUT AND SEVERAL OTHER SALMONIDS

HOW: GENERAL ATTRACTOR

HOOK: 4 TO 12 SALMON SINGLE
TAG: FLAT GOLD TINSEL
BODY: BLACK FLOSS RIBBED WITH OVAL GOLD TINSEL
WING: BUCKTAIL, ORANGE THEN YELLOW THEN BLACK

Rat-faced McDougal

WHAT A WONDERFUL NAME! Whenever you need a good dry fly that floats well even after taking a few fish then look no further than the Rat-faced McDougal. In a range of sizes it will tempt most freshwater fish and is probably best used on moving water. A regular player towards the end of the mayfly hatch on English chalk streams.

WHERE: NEARLY WORLDWIDE

WHEN: SPRING TO AUTUMN

WHAT: ALL TROUT, GRAYLING, PANFISH

HOW: A GENERAL PATTERN THAT SUGGESTS MANY ADULT FLIES

HOOK: 6 TO 14 STANDARD SHANK
TAIL: LIGHT BROWN ELK
BODY: LIGHT GREY DEER HAIR SPUN AND CLIPPED
WINGS: GRIZZLE HEN HACKLE TIPS
HACKLE: LIGHT GINGER COCK

Hawthorn

WHEREVER YOU MAY FISH there will always be insects which fall onto the water. This imitation of the hawthorn is a UK pattern for the month of May, but similar insects occur throughout the world and a large, blackish fly with shiny wings will rarely be refused. Warm, sunny days are usually best and if you can be just downwind of shrubbery you will often find that Mother Nature has already done the ground baiting!

WHERE: WORLDWIDE IN FRESHWATER

WHEN: SPRING AND EARLY SUMMER

WHAT: TROUT, GRAYLING, BLUEGILL, SMALLMOUTH BASS

HOW: SPECIFICALLY IMITATES THE HAWTHORN BUT A GENERAL PATTERN ANYWHERE

HOOK: 10 OR 12 STANDARD SHANK
BODY: DYED BLACK FEATHER FIBRE
HACKLE: BLACK COCK
WING: THREE LARGE CDC PLUMES AND A FEW FIBRES OF PEARL CRYSTALFLASH
LEGS: TWO BLACK FEATHER FIBRES

Damsel Wiggle Nymph

THIS EARLY TYING TECHNIQUE, DESIGNED to simulate the wiggle of a damsel nymph's abdomen, comes into its own when large or small mouth bass make short work of a similar nymph tied with a marabou tail. The fly actually needs to be retrieved quite quickly in stillwater to build up enough water pressure to make the tail section wiggle. In a river, the current does the work for you.

WHERE: STILLWATERS AND SLOWER RIVERS IN TEMPERATE REGIONS

WHEN: SUMMER

WHAT: TROUT, LARGE AND SMALLMOUTH BASS, BLUEGILLS

HOW: DAMSEL NYMPH IMITATION

HOOK: 8 TO 12 STANDARD SHANK WITH MONO LOOP AND EXTRA HOOK SHANK
TAIL: THREE COCK HACKLE POINTS
ABDOMEN: MIX OF OLIVE, ORANGE AND BLUE SEALS FUR RIBBED WITH OVAL GOLD TINSEL
HACKLE: OLIVE PARTRIDGE
THORAX: CASE PHEASANT TAIL FIBRES
EYES: MINI LEAD DUMBBELLS

Gray Wulff

LEE WULFF, who created the Wulff series of flies, justly deserves his iconic status in the fly fishing world. You can fish them dry, slightly soggy, wet or skated and they will catch all manner of fish. However, as a dry fly during hatches of the larger mayflies, the original takes some beating. Tied down to a size 16, it makes a brilliant general-purpose dry fly.

WHERE: WORLDWIDE IN RIVERS AND STILLWATER IN TEMPERATE ZONES

WHEN: ALL YEAR BUT BEST IN SPRING AND SUMMER

WHAT: TROUT, GRAYLING, SALMON, SEA TROUT, STEELHEAD, CHAR AND JUST ABOUT ANY FRESHWATER SPECIES

HOW: A GENERAL-PURPOSE DRY AND AN EXCELLENT MAYFLY IMITATION

HOOK: 8 TO 16 STANDARD SHANK TO 2X SHANK
TAIL: GREY SQUIRREL TAIL FIBRES
BODY: MUSKRAT UNDERFUR OR NATURAL RABBIT UNDERFUR
WING: GREY SQUIRREL TIED FORWARD AND SEPARATED, DEER ON SMALLER SIZES
HACKLE: MEDIUM BLUE DUN COCK HACKLE

Seducer

A MARVELLOUS SALTWATER FLY which provides the illusion of bulk without the weight. This is an old pattern but when tied in various colours will catch many saltwater species. This pattern needs to be tied large to be really effective. Fish the seducer series with absolute confidence.

WHERE: WORLDWIDE IN SALTWATER, BUT GENERALLY BEST SUITED TO THE TROPICS

WHEN: ALL YEAR DEPENDING ON SPECIES LOCATION

WHAT: TARPON, REDFISH, SNOOK, JACK (TREVALLY), DORADO, NILE PERCH, TAIMEN, BARRAMUNDI

HOW: GIVES AN ILLUSION OF LIFE AND INDUCES A STRIKE ACTION FROM PREDATORS

HOOK: 2/0 OR 3/0 3X SHANK

TAIL: THREE PAIRS OF YELLOW SADDLE OR SCHLAPPEN FEATHERS ON EACH SIDE AND TIED TO FLARE OUT WITH A GRIZZLE HACKLE ON EITHER SIDE

BODY: FULLY PALMERED WITH YELLOW THEN GRIZZLE THEN YELLOW LONG-FIBRED HACKLES

Mackay

THE MACKAY IS ONE OF THE HOT little nymphs that came from Scotland in the late 1990s. Very much a stillwater fly in conception, I'm sure it would work in rough streams especially early and late in the season. I can also see it being a good sea trout fly for low, clear water. It works just as well for wild fish as for stock fish. It has a variety of colour options, and adding marabou, Crystalflash and Glo-brite to a nymph tying adds special appeal to fish.

WHERE: STILLWATER IN TEMPERATE REGIONS

WHEN: ALL YEAR

WHAT: TROUT, BUT GOOD FOR MANY OTHER SPECIES AS WELL

HOW: GENERAL ATTRACTOR

HOOK: 10 TO 8 STANDARD SHANK
TAIL: BLACK MARABOU WITH A FEW STRANDS OF PEARL CRYSTALFLASH
BODY: HARE'S EAR RIBBED WITH OVAL GOLD TINSEL
THORAX: HARE'S EAR WITH PHEASANT TAIL FIBRES OVER
BODY AND HEAD: TUFTS OF ORANGE AND WHITE GLO-BRITE FLOSS

Bare Bones Buzzer

WHERE: WORLDWIDE IN STILLWATER

WHEN: BEST FROM SPRING TO AUTUMN AND USUALLY ON BRIGHTER DAYS

WHAT: PRINCIPALLY TROUT BUT MOST FRESHWATER SPECIES WILL TAKE IT

HOW: SUGGESTS THE PUPAL STAGE OF THE CHIRONOMID BUZZER

HOOK: CURVED SHANK, GOLD COLOUR
BODY: FLEXI-FLOSS RIBBED UP SHANK AND THEN OVERLAPPED TO FORM THORAX
TO MAKE THE BUZZER: TRAP THE FLOSS END IN THE VICE WITH THE HOOK, MAKING THE RIB AND THORAX THEN HANGING HACKLE PLIERS ON THE FLOSS END. APPLY A LAYER OF SUPERGLUE, ALLOW TO DRY, TRIM OFF ENDS AND THEN APPLY TWO MORE LAYERS OF SUPERGLUE.

ONE DAY I SAW an angler doing very well with just copper wire wrapped around a curved hook during a buzzer (chironomid) hatch and from that I evolved this minimalist pattern fashioned from Flexi-floss, a coloured hook and superglue. The result was a fly which is taken positively, especially on sunny days. I just wish I had had it in my fly box 30 years ago when I fished stillwaters for buzzer-feeding trout.

Poxy Bug

AN ODD LITTLE FLY intended for small, clearwater ponds where individual trout can be seen and targeted. The lead wire gives a suggestion of segmentation and the marabou provides a degree of movement sufficient to fool stocked trout into thinking that it is edible. The fish will accept this pattern so quietly that if it were not for the fact that it is a sighted take the angler would have no idea it had been taken. Colour changing works and really difficult fish will sometimes literally pounce on a different colour having ignored several others.

WHERE: SMALL, STOCKED STILLWATERS IN THE UK, EUROPE AND SOME IN THE USA

WHEN: BEST IN SUMMER WHEN THE SUN IS HIGH ALLOWING GOOD VISION INTO THE WATER

WHAT: STOCKED RAINBOW AND BROWN TROUT

HOW: POSSIBLY SUGGESTS A NYMPH BUT MAYBE IT'S JUST A TRIGGER OF SHAPE AND COLOUR

HOOK: 10 TO 14 STANDARD SHANK
TAIL: SHORT TUFT OF MARABOU (OLIVE, BLACK, WHITE, ORANGE, CORAL, RED)
BODY: LEAD WIRE COATED WITH RAPID SETTING EPOXY GLUE AND STAINED OLIVE
HEAD: A SMALL YELLOW EYE SPOT WITH EPOXY OVER

Orange Mini Muddler

YOU CAN TURN ANY SORT OF MUDDLER into a miniature version and use it as a fry or caddis (sedge) imitation or simply as an attractor. Muddlers work in the surface or on a sunk line and I believe that their success is due to the disturbance caused by the fat head of deerhair which creates all sorts of underwater vibration, which they pick up in the sensors in the lateral line.

WHERE: WORLDWIDE IN RIVERS AND STILLWATER

WHEN: ALL YEAR

WHAT: TROUT AND MOST PREDATORY AND INSECT-EATING FISH

HOW: CAN SUGGEST MANY THINGS DEPENDING ON THE COLOUR USED

HOOK: 10 TO 12 STANDARD SHANK
TAIL: ORANGE CRYSTALHAIR
BODY: ORANGE FLOSS WITH OVAL SILVER TINSEL RIB
WING: ORANGE SQUIRREL WITH ORANGE CRYSTAL HAIR
HEAD: DEERHAIR SPUN AND CLIPPED

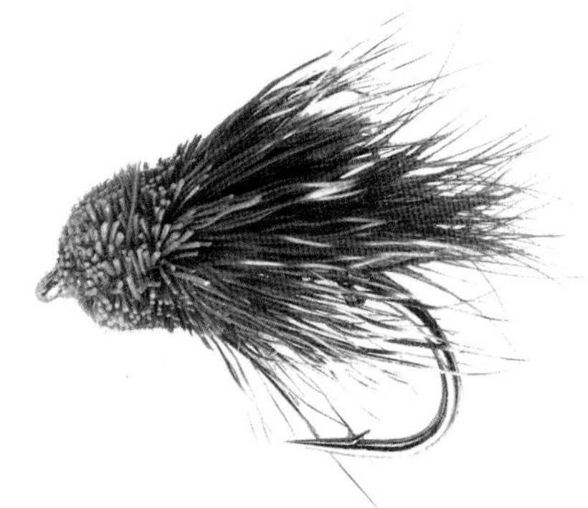

CDC and Elk

CADDIS (SEDGE) FLIES ARE VITALLY IMPORTANT to the fly fisher because they are a worldwide clan with literally hundreds of members. This version of the classic Elk Hair Caddis gives us a general-purpose fly which floats well and is simple to tie. Yet another fly which relies on the high-floating qualities of CDC plumes.

WHERE: WORLDWIDE IN RIVERS AND STILLWATER, BUT MOSTLY IN TEMPERATE REGIONS

WHEN: SUMMER TO AUTUMN

WHAT: TROUT, CUTTHROAT, SMALLMOUTH BASS

HOW: ACCURATELY REPRESENTS AN ADULT CADDIS (SEDGE)

HOOK: 12 TO 16 STANDARD SHANK FINE WIRE
BODY/HACKLE: ONE CDC FEATHER
WING: FINE, BLACK-TIPPED DEERHAIR

Blue Winged Olive Nymph

THIS INSECT OF THE alkaline streams has a life cycle that we do not fully understand. One year it will hatch in its thousands, only to be absent altogether for several years. Although the adult is the most imitated stage, the nymph is undeniably effective and this modern approach can frequently turn an otherwise slow day into a red-letter one. Remember that even chalkstream fish take much of their food below the surface.

WHERE: CHALK (LIMESTONE) STREAMS WORLDWIDE IN TEMPERATE REGIONS

WHEN: LATE SPRING TO AUTUMN

WHAT: TROUT, GRAYLING

HOW: BLUE WINGED OLIVE NYMPH IMITATION

HOOK: 14 TO 16 STANDARD SHANK
TAIL: WOOD DUCK FIBRES
BODY: MUSKRAT UNDERFUR
THORAX: RUST SEAL'S FUR WITH PEARL WING CASE OVER

Scintillator

WHERE WOULD WE BE WITHOUT BEADS? I really like this fly for streamy water in shallow limestone creeks or freestone rivers which have lots of bubble and life. The pearl bead probably suggests the stage immediately before the insect hatches. Gradually becoming accepted for stillwater fishing, it works best where the water is clear. Fish it in the upper layers during late afternoon or early evening as the hatch begins.

WHERE: SHALLOW, STREAMY WATER IN RIVERS IN TEMPERATE AND SUB-ARCTIC

WHEN: SUMMER TO AUTUMN

WHAT: TROUT, GRAYLING,

HOW: SUGGESTS AN EMERGING CADDIS (SEDGE) PUPA

HOOK: 14 TO 16 STANDARD SHANK
ABDOMEN: PALE OLIVE (OR BLACK, BROWN OR BRIGHT GREEN) ANTRON
BODY: PEARL BEAD
HACKLE: GREY SPECKLED MALLARD OR GREY PARTRIDGE
HEAD: LIGHT BROWN OSTRICH HERL

Cutwing Callibaetis PMD

MAYFLIES ARE AN INDICATOR OF RIVER QUALITY as well as being a prime food source for trout. This beautiful little fly, the Pale Morning Dun, is so very important in the US and this tying works well on many other locations where small, pale patterns are needed. The trend of maintaining native bred trout stocks without recourse to heavy stocking purely for sport, will see a gradual return to more imitative fly tying. Such true-to-life patterns will once again become essential on waters where currently just about anything will take the stock fish.

WHERE: RIVERS WORLDWIDE IN TEMPERATE REGIONS

WHEN: SPRING THROUGH TO FALL
WHAT: TROUT GRAYLING

WHAT: BROWN AND RAINBOW TROUT

HOW: IMITATIVE DAY FLY

HOOK:18 TO 12 FINE WIRE STANDARD SHANK
TAIL: CREAM YELLOW MICRO FIBBETS
BODY: CREAM POLYPROPYLENE DUB WITH CLEAR NYLON RIB
HACKLE: CREAM COCK
WINGS: PRECUT WING FIBRE

Danny's Redfish Special

REDFISH ARE A GOOD-LOOKING FISH with an excellent fighting reputation and are much sought-after by fly fishers. Many redfish patterns use red and yellow as their base, and this colour combination also works well for sea trout (marine fish not the sea-run brown trout). Any fly tied with cactus chenille will have a softer landing and a slower sink rate than the same one tied with rayon chenille.

WHERE: TROPICAL SALTWATER AROUND THE EAST COAST OF THE USA

WHEN: ALL YEAR, BUT SEASONAL MIGRATIONS

WHAT: REDFISH, SEA TROUT, SNOOK

HOW: AN ALL-PURPOSE ATTRACTOR

HOOK: 1 TO 1/0 STAINLESS O'SHAUGHNESSY. FISH THIS FLY HOOK POINT UP
BODY: BRIGHT YELLOW CACTUS CHENILLE
WING: DARK YELLOW BUCKTAIL WITH ORANGE OVER AND THEN COPPER CRYSTALFLASH

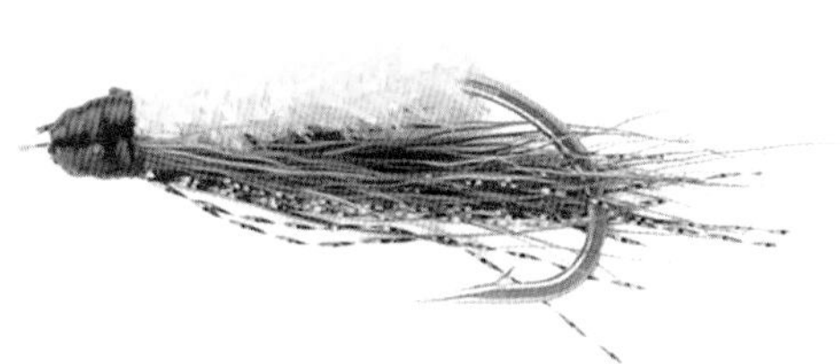

Cove Pheasant Tail

THE IMPORTANCE OF THE CHIRONOMID cannot be over-emphasized for stillwater fishing where the fish feed very heavily on at all stages of the insect.

WHERE: WORLDWIDE IN STILLWATER

WHEN: ALL YEAR BUT SPRING TO EARLY SUMMER IS BEST

WHAT: TROUT, SMALLMOUTH AND LARGEMOUTH BASS, SOMETIMES CARP

HOW: IMITATES THE STAGE OF THE CHIRONOMID

HOOK: 6 TO 10 2X NYMPH SHANK
BODY: PHEASANT TAIL FIBRES TIED ROUND THE BEND AND RIBBED WITH FINE COPPER OVAL
THORAX: RABBIT UNDERFUR WITH PHEASANT TAIL FIBRES OVER

This pattern evolved in the mid-1960s to imitate the pupal stage. When fished close to the bottom from the bank fly cast it will catch extremely well. Named after stillwater specialist Arthur Cove, this simple nymph uses common materials in a new format. Retrieve the Cove Nymph very slowly along the bottom for optimum results.

Baby Doll

THIS SIMPLY TIED LURE cashes in on the trout's ability to see the effects of ultra-violet light. The white nylon baby wool surrounds itself with a light blue halo which trout find irresistible. Once the fly has become stained, its powers fail. Throw it away and tie on a clean fly.

WHERE: WORLDWIDE IN STILLWATER, RIVERS AND COASTAL WATERS

WHEN: ANY TIME OF THE YEAR

WHAT: ALL PREDATORY SPECIES, EVEN CARP AT TIMES

HOW: MAYBE RESEMBLES A SMALL FISH

HOOK: 4X TO 14 4X LONG SHANK OR 2X NYMPH SHANK OR STANDARD SHANK TAIL, BODY AND BACK: WHITE NYLON BABY WOOL

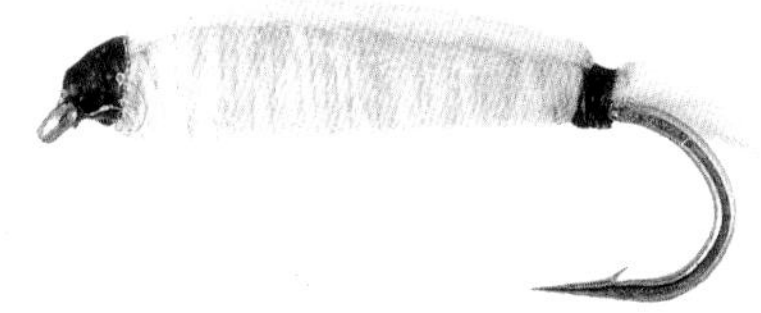

Everglow Serpent

FLY FISHING IN SALTWATER has been the fastest-growing aspect in worldwide fly fishing in recent years, but heavier than usual tackle is required to cast out the larger and bulkier flies on a windy day. This is a lovely fly for calmer inshore and estuary work. It is easy to cast and has wonderful movement. Fluorescent materials make the lure easier to spot in poor light or murky water.

WHERE: WORLDWIDE IN SALTWATER

WHEN: ALL YEAR

WHAT: MOST PREDATORY FISH

HOW: COLOUR AND MOVEMENT ARE KEY FACTORS

HOOK: 4X TO 1/0 STAINLESS O'SHAUGHNESSY
TAIL: CHARTREUSE RABBIT STRIP
BODY: EVERGLOW TUBING WITH PAINTED GILLS AND EYE THEN EPOXY RESIN

Floating Perch

WHEN RESERVOIR TROUT CHARGE INTO SHOALS of tiny fish they stun or damage far more that they actually eat right away. The crippled fry then float to the surface where they make easy picking for any cruising trout. Probably best fished around weed beds, this pattern requires stealth and patience. Use a strong leader, at least 4.5 kg (10 lbs), and hold the fish hard to stop them getting fouled up. This is a marvellous fly too for almost all predatory fishes.

WHERE: JUST ABOUT ANY STILLWATER IN TEMPERATE REGIONS

WHEN: FRY TIME WHICH IS USUALLY IN THE FALL

WHAT: TROUT AND ANY PREDATORY SPECIES

HOW: SUGGESTS A DEAD OR DYING BABY FISH

HOOK: 2 TO 6 4X TO 6X SHANK
BODY: SPUN WHITE DEER HAIR CLIPPED AND THEN PANTONE PEN TO IMITATE PREY SPECIES
EYES: STICK ON PLASTIC DOLL EYES
TAIL: MARABOU SOMETIMES A BIT OF CRYSTAL HAIR TOO

Black Gnat

AN OLD-TIMER THAT WILL REMAIN A FIRM FAVOURITE when many of today's patterns have been forgotten. It follows the golden rule that a small, simple black fly will work in just about any situation wherever one fishes. An essential for early season work on rivers when the natural black gnat is most abundant, it is an excellent all-purpose search fly for rain-fed rivers (freestone streams) and useful for fish which are clearly feeding but, not on any one specific fly. Make sure you have a range of sizes.

WHERE: WORLDWIDE IN STILLWATER AND RIVERS

WHEN: ALL YEAR BUT BEST FROM SPRING TO AUTUMN

WHAT: TROUT, GRAYLING, CHAR, CUTTHROAT TROUT, SMALLMOUTH BASS

HOW: SPECIFICALLY IMITATES A BLACK GNAT BUT ALSO A GENERAL SEARCH PATTERN

HOOK: 10 TO 20 STANDARD SHANK
TAIL: BLACK COCK HACKLE FIBRES
BODY: BLACK RABBIT OR POLYPROPYLENE DUBBING
WING: GREY MALLARD QUILL OR STARLING IN SMALL SIZES
HACKLE: BLACK COCK

Elk Hair Caddis

EASY TO PRODUCE IN A NUMBER OF COLOUR VARIATIONS to match the hatch, this is deservedly an extremely popular fly for which we must thank master American fly tier Al Troth. Caddis (sedge) are terribly important, more so in rivers than lakes, and you must be prepared to fish the rise to this insect as it can give some of the best sport of the season. It is such a good fly that you can fish it even when there isn't a hatch as the fish will often snack off what appears to be a single, lonely adult. If grayling come short, I sometimes trim the hackle to make it sit lower in the water.

WHERE: WORLDWIDE IN RIVERS AND STILLWATER

WHEN: SUMMER TO AUTUMN

WHAT: TROUT, CHAR, GRAYLING, LAKE TROUT, SMALLMOUTH BASS, BLUEGILL

HOW: SUGGESTS AN ADULT CADDIS (SEDGE)

HOOK: 10 TO 16 STANDARD SHANK FINE WIRE
BODY: DUBBED POLYPROPYLENE YARN OR SEAL'S FUR
HACKLE: PALMERED RED GAME
WING: ELK HAIR

Gotcha

FISH OVER LIGHT-COLOURED FLATS and this pattern is a must. I used it the first time I fished bonefish in the Bahamas, substituting plastic beads for the more common bead chain eyes. Most of the time the water is really shallow and you don't need a heavy fly. The casting is easier and the presentation softer than with a chain-eyed version. Catching bonefish is a challenge. Try it and you'll be amazed at the sheer power of a modest 1.8 kg (4 lb) bonefish.

WHERE: TROPICAL SEAS AROUND THE EQUATOR AND MOSTLY ON THE FLATS

WHEN: ALL YEAR

WHAT: PRINCIPALLY BONEFISH BUT MANY FLATS' DWELLERS WILL TAKE IT TOO

HOW: SUGGESTS A SAND-LIVING SHRIMP

HOOK: 2 TO 6 SALTWATER O'SHAUGHNESSY. FISH THIS FLY HOOK POINT UP
TAIL: BUNCH OF PEARL FLASHABOU FIBRES
BODY: PEARL BRAID
WING: SHRIMP-COLOUR POLAR HAIR WITH FIBRES OF ORANGE CRYSTAL HAIR OVER
EYES: PINK PEARL PLASTIC BEAD CHAIN
HEAD: TIED SLIGHTLY LONG AND WITH PINK THREAD

French Partridge Mayfly

TROUT OFTEN PREFER THE HATCHING STAGE of mayfly and this pattern can be fished semi-submerged to imitate this. With large dry flies like this it is unwise to fish too light or too long a leader. The beautiful flank feather of the French, Red-legged or Hungarian Partridge is perfect for this fly, and tied well, makes for a classic pattern and highly effective fly.

WHERE: IN SPRING CREEKS, CHALK STREAMS, LIMESTONE LOUGHS OR SMALL STILLWATERS

WHEN: DURING THE MAYFLY HATCH

WHAT: RAINBOW, BROWN, BROOK AND CUTTHROAT TROUT, GRAYLING

HOW: SUGGESTS THE ADULT OR HATCHING STAGE OF THE MAYFLY

HOOK: 8 TO 12
TAIL: THREE OR FOUR FIBRES OF COCK PHEASANT CENTRE TAIL
BODY: TAN RAFFENE PALMERED WITH AN OLIVE COCK HACKLE AND RIBBED WITH RED THREAD AND GOLD WIRE
HACKLE: FRENCH PARTRIDGE FLANK FEATHER

Lumi Smelt

I WILL NEVER FORGET WATCHING GIANT RAINBOW TROUT crashing into smelt in Lake Okataina in New Zealand. They were much too far offshore for me to reach and how I wanted to be on a boat that day! Little bait fish are very important in both fresh and saltwater situations with the various smelt species being a regular target. These food fish can be ciscos in Canada, roach in the UK, ide in Europe or salmon smelt in Alaska. This fly imitates them all and works well in most situations.

WHERE: WORLDWIDE IN FRESHWATER LAKES AND SALTWATER

WHEN: ALL YEAR

WHAT: ALL PREDATORY SPECIES INCLUDING TROUT AND BASS

HOW: THE IDEAL SMALL BAIT FISH IMITATION

HOOK: 6 TO 8 NICKEL 2X SHANK
WING: WHITE FISHAIR WITH ULTRA-VIOLET PEARL CRYSTAL HAIR AND RED CRYSTAL HAIR
BODY: RAPID SETTING EPOXY GLUE OVER WING ROAT AND EYE

Bob's Bits

MANY YEARS AGO I wrote a column for a UK fishing weekly and once questioned how someone could possibly take two hours to play a 3.2 kg (7 lb) reservoir brown trout. What I didn't know was that it had been hooked on this little gem of a fly, and that for its creator, Bob Worts, it was then his lifetime's best fish. I now have nothing but praise for this fantastic emerger – it really does fool the fish and when chironomids are hatching you can do little better than fish this simple fly. Best fished static in stillwater. Carry versions in different colours to match the hatch of the day.

WHERE: STILLWATER AND SLOWER RIVERS IN TEMPERATE REGIONS

WHEN: SPRING TO AUTUMN

WHAT: TROUT, GRAYLING

HOW: SUGGESTS THE HATCHING STAGE OF THE CHIRONOMID

HOOK: 10 TO 14 STANDARD SHANK FINE WIRE
BODY: BRIGHT RED SEAL'S FUR
WING: A FEW WHITE FEATHER FIBRES
HACKLE: RED GAME COCK, VERY SPARSE ON TOP OF HOOK ONLY. VARIANTS ARE OLIVE, GINGER AND ORANGE

Minkie

WHERE: THROUGHOUT THE WORLD IN STILLWATERS

WHEN: ALMOST ANYTIME BUT ESPECIALLY AT FRY TIME

WHAT: TROUT AND ANY PREDATORY FISH

HOW: A SUGGESTIVE SMALL FISH IMITATION WITH FANTASTIC MOVEMENT

HOOK: 10 TO 6 LONG SHANK(4X)
BODY: BROWN WOOL, VARIANTS USE PEARL OR SILVER FRITZ
WING: A 1/8" STRIP OF BROWN MINK TWICE SHANK LENGTH TIED DOWN MATUKA STYLE WITH GOLD WIRE RIBBING CHEEKS JUNGLE COCK EYE FEATHER
HACKLE: A FEW FIBRES OF SILVER MALLARD OFTEN TIED WITH SOME LEAD WIRE WEIGHT AT THE HEAD END

DAVE BARKER IS AN ACE RESERVOIR ANGLER in the UK and deserves the credit for developing this deadly fry pattern. Mink pelt has an altogether more sinuous movement when tied zonker style than any other hair and predatory fishes just can't resist it's appeal. The original used natural brown mink but silver, white and grey are essential options. Works best around weedbeds or structure but can also be very effective fished with a floating line and long leader over open water with a stop start retrieve. As with many fry patterns it will attract a small following of fry until the attack comes leaving it alone and vulnerable!

Go To Joe

INVENTOR AND FLORIDA GUIDE, STEVE HUFF, reckons this is a winner for spooky, tailing bonefish. This is a fly which combines a bit of glitter with an overall illusion of shape and movement that makes a great shrimp imitation. Fish often only need to see a basic impression of food rather than exact copy to trigger a take. I have the feeling that if this pattern were adapted into an Atlantic salmon fly it would be equally successful. Note the interesting use of a soft grizzle hackle feather to gain movement. Use feathers from an inexpensive cape.

WHERE: TROPICAL SALTWATER FLATS

WHEN: YEAR ROUND

WHAT: BONEFISH, PERMIT, REDFISH, SEATROUT

HOW: SHRIMP IMITATION

HOOK: 2 TO 4 SALTWATER O SHAUGHNESSY
TAIL: PEACOCK HERL AND GRIZZLE SADDLE TIPS
BODY: ROOT BEER FRITZ
EYES: BURNED MONO
HACKLE: SOFT GRIZZLE

Flashback Hare's Ear Red

HOLOGRAPHIC TINSEL has added a new dimension to many fly patterns, and although I use several different colours it is the red tinsel that far out-fishes the others. This is very good for winter grayling in clear water, but is really intended for slightly coloured rivers and stillwaters where a small amount of shine works really well. It needs to be well-weighted and is best fished dead drift close to the bottom. Try it in rough streams and freestone rivers for trout early in the season.

WHERE: WORLDWIDE IN RIVERS IN TEMPERATE REGIONS

WHEN: ALL YEAR

WHAT: TROUT, GRAYLING

HOW: A GENERAL-PURPOSE NYMPH PATTERN

HOOK: 8 TO 12 STANDARD SHANK
TAIL: FIBRES OF NATURAL BROWN PARTRIDGE
BODY: DARK HARE'S EAR DUBBED THICKLY AND RIBBED WITH OVAL COPPER TINSEL
THORAX: SAME AS BODY BUT WING CASE OF RED HOLOGRAPHIC TINSEL
HACKLE: BROWN PARTRIDGE

Compara Dun

THIS SIMPLE TYING has all the right trigger points for a feeding trout. It sits in the surface film, has a visible tail, a rough body and the illusion of emergent wings. For us, it has the bonus of being easy to tie, is made from cheap material and can be colour-adapted to suggest many of the smaller mayflies. Plus, it is light and easy to cast and floats supremely well with the deerhair wings being easy to see. You will find time and again that trout want a fly right in the surface film and not on it or under it.

WHERE: RIVERS AND SOME STILLWATER IN TEMPERATE REGIONS

WHEN: SPRING TO AUTUMN

WHAT: TROUT, GRAYLING

HOW: GENERAL PURPOSE DAY FLY

HOOK: 16 TO 10 STANDARD SHANK FINE WIRE
TAIL: PALE BLUE DUN COCK HACKLE FIBRES OR MICRO FIBBETTS
BODY: MEDIUM OLIVE ANTRON
WINGS: NORMALLY DEER OR ELK BUT HERE ULTRA LIGHT CDC FEATHERS WERE USED WITH A BLUE DUN HACKLE WOUND THROUGH AND THEN CLIPPED
HEAD: ANTRON MEDIUM OLIVE

Hotspot Pheasant Tail

EVER SINCE DAYLIGHT FLUORESCENT MATERIALS (DFM) made their way into fly dressing, they have enhanced many otherwise drab patterns. You should know that most fish see ultra-violet (UV) in a way that we do not fully understand – their eyes certainly have more UV receptor cones than we do – and DFM behaves very differently under UV – it literally glows. Used sparingly, as in the thorax of this fly, it really can make a difference. I like red for spring, green for summer and orange for autumn when, it is snapped up by brown trout in stocked stillwaters.

WHERE: WORLDWIDE IN RIVERS AND STILLWATER IN TEMPERATE REGIONS

WHEN: ALL YEAR

WHAT: TROUT, GRAYLING

HOW: A GENERAL-PURPOSE NYMPH PATTERN WITH A HIGHLIGHT

HOOK: 10 TO 14 STANDARD SHANK
TAIL: COCK PHEASANT TAIL FIBRES
BODY: COCK PHEASANT TAIL FIBRES WITH COPPER WIRE RIB
THORAX: ORANGE DFM FLOSS WITH PHEASANT FIBRES OVER

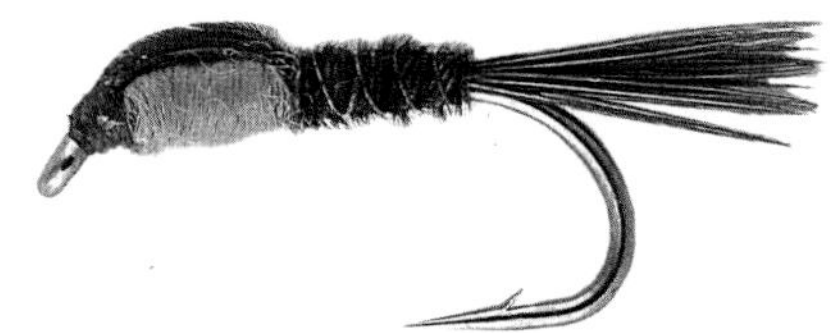

Last Hope

YOU KNOW THE SITUATION, it's a summer evening, the light is fading fast, the trout are taking something really small as though it's their last ever meal and you can maybe see well enough for one last fly change. I bet that's how the Last Hope got its name. Fortunately, it has proved to be the saviour on many such an occasion on both rivers and lakes. You must fish these tiny flies with a 2 or 3 weight rod and a 1 kg (2 lb) leader. Anything stronger and you risk pulling the fine wire hook straight and losing that hard won fish. You need to cast accurately and preferably at short range to get the best from the Last Hope. While designed to take trout at twilight, it will also tempt small coarse fish species in and around weed beds on a bright day.

WHERE: RIVERS AND STILLWATERS IN TEMPERATE REGIONS

WHEN: THE WARMER MONTHS ESPECIALLY LATE IN THE DAY

WHAT: TROUT AND MANY OTHER SPECIES

HOW: SURFACE FEEDING TROUT AT TWILIGHT

HOOK: 16 TO 22 FINE WIRE
TAIL: WHITE COCK HACKLE FIBRES
BODY: SINGLE WHITE FEATHER FIBRE
HACKLE: VERY SHORT WHITE COCK

Living Damsel

PLAITING MARIBOU FIBRES gives a degree of strength as well as some stiffness, and is a great way of making a detached body.

WHERE: STILLWATER IN TEMPERATE REGIONS

WHEN: EARLY SUMMER TO AUTUMN IS BEST

WHAT: TROUT, SMALLMOUTH AND LARGEMOUTH BASS, BLUEGILL, CARP

HOW: SUGGESTS THE LARVAL STAGE OF A DAMSEL FLY

HOOK: 10 TO 12 STANDARD SHANK
TAIL: PLAITED MARABOU FIBRES
BODY: GOLDEN OLIVE SYNTHETIC FUR WITH OVAL GOLD TINSEL RIB
BACK: PHEASANT TAIL FIBRES
EYES: LEADED DUMBBELLS WITH BODY DUBBING WOUND AROUND

This golden olive tying is sometimes better than the conventional pale olive used when trying a Damsel Nymph. I wonder if the fish see it as a nymph immediately after it has changed its skin for the next growth stage? Using the dumbbell eyes for weight also adds to the effect as damsel larvae have prominent eyes.

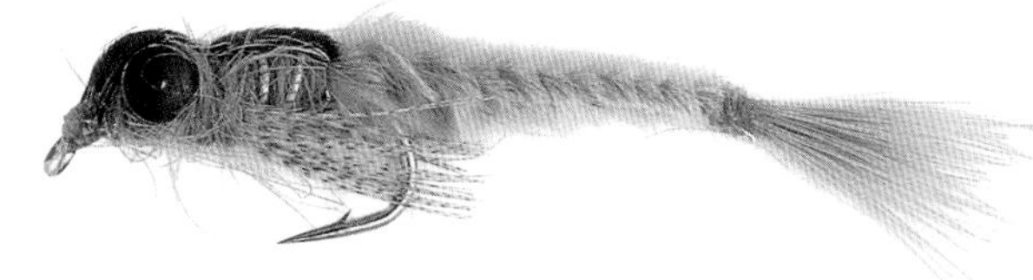

Maggot

FLY FISHERS SHOULD ALWAYS BE OBSERVANT OPPORTUNISTS, and a couple of Maggot Flies hidden deep in your box will one day serve you well. All things die, and when they do, their remains are consumed by maggots which may then end up in the water. Think about the sheep carcass lodged just above the flood line, the salmon carcass on the gravel bar; all part of nature's larder and never ignored by hungry fish. Coarse fishers throughout the world use the maggot as bait even where fish have never seen them. Why? Because just about any fish will eat them.

WHERE: WORLDWIDE IN RIVERS OR STILLWATER

WHEN: USUALLY SUMMER AND EARLY AUTUMN

WHAT: TROUT, GRAYLING, WHITEFISH, CHAR, SMALLMOUTH AND LARGEMOUTH BASS

HOW: IMITATES THE LARVAL STAGE OF THE COMMON HOUSE FLY

HOOK: 10 TO 14 STANDARD SHANK
BODY: OFF-WHITE YARN OR DUBBING RIBBED WITH FINE CLEAR NYLON

Black Stonefly

WHERE: WORLDWIDE IN FREESTONE RIVERS AND SOME LAKES, USUALLY IN THE HIGH ARCTIC

WHEN: LATE SPRING TO SUMMER

WHAT: TROUT, LAKE TROUT, GRAYLING, SMALLMOUTH BASS

HOW: SUGGESTS THE LARVAL STAGE OF STONEFLY

HOOK: 6XÍ TO 10 2X NYMPH OR 4X LURE SHANK
TAIL: TWO BLACK GOOSE BIOTS
BODY: A BLEND OF BLACK RABBIT FUR AND BLACK SEAL'S FUR WITH HINTS OF ORANGE, CLARET, PURPLE AND BROWN SEAL'S FUR MIXED IN THEN RIBBED WITH BLACK SWANNUNDAZE
THORAX: SAME AS BODY BUT WITH THREE WING CASES OF CLIPPED BLACK TURKEY QUILL
HEAD: SAME AS BODY

THE HATCHING OF THE STONEFLY is one of the most revered and exciting times on North American rivers. The insect is huge and can make the most cautious of fishes lose its cool. Many species of stonefly occur throughout the world and black is always a safe colour to use if you aren't sure which species is most likely to be found. This fly is also an excellent search pattern for deeper water in rivers and some lakes. The biggest sized fly is often taken by large grayling in water where nothing resembling it occurs naturally. It is a big fly so use a suitable sized rod and line – this isn't one for size 3 outfits!

Howitts Done

CHRIS HOWITT OF ENGLAND HAS REPRESENTED HIS COUNTRY many times at International level. A true all-rounder, if he puts his name to a fly you can bet it is one of the best for its purpose. He ties this parachute style emerger in a range of colours to match hatching chironomids. When cast to rising fish from a free drifting boat, it is an outstanding fly. Equally good as a river fly, Chris rates it highly for grayling and you will love its positive ride position in the surface.

WHERE: STILLWATERS AND RIVERS IN TEMPERATE REGIONS

WHEN: SPRING THROUGH FALL

WHAT: TROUT, GRAYLING, BLUEGILLS, CARP

HOW: EMERGING CHIRONOMID IMITATION

HOOK: 10 OR 12 STANDARD SHANK
BODY: DUBBED TAN SEAL'S FUR
THORAX: DUBBED GINGER SEAL'S FUR AROUND THE PARACHUTE POST
WING: AND POST ELK HAIR
HACKLE: RED GAME COCK

No Hackle

THIS DRY FLY/EMERGER IS UNLIKE ANY OTHER PATTERN and was a clear result of a fresh look at artificial flies by innovative American tiers Doug Swisher and Carl Richards. A partially hatched mayfly is frequently a selective food item for limestone river trout who have such a rich diet that they can become super choosy and will feed only on a specific stage of a hatch. You need to be an observer of Nature rather than just a flogger of the water. Time taken to study how the fish are feeding, and what insect has captured their imagination will make you a far better angler.

WHERE: WORLDWIDE IN LIMESTONE RIVERS WHEREVER MAYFLY HATCH

WHEN: USUALLY BEST IN SPRING AND SUMMER

WHAT: TROUT, GRAYLING

HOW: SUGGESTS THE HATCHING STAGE OF A MAYFLY

HOOK: 14 TO 20 STANDARD SHANK FINE WIRE
TAIL: DUN HACKLE FIBRES TIED TO SEPARATE [PLEASE CLARIFY]
BODY: FINE RABBIT DUBBING OR OTHER TO MATCH THE HATCH
WINGS: NATURAL GREY MALLARD QUILL

Henry's Fork Hopper

EVERYONE SHOULD TRY HOPPER FISHING in mid-summer. Some of my earliest trout fishing experiences were with natural grasshoppers on small streams and only in the latter years I have fished the artificial. Some of the very best hopper fishing is in the American West and the beautiful rivers of Chile and Patagonia, but this fly will work just about anywhere. Try for a firm "splat" to imitate the disturbance as the natural grasshopper hits the water. The occasional twitch should get the fish's nerves on edge and involve an explosive take.

WHERE: WORLDWIDE IN RIVERS IN TEMPERATE REGIONS

WHEN: MID-SUMMER

WHAT: TROUT, SMALLMOUTH AND LARGEMOUTH BASS

HOW: SUGGESTS A SMALL SPECIES OF GRASSHOPPER

HOOK: 8X TO 12 2X SHANK
BODY: WHITE DEERHAIR RIBBED WITH YELLOW THREAD
UNDERWING: YELLOW ELK HAIR
OVERWING: BROWN SPECKLED HEN SADDLE FEATHER VARNISHED
HEAD: ELK TIED BULLET STYLE

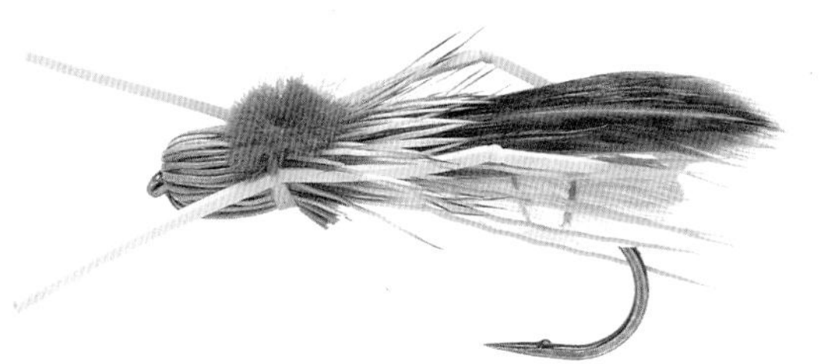

Peeping Caddis

WEIGHTED TO FISH HARD ON THE BOTTOM, exactly where it should be, this is a very smart way of imitating a caddis (sedge) larva just taking a peek out of its home. A great fly for freestone streams at just about any time of year, but requires a degree of skill to avoid being snagging the bottom. Pitch the fly into rough water and let it sweep into pockets between the stones. This search casting demands a great amount of concentration and accuracy.

WHERE: FREESTONE STREAMS IN TEMPERATE AND SUB-ARCTIC REGIONS

WHEN: ALL YEAR

WHAT: TROUT, GRAYLING, WHITEFISH

HOW: IMITATES A CADDIS (SEDGE) LARVA

HOOK: 10X 2X SHANK
TAIL: GREEN OR ORANGE FLUORESCENT NYLON WOOL BURNT TO SEAL
HACKLE: BROWN PARTRIDGE
BODY: THICKLY DUBBED HARE'S EAR
HEAD: SPLIT SHOT PINCHED ONTO NYLON AND WHIPPED ONTO HOOK

Orange Otter

AN UNUSUAL STYLE OF TYING FOR A DRY FLY, and although I'm not sure of its origins, it works well on grayling and trout throughout Europe. I have friends who swear by it for both Labrador brook trout and Western State cutthroat trout. Originally tied with dyed otter's fur, seal's fur is now used in Europe as the otter is protected. This fly sits up very well in streamy water and is easy to see. I am very fond of orange dry or emerger patterns as I'm positive that the bright colour provides a trigger for a surface – feeding fish.

WHERE: ORIGINALLY IN EUROPEAN RIVERS BUT WORKS IN MANY WATERS IN TEMPERATE REGIONS

WHEN: ALL YEAR, EVEN WHEN NO FLY ARE HATCHING

WHAT: TROUT, GRAYLING, CUTTHROAT

HOW: A GENERAL-PURPOSE DRY FLY

HOOK: 14 TO 16 STANDARD SHANK
TAIL: RED GAME COCK HACKLE FIBRES
BODY: ORANGE SEAL'S FUR
HACKLE: RED GAME COCK TIED IN THE MIDDLE OF THE BODY

Minkie Booby

MICKY BEWICK OF THE UK made the Booby his style of fly for concrete bowl reservoirs. His casting style with a fast-sinking shooting head brings an effortless 40 metres (120 feet). In winter, you need to reach a certain depth to find the fish. The Minkie Booby should be fished very slowly or left static. Quite why trout will take a stationary fly is a puzzle. Fry feeders in autumn absolutely love it. It would work well in the lakes of New Zealand and on lake trout in the northern hemisphere.

WHERE: STILLWATER IN TEMPERATE REGIONS

WHEN: ALL YEAR

WHAT: TROUT, LAKE TROUT

HOW: A VERY ODD LURE WITH AN INEXPLICABLE APPEAL

HOOK: 6 TO 10 2X SHANK
TAIL: STRANDS OF PEARL CRYSTALFLASH AND A STRIP OF WHITE OR GREY MINK
BODY: PEARL TINSEL WITH THE MINK STRIP ALONG ON TOP WITH SILVER WIRE RIB
HEAD: ETHAFOAM CYLINDER , TRIMMED AND SILVER AND BLACK EYES STUCK ON

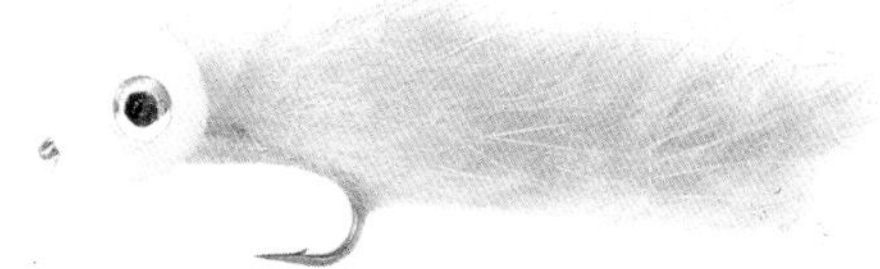

Polar Fibre Minnow

A BRILLIANT BAIT FISH PATTERN made all the more deadly because of the way it is built on the incurved hook making the the fly seem on an even keel. So many fly patterns actually fish at odd angles and not as we perceive them to be that this really is a breakthrough. Using Polar Fibre too is an excellent way of making a sturdy but very lightweight fly which can be cast without using heavy fly rods. Like so many good bait fish patterns this one can be tied to copy a specific species.

WHERE: SALTWATER WORLDWIDE, TROPICAL TO TEMPERATE

WHEN: YEAR ROUND

WHAT: ALL PREDATORY SPECIES

HOW: BAITFISH IMITATION

HOOK: 4 TO 3/0
WING: LAYERS OF POLAR FIBRE KICKED UP AWAY FROM HOOK SHANK
HEAD: STICK ON EYE AND SOFTEX OVER

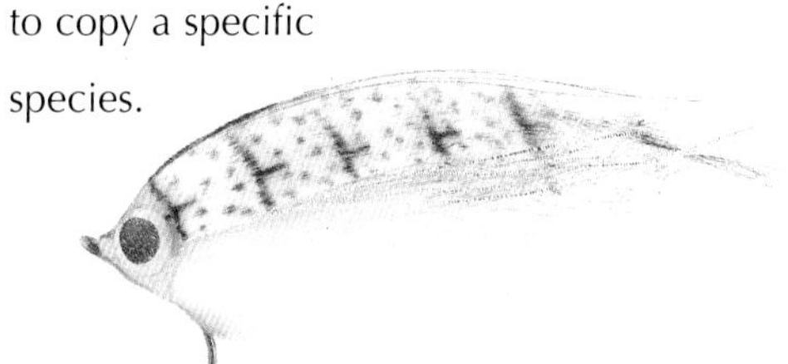

Red Tag

EASY TO TIE, THE RED TAG is wonderfully effective for both trout and grayling. It is one of the must-have patterns for fishing in the shallow and fertile lakes of Tasmania; it is also deadly for late autumn grayling in the UK. Mongolian grayling just love this fly. Reckoned by many to be one of the first fly patterns ever recorded, the Red Tag may seem to be old-fashioned, but nevertheless it remains a very good fly.

WHERE: WORLDWIDE IN RIVERS AND LAKES

WHEN: ALL SEASON, BUT ESPECIALLY GOOD WHEN THE WATER IS RUFFLED BY WIND

WHAT: TROUT, GRAYLING, CHAR

HOW: A GENERAL PURPOSE DRY OR WET FLY

HOOK: 8 TO 16 STANDARD SHANK (SOMETIMES TIED AS A TANDEM)
TAG: RED WOOL
BODY: PEACOCK HERL
HACKLE: RED GAME COCK

Quill Gordon

MANY OF MY EARLY FLY TYING ORDERS were for the classic dry flies, and I really do believe they are the mainstay of dry fly fishing on rivers wherever mayfly occur. This one by Theodore Gordon is a great pattern for when darker flies are hatching or for times when the light is constantly changing when stormy clouds scud across the sky and a stiff wind ripples the river surface. It needs to be tied in proportion and with good-quality hackles to get it to sit up on the water's surface. Have a range of sizes as this pretty fly will cover many species of mayfly.

WHERE: WORLDWIDE IN RIVERS IN TEMPERATE REGIONS

WHEN: SPRING TO AUTUMN

WHAT: TROUT, GRAYLING, CUTTHROAT, SMALLMOUTH BASS

HOW: SUGGESTS AN ADULT MAYFLY

HOOK: 12 TO 16 STANDARD SHANK FINE WIRE
TAIL: DARK BLUE DUN COCK HACKLE FIBRES
BODY: STRIPPED PEACOCK QUILL VARNISHED OR SUPERGLUED
WING: LEMON WOODDUCK FLANK
HACKLE: DARK BLUE DUN COCK

Grey Duster

THIS FLY IMITATES SO MANY DIFFERENT INSECTS THAT I certainly wouldn't want to be without a few of them in my box. I like a parachute version tied with a white post for visibility in poor light, but may be related to my poor eyesight! A great pattern if you aren't sure what to try, it is particularly good for wary brown trout in shallow water. It is a favourite for the South Island of New Zealand and some of Australia's prime rivers, especially in Tasmania.

WHERE: WORLDWIDE IN RIVERS OR STILLWATER

WHEN: ALL YEAR, BUT WARMER MONTHS ARE BEST

WHAT: TROUT, GRAYLING, CHAR, BLUEGILL

HOW: A BROAD-SPECTRUM, NON-SPECIFIC PATTERN

HOOK: 12 TO 18 STANDARD SHANK LIGHT WIRE
BODY: BLUE UNDERFUR FROM RABBIT OR MUSKRAT
HACKLE: WELL-MARKED BADGER COCK

Rusty Rat

FLIES FOR ATLANTIC SALMON ARE IN A CLASS OF THEIR OWN – show them to any fly fisher and you can guarantee that they will be handled more carefully than any other type of fly. While the rats have a special following among anglers on the eastern seaboard of the US and in Iceland, but of course will work anywhere that this majestic fish occurs. Use the Rusty Rat any time when the water is low and clear.

WHERE: ATLANTIC SALMON RIVERS IN THE NORTHERN HEMISPHERE

WHEN: USUALLY SUMMER TO AUTUMN

WHAT: ATLANTIC SALMON AND SEA TROUT

HOW: GENERAL-PURPOSE FLY

HOOK: 2 TO 10 SALMON IRON
TAG: FINE OVAL GOLD TINSEL
TAIL: PEACOCK SWORD
BODY: REAR YELLOW FLOSS, FRONT PEACOCK HERL, ALL RIBBED WITH OVAL GOLD
WING: GREY FOX GUARD HAIRS
HACKLE: GRIZZLE COCK
CHEEKS: JUNGLE COCK

Hare and Cream

THIS MID-SUMMER PATTERN is best for stillwater rainbow trout which have been feeding in the open water on daphnia and very small insect larvae. Developed within the competition circuit it uses the amazing attraction of dubbed hare's fur with the mobility of marabou. Try it on the hot, bright days with a slow-sinking line and a very slow retrieve.

WHERE: STILLWATER IN TEMPERATE REGIONS

WHEN: SUMMER

WHAT: TROUT

HOW: AN ALL-PURPOSE PLANKTON FLY

HOOK: 12 TO 16 STANDARD SHANK
TAIL: OFF-WHITE OR VERY PALE PINK MARABOU
BODY: HARE'S EAR WITH FLAT PEARL FLASHBACK AND SILVER WIRE RIB

Muddled Daddy

IT'S THE GOOD OLD MIX of a hare's ear colouration with the straggly legs of knotted pheasant tail and the bumbling fuss of a deerhair head which makes this unlikely fly such a hit with trout, grayling, char and many other species. Struggling through the surface, fished deep in the water, and even skated, it will bring slashing takes. I fish this fly all over the world and it's a favourite dropper for lake grayling. Indeed, I have patterns that have caught so many fish that the hook is now brightly polished instead of bronze.

WHERE: WORLDWIDE IN RIVERS AND STILL WATERS

WHEN: SUMMER TO AUTUMN

WHAT: TROUT AND GRAYLING

HOW: CRANE FLY IMITATION AT ALL LEVELS

HOOK: SIZE 8 TO 12 2X LONGSHANK
BODY: HARE'S EAR FUR RIBBED OVAL GOLD
LEGS: KNOTTED PHEASANT TAIL
HOOD AND WING: CLIPPED NATURAL DEERHAIR

Sawyer's Pheasant Tail

WHERE: WORLDWIDE IN RIVERS AND IS EFFECTIVE IN LAKES TOO

WHEN: ALL YEAR BUT BEST LATE SPRING TO AUTUMN

WHAT: TROUT, GRAYLING, CHAR, WHITEFISH, LENNOX, AND JUST ABOUT ANY FRESHWATER FISH

HOW: SUGGESTS AN EPHEMERID NYMPH

HOOK: 12 TO 16 STANDARD SHANK
TAIL: FIBRES OF COCK PHEASANT CENTRE TAIL
BODY: PHEASANT FIBRES TWISTED WITH FINE COPPER WIRE
THORAX: BALL OF COPPER WIRE AND PHEASANT FIBRES WITH CASE OVER THE TOP OF PHEASANT
NOTE: THE COPPER WIRE IS THE TYING THREAD IN THIS UNUSUAL PATTERN

POSSIBLY THE MOST USED NYMPH. Used mainly in clear, limestone rivers as an impression of many natural nymphs. Frank Sawyer's little nymph is particularly good when used for the induced-take technique where rod lift causes the fly to lift sharply in the water in front of a visible trout. The fish just can't seem to resist and take the fly.

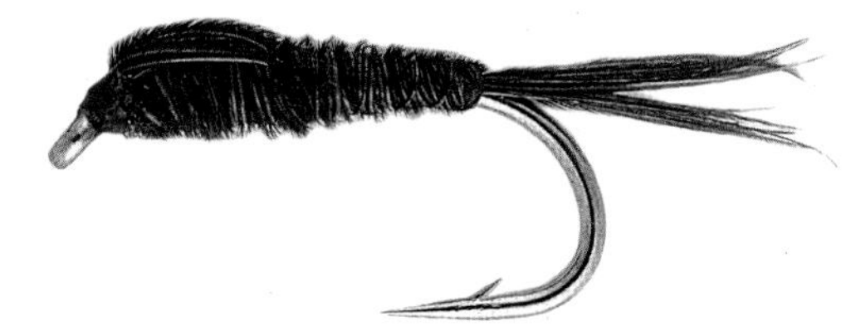

Caddis Larva

OF COURSE THIS FLY WORKS, it's so wonderfully realistic and sometimes it feels as though you are fishing bait instead of an imitation. Fantastic for grayling and freestone river trout. You can have a real blast fishing ultra small brooks with a 2- or 3-weight rod and pitching this fly into little pots and runs. Fish don't have to be big to be fun. Where I learnt my river fishing a 0.34 kg (12 oz) brown was a monster and I hope I never lose the thrill of catching fish from such places. Tie this one up in brown and amber too.

WHERE: FREESTONE STREAMS IN TEMPERATE AND SUBARCTIC REGIONS

WHEN: SPRING THROUGH FALL

WHAT: TROUT, GRAYLING, CUTTHROAT AND WHITEFISH

HOW: SUGGESTS BAIT

HOOK: 12 TO 16 2X SHANK
BODY: ANTRON GREEN
HEAD: GOLD BEAD

Surf Candy

A FABULOUS FLY FOR SALTWATER. The perfect sand eel imitation and I really can't emphasize how important it is to have this one in the fly-box. How I wish I had known of this fly when I fished for European bass off the Cornish coast in the UK more than forty years ago. Bob Popovic's fly is a stunner and he continues to come up with ever-more creative patterns using epoxy as the binding ingredient. This is a must-have pattern when fish are patrolling the surf looking for sand eels dislodged from their homes by the waves.

WHERE: WORLDWIDE IN SALTWATER

WHEN: ALL YEAR

WHAT: ALMOST ANY SALTWATER SPECIES

HOW: IMITATES A SAND EEL

HOOK: 1/0 O'SHAUGHNESSY
WING: WHITE OCEAN HAIR OR SIMILAR WITH OLIVE ON TOP
SIDES: WIDE PEARL MYLAR AND BAND OF RED FLOSS
EYES: GREEN AND BLACK STICK ON
HEAD: CLEAR EPOXY

Yellow Dolly

I DON'T KNOW HOW DEREK KNOWLES came to invent this fly, but it most definitely stirs up stale Atlantic salmon. When the water is warm and low you grease this fly, cast square across and wake it over the fish's head. Amazingly, the occasional fish will attack the fly. I often get results by stripping large 'tadpole' patterns square over a fish's nose so there is clearly something about this approach which can provoke a salmon into making an attack.

WHERE: RIVERS WHERE ATLANTIC SALMON OCCUR

WHEN: CONDITIONS OF LOW, WARM WATER

WHAT: ATLANTIC SALMON AND MAYBE STEELHEAD

HOW: SURFACE LURE

HOOK: SMALL TREBLE, 14 OR 16
BODY: RED PLASTIC TUBING
HACKLE: A VERY SHORT, CLIPPED SKIRT OF YELLOW BUCKTAIL WITH A SHORTER SKIRT OF BLACK BUCKTAIL OVER

Shrimper

SCUD, GAMMARUS AND FRESHWATER SHRIMP are the same thing, occur worldwide and are a vital part of a fish's diet. The shrimp is a curious little humpbacked creature that scuttles around in the bottom detritus and often swims on its side in looping runs of 30 cm (a foot) or so. It also has a habit of freely drifting with the current as though relocating itself. It's the carotene pigmentation in the natural shrimp that gives the attractive pink and red colouration to the flesh of salmonids. Fish the artificial fly to mimic the real shrimp's habits and you will do very well.

WHERE: WORLDWIDE IN STREAMS, LAKES AND PONDS

WHEN: ALL YEAR

WHAT: TROUT, GRAYLING, CHAR, SMALLMOUTH AND LARGEMOUTH BASS, BLUEGILL, CARP

HOW: CLOSE COPY OF SHRIMP (SCUD)

HOOK: 8 TO 14 CURVED SHANK
BACK: CLEAR POLYTHENE STRIP
BODY: LEAD STRIP ALONG BACK THEN DUBBED OLIVE SEAL'S FUR WITH A PALMERED OLIVE HEN HACKLE THEN ALL IS RIBBED WITH MEDIUM COPPER WIRE
NOTE: A PINK VERSION IS VERY GOOD TOO

Appetiser

THE APPETISER WAS INVENTED by Bob Church, whose pioneering work on UK reservoirs in the 1960s produced many new flies and techniques. Bob tied the fly to represent the fry of roach (a silvery fish with colour in its fins and not the similarly named fish in US lakes). It's a marvellous small fish pattern which can be tied on a tandem hook format for larger, grown-on trout as well as predators such as pike, perch and zander. Most often fished on a sinking line with a stripping action, the Appetiser doubles up as an all-purpose attractor as it works where no small bait fish exist. It can be very good when fished slowly just under the surface at dusk.

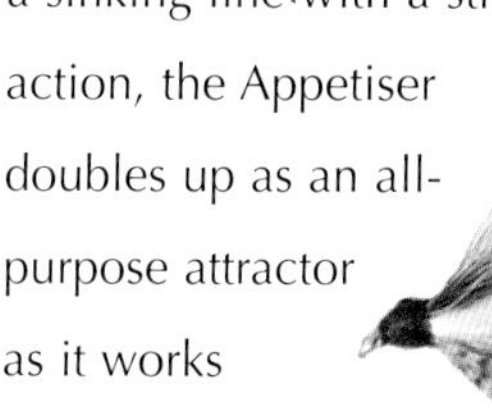

WHERE: WORLDWIDE IN STILLWATER

WHEN: ALMOST ANY TIME OF YEAR BUT PARTICULARLY WHEN FRY ARE ABUNDANT

WHAT: TROUT AND ANY PREDATORY FISH

HOW: A SPECIFIC SMALL FISH IMITATION THAT DOUBLES AS A GENERAL ATTRACTOR

HOOK: 10 STANDARD SHANK TO 6 4X LONG SHANK TO TANDEM RIG
TAIL: MIX OF SILVER MALLARD FIBRES, HOT ORANGE AND BRIGHT GREEN COCK HACKLE FIBRES
BODY: WHITE CHENILLE WITH OVAL SILVER TINSEL RIB
HACKLE: SAME AS TAIL AND TIED FALSE
WING: WHITE MARABOU OVERLAID WITH FIBRES OF GREY SQUIRREL TAIL

Bead Egg

WHERE: EVOLVED WITHIN BRISTOL BAY STREAMS IN ALASKA BUT COULD BE USED ELSEWHERE

WHEN: AT SPAWNING TIME WHEN OTHER FISH, NOTABLY SOCKEYE SALMON, ARE EGG LAYING

WHAT: PRINCIPALLY RAINBOW TROUT BUT ALSO GRAYLING AND CHAR

HOW: EXACT IMITATION OF AN EGG

HOOK: A 6MM TRANSLUCENT, FLUORESCENT ORANGE BEAD PAINTED WITH TWO OR THREE COATS OF PEARL NAIL VARNISH. COLOUR VARIES WITH STAGE OF EGG LAYING
NOTE: THE BEAD IS THREADED ON THE LINE AND HELD WITH A STOP KNOT 12 CM (4 INCHES) FROM A SIZE 10 SHORT SHANK HOOK WITH A TINY TUFT OF WHITE MARABOU TIED ON. THE FISH TAKES THE EGG AND THE HOOK BECOMES FAST IN THE SIDE OF THE MOUTH

I AM NOT SURE THAT THIS IS STRICTLY classed as a fly, but it does imitate trout food and is intrinsically no different to a roe bug. Alaska's rainbow trout are very long-lived, but due to their aggressive feeding habits on eggs they are repeatedly caught by anglers. They are a very valuable sportfish and must be protected, hence this pattern and its rig is valuable as it ensures the fish is hooked around and not inside its jaw where damage and possible death would result. It may be contentious to include this fly, but it is very effective.

Palmered Bunny

A VARIATION TO THE ZONKER THEME, this highly valuable fly is ideal for saltwater situations but also extremely good for fresh run silver salmon that require a combination of colour, flash and movement to make a strike. Make up a range in the prime silver colours of pink, black, purple, blue and especially hot green. Any deep, fastwater situation lends itself to this fly and most predators will take it. The heavy dumbell eyes give this style of fly tremendous action. Tigerfish, nile perch and barramundi love this one, but do be careful when casting as the weight makes it travel low down and it's all too easy to hit the back of your head!

WHERE: WORLDWIDE ON RIVERS, STILWATERS AND SALTWATER

WHEN: YEAR ROUND

WHAT: ALL PREDATORS, EXCELLENT FOR COHO, BARRAMUNDI, TIGERS, PEACOCK BASS.

HOW: IT'S THE COLOUR, MOVEMENT AND ACTION THAT TRIGGER AN ATTACK

DRESSING: HOOK E 2 TO 3/0 SALMON IRON TO SALTWATER O'SHAUGNESSY
TAIL: STRIP OF RABBIT SKIN WITH APPROPRIATE COLOUR CRYSTALHAIR AND FLASHABOU
BODY: FRITZ WITH PALMERED RABBIT STRIP
HACKLE: LONG FIBRED SOFT COCK SADDLE
HEAD: DUMBELL EYES

Fur Thorax Caddis Pupa

I HAVE WORKED FOR YEARS WITH PETER GATHERCOLE on many fishing assignments for magazines and know only too well that I will never be the fly tier that he is. I wanted to include this stillwater special from his inventive vice, which is the perfect summer evening fly. Trout feeding on caddis (sedge) pupa make distinctive heavy swirls and bow waves as they chase the ascending and surprisingly active insect prior to the hatch beginning. Use a floating line and a long leader with long smooth pulls in the early evening and then slow the speed to a crawl just as dusk settles in.

WHERE: WORLDWIDE IN STILLWATER IN TEMPERATE REGIONS

WHEN: BEST FROM MID-SUMMER TO AUTUMN

WHAT: TROUT

HOW: COPIES THE HATCHING STAGE OF A CADDIS (SEDGE)

HOOK: 12 TO 16 CURVED SHANK
BODY: AMBER SEAL'S FUR OR SYNTHETIC WITH CLEAR NYMPH GLASS OVER AND THEN RIBBED WITH GOLD WIRE
WING BUDS: SLIPS OF GREY MALLARD
HACKLE: BROWN RABBIT SPUN AND CLIPPED ALONG THE BACK

Black Ghost

FLY FISHING IS NOT ALWAYS ABOUT BEING IMITATIVE. Predatory fish will react to many differing stimuli such as colour, movement, shape and size and will frequently take a lure for reasons we cannot fathom. The Black Ghost is one such fly in that it can often produce the goods in water coloured with suspended silt, but can also be effective at many other times. I particularly like it when the light is poor, for example late in the evening or when the sky is overcast.

WHERE: WORLDWIDE IN RIVERS, STILLWATER AND ESTUARIES

WHEN: ALL YEAR

WHAT: TROUT, CHAR, PIKE, SMALLMOUTH, LARGEMOUTH AND PEACOCK BASS, WALLEYE, BARRAMUNDI, STRIPED BASS AND ALMOST ANY PREDATORY FISH

HOW: NON-SPECIFIC LURE

HOOK: 6 TO 10 4X LONG SHANK
TAIL: YELLOW COCK HACKLE FIBRES
BODY: BLACK FLOSS RIBBED WITH FLAT SILVER TINSEL
WING: PAIR OF WHITE COCK HACKLES (USE POLAR FIBRE IN SALTWATER)
HACKLE: LONG FIBRES YELLOW COCK
CHEEK: OPTIONAL JUNGLE COCK

Booby

I DON'T THINK I WILL EVER UNDERSTAND TROUT, and in particular why they will take a Booby fished on a short leader with a very fast sinking line which will anchor it just off the bottom of the lake or pond. Surely, anything in its right mind would take just one look and swim off in the opposite direction. But no, even wild and mature trout will devour these flies to such an extent that surgery is required to remove them from the fish's stomach. Although this cannot be used for catch and release, this fly is unbelievably effective. It is often best fished with a series of slow pulls but is also very good when stripped through the surface.

WHERE: WORLDWIDE IN STILLWATER

WHEN: ANY TIME, EVEN WHEN SEVERELY COLD

WHAT: TROUT, PIKE, WALLEYE, LARGEMOUTH AND SMALLMOUTH BASS

HOW: A RATHER ODD SORT OF ATTRACTOR

HOOK: 8 TO 12 STANDARD SHANK
TAIL: BUNCH OF MARABOU FIBRES
BODY: SEAL'S FUR WITH OVAL TINSEL RIB
WING: MARABOU FIBRES
EYES: ETHAFOAM CYLINDER LASHED ON IN A FIGURE-OF-EIGHT STYLE WITH EYES PAINTED OR STUCK ON THE ENDS

Olive Cactus

THERE ARE MANY FLY FISHERS who begin to fish for stocked trout in small ponds and have immediate success with this type of fly. Often they are content to fish no other way. They must believe that trout live on a diet of fritz, marabou and gold beads! Fritz (cactus chenille, ice chenille or estaz) has made it very easy to tie a fish-catching fly. It can be used to highlight a pattern or dominate the dressing, but its reflective properties really do work and trout the world over think it's the best thing since sliced bread.

WHERE: WORLDWIDE IN RIVERS AND LAKES, BUT MOSTLY IN STOCKED FISHERIES

WHEN: ALL YEAR

WHAT: ALL SPECIES OF TROUT AND ANY PREDATORY FISH

HOW: COMBINES THE MOVEMENT OF MARABOU WITH GLITTER

HOOK: 12 TO 6 2X NYMPH SHANK
TAIL: BUNCH OF OLIVE MARABOU FIBRES
BODY: OLIVE FRITZ
HEAD: GOLD BEAD

Elver Fly

PERHAPS MORE MODERN MATERIALS WORK BETTER, but there is no other feather quite like the one plucked from the vulturine Guinea Fowl, and it was only when I was able to see this fly being fished that I fully appreciated its unique appeal. Perched high above the Hafralonsa in Iceland I watched Sir Richard Leigh fish down a long pool with an Elver Fly. It looked fantastic as it wiggled around and over rocks with every fish in the run taking a look at it even though Sir Richard had no idea what was happening. For fresh fish just in from the sea it's a winner.

WHERE: SALMON RIVERS WORLDWIDE IN TEMPERATE AND SUBARCTIC REGIONS

WHEN: ALL YEAR BUT BEST IN SUMMER AND AUTUMN

WHAT: ATLANTIC SALMON, SEA TROUT, CHAR, STEELHEAD

HOW: SUGGESTS A SAND EEL

HOOK: 6 TO 10 SINGLE OR DOUBLE SALMON
BODY: BLACK FLOSS RIBBED WITH FLAT SILVER TINSEL
WINGS: TWO LONG, STRIPED VULTURINE GUINEA FOWL FEATHERS
CHEEK: JUNGLE COCK
HACKLE: COBALT BLUE VULTURINE GUINEA FOWL

Cruncher

IN MY DAYS OF COMPETITION FLY FISHING I had many memorable encounters with John Dawson and Martin Cairncross, who both hail from the Bristol area of the UK. These two top fly fishers evolved many variants to existing patterns and techniques in their quest for success. Altering the accepted concept of the simple Pheasant Tail Nymph they used the pale, almost straw coloured, centre tail feathers, as opposed to the richer, reddish brown more often favoured, and then tied the Greenwell hen hackle to achieve 'kick' against the thorax. Nymphing trout on stillwaters are suckers for this pretty fly.

WHERE: STILLWATERS IN TEMPERATE CLIMES

WHEN: ALL YEAR

WHAT: RAINBOWS AND BROWNS IN STILLWATERS

HOW: CHIRONOMID IMITATION

HOOK: 10 TO 14 STANDARD SHANK
TAIL: HONEY COCK HACKLE FIBRES
BODY: PALE COCK PHEASANT CENTRE TAIL WITH FINE SILVER WIRE RIB
THORAX: PEACOCK HERL
HACKLE: GREENWELL HEN

Hairwing No Hackle

PROPERLY FISHED, this fly will sit almost entirely submerged with just the hairwing fibres sticking up above the surface. I say 'properly fished' because you must cast to achieve a delicate landing or it will sink on impact. I sometimes 'Gink' the hair, especially after the first fish or if the water has a bit of chop on the surface. This is an emerger for mayfly hatches. I cannot stress how important the emerger style of pattern is to the fly fisher's armoury.

WHERE: WORLDWIDE IN RIVERS IN TEMPERATE REGIONS

WHEN: SPRING TO AUTUMN

WHAT: TROUT, GRAYLING, CUTTHROAT

HOW: SUGGESTS AN EMERGING MAYFLY

HOOK: 14 TO 20 STANDARD SHANK FINE WIRE
TAIL: DUN COCK HACKLE FIBRES
BODY: OLIVE SUPERFINE POLYPROPYLENE DUB
WING: DEERHAIR

CDC Biot Comparadun

DRY FLIES TIED COMPARADUN STYLE sit high in the surface film and suggest a newly hatched drying its wings before taking to the air. There are few better patterns for fly fishing a limestone river, when ephemerids are hatching in their millions. This pattern imitates the blue-winged olive, an insect common in the Americas and throughout Europe. fly fishers regard a blue-winged olive hatch as a special event in their fishing year.

WHERE: LIMESTONE RIVERS AND STREAMS IN TEMPERATE REGIONS

WHEN: SPRING TO AUTUMN

WHAT: TROUT, GRAYLING, CUTTHROAT, CHAR, SMALLMOUTH BASS

HOW: SUGGESTS THE HATCHING STAGE OF A SMALL EPHEMERID

HOOK: 14 TO 20 STANDARD SHANK FINE WIRE
TAIL: TIED SPLIT USING DUN BETT'S TAIL FIBRES
BODY: OLIVE GOOSE OR TURKEY BIOT
WINGS: NATURAL CDC FEATHER WITH FIBRES OF MALLARD GREY SPECKLED SHOULDER
THORAX: TAN FINE POLYDUB

Civil War Fly

THIS TEENY NYMPH variant was named by Darren Bell, who has often guided me in Alaska for steelhead. I made it to resemble the old classic sea trout fly, the Teal Blue and Silver (see page 397) and it worked superbly on the migratory rainbow trout. Char love it too, and although I believe it is often taken to be a small fish it also matches the colour of some caddis (sedge) pupae found in northern streams. I have fished it with success for sea trout in Sweden and bass around English coastlines.

WHERE: RIVERS AND SALTWATER IN COLDER CLIMATES

WHEN: ALL YEAR BUT BEST WHEN PREDATORY FISH ARE PRESENT

WHAT: STEELHEAD, SEA TROUT, SALMON, CHAR, BASS

HOW: SUGGESTS A SMALL BAIT FISH

HOOK: 6 TO 2 SALMON IRON
TAIL: COCK PHEASANT BLEACHED AND DYED PALE GREY WITH FIBRES OF PALE BLUE CRYSTALHAIR
BODY: REAR HALF SAME AS TAIL
BEARD HACKLE: FIRST ONE IS FIBRES OF GREY PHEASANT
THORAX: BLUE PHEASANT TAIL WITH END FIBRES PULLED OVER TO MAKE SECOND BEARD HACKLE

Fat Freddy

THIS IS THE BIGGEST EGG FLY EVER and is intended for king salmon, which will undoubtedly take single eggs or bunches of egg, maybe from aggression, curiosity or more likely territorial defence of their own eggs. King salmon are monsters on a fly rod and anything over 18 kg (40 lbs) are extremely difficult to land. This fly needs to be fished with at least a Teeny T300 flyline to get it down where it is fished on the dead drift. It is usually best in glacial streams and especially when the fish are beginning to prepare their redds. (A 'redd' is a kind of nest that trout and salmon lay their eggs in).

WHERE: ALASKAN RIVERS AND ALSO DOWN THROUGH BRITISH COLUMBIA, WASHINGTON AND OREGON, THE GREAT LAKES AND SYSTEMS IN NEW YORK STATE

WHEN: JULY FOR ALASKA

WHAT: KING (CHINOOK) SALMON BUT ALSO CHUM, COHO AND STEELHEAD

HOW: SUGGESTS AN EGG CLUSTER

HOOK: 2/0 TO 2 SALMON IRON
BODY: GLO BUG YARN, SALMON EGG COLOUR WITH TUFT OF WHITE MARABOU EACH END

Dabbler

A NEWCOMER TO THE IRISH LOUGHS IT IS TESTED with great success in competitive events. It has an excellent reputation as a fly capable of raising wily old brown trout. Like so many of the well hackled flies it fishes best when there is a good wave and poor light. The Dabbler can be fished on floating or sinking lines and is frequently fast stripped and then dibbled on the surface before being recast. It's as though the fly arouses interest for a chase and then when it seemingly struggles at the surface it is altogether too much for a trout to resist. Fish it in any wild location with every confidence.

WHERE: LARGE STILLWATERS IN TEMPERATE REGIONS

WHEN: BEST FROM LATE SPRING THROUGH TO AUTUMN

WHAT: PRIMARILY BROWN TROUT BUT ALSO RAINBOW, SEA TROUT AND ATLANTIC SALMON

HOW: A NON SPECIFIC PATTERN THAT AROUSES GREAT INTEREST

HOOK: 8 TO 12 STANDARD SHANK
TAIL: COCK PHEASANT CENTRE TAIL FIBRES
BODY: GOLDEN OLIVE SEALS FUR PALMERED THROUGH WITH A RED GAME COCK HACKLE
HACKLE: RED GAME COCK WOUND FULL
WING: BRONZE MALLARD TIED ON TOP AND AT THE SIDES AS THOUGH VEILING THE FLY

Cormorant

AN EXCEEDINGLY SIMPLE TYING that evolved from the reservoir competition scene and whose name reflects its efficiency!

Equally deadly, the cormorant fly is a first-class modern wet fly and is equally at home in rivers or stillwaters for wild and reared fish. Keep it small and sparse it will be especially deadly on windy, overcast days. There are red or pearl body options.

WHERE: RIVERS AND STILLWATER IN TEMPERATE AND SUB-ARCTIC REGIONS

WHEN: ALL YEAR

WHAT: TROUT

HOW: PROBABLY AN CHIRONOMID INTERPRETATION

HOOK: 10 STANDARD SHANK
BODY: PEACOCK HERL
WINGS: BLACK MARABOU

Terry's Terror

WHERE: WORLDWIDE IN RIVERS

WHEN: ANY TIME BUT BEST IN THE EVENING OR ON OVERCAST DAYS

WHAT: TROUT, GRAYLING

HOW: GENERAL-PURPOSE DRY FLY BUT VERY GOOD AT CADDIS (SEDGE) HATCH

HOOK: 10 TO 14 STANDARD SHANK
TAIL: MIX OF YELLOW AND ORANGE GOAT HAIR CLIPPED SHORT
BODY: PEACOCK HERL RIBBED WITH FLAT COPPER TINSEL
HACKLE: RED GAME COCK

INITIALLY USED DURING HATCHES OF OLIVE MAYFLIES on English chalk streams, it is regarded as a useful pattern for the late evening caddis (sedge) hatch. It is much used on the rough streams of South America and New Zealand where it is a general dry fly attractor. It always seems best on overcast, slightly blustery days when the gleam of copper and the bright tail serve to attract a trout's attention.

Woolhead Sculpin

SCULPINS (CALLED BULLHEADS IN EUROPE) are eaten by many species of fish. This grubby looking little beastie spends its life scuttling around the river bed and provides a very tasty mouthful for a trout out on the prowl. Sculpins can move surprisingly quickly over short distances and the artificial fly needs to be fished hard on the bottom with a jerky retrieve for best results. The Woolhead Sculpin is best for close-range casting where you can use its denser materials to fish nearer to the bottom. I have shown the olive version, but am also very fond of an all-black one.

WHERE: WORLDWIDE IN TEMPERATE AND ARCTIC REGIONS MOSTLY IN RIVERS

WHEN: ALL YEAR

WHAT: TROUT, CHAR, LAKE TROUT, GRAYLING, PIKE, SMALLMOUTH AND LARGEMOUTH BASS, WALLEYE

HOW: EXCELLENT IMITATION OF A SCULPIN (BULLHEAD)

HOOK: 4 TO 6 4X LONG SHANK
OLIVE RABBIT FUR STRIP WITH A LITTLE OLIVE CRYSTALFLASH
BODY: OLIVE RABBIT FUR PALMERED
FINS: OLIVE HEN HACKLES
HEAD: OLIVE LAMB'S WOOL SPUN AND CLIPPED

Jelly Fry

NEWLY-HATCHED FRY GANG TOGETHER IN LARGE SHOALS for safety in numbers, but are still easy prey for trout and bass which engulf them several at a time. The main course over, the predator then cruises the scene of the attack to pick up the cripples. The fragile little bodies quickly break down in the fish's gut to resemble a jelly with eyes – hence the name. Cast this little fly into areas of fry feeding and wait for the take; it's just like fishing to emerger feeders but can often yield some of the very best specimens.

WHERE: WORLDWIDE IN STILLWATER AND SLOW RIVERS

WHEN: EARLY SUMMER ONWARDS

WHAT: TROUT, BASS

HOW: IMITATES A NEWLY HATCHED AND DYING FRY

HOOK: 12 STANDARD SHANK
BODY: FLAT SILVER TINSEL WITH FINE FLAT PEARL RIB AND SINGLE LAYER PVC STRIP
WING: CDC
HEAD: PEACOCK HERL

Griffith's Gnat

WHEN MIDGES HATCH AND SKITTER about on the surface this pattern will take fish after fish. It is very good on streams especially for grayling in mid-afternoon. It also works well on stillwater, particularly if you cast under bank-side vegetation. When midges get stuck in the surface tension along the downwind shorelines a cunning old trout will often sip them close to the land. This is the fly to cast at those shallow water cruisers, but be very careful with your casting! This is best done by laying ambush and casting so your leader is on the bank.

WHERE: WORLDWIDE IN RIVERS AND STILLWATER

WHEN: SUMMER TO AUTUMN

WHAT: TROUT, GRAYLING, CUTTHROAT, CHAR, SMALLMOUTH BASS

HOW: SUGGESTS AN ADULT MIDGE

HOOK: 18 TO 24 STANDARD SHANK FINE WIRE
BODY: PEACOCK HERL
HACKLE: GRIZZLE COCK PALMERED THROUGH BODY

Deep Sparkle Pupa

CADDIS (SEDGE) PUPAE are usually a mess of shuck and body parts as they hatch. The initial stages are set off by the release of gases to break the pupal shroud. This was always a tough thing to copy until Gary La Fontaine used antron yarn to create a bubble effect around the body of a fly. This superbly suggested the commencement of the hatch. I think this pattern is much better suited to rivers with the swirl and confusion of currents and, tied in a range of colours and sizes, it will serve you very well wherever you might be faced with a caddis hatch.

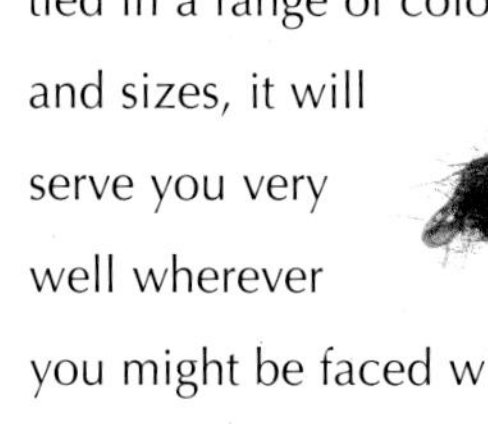

WHERE: WORLDWIDE IN TEMPERATE AND SEMI-ARCTIC REGIONS IN RIVERS AND STILLWATER

WHEN: LATE SPRING TO AUTUMN

WHAT: TROUT, GRAYLING, CHAR, CUTTHROAT

HOW: SUGGESTS THE CADDIS (SEDGE) PUPA BEGINNING TO HATCH

HOOK: 12 TO 18 STANDARD SHANK
UNDERBODY: GREEN ANTRON DUB
OVERBODY: GREEN ANTRON YARN
LEGS: MALLARD FLANK FEATHERS
HEAD: GREY RABBIT DUBBING

Blakestone's Buzzer

DEFINITELY ONE OF THE MOST successful patterns for imitating chironomid pupae. One of my greatest thrills as an instructor is to give someone a 5-weight outfit with a 4.5-metre (15-foot) leader and one of these Buzzers on a spring day when the surface is ringed with feeding trout. Pitch the fly out, watch the leader straighten and a fish is on. It never ceases to amaze me that a trout will take such a sparse pattern. If you use black in spring, olive in summer and red in winter this pattern will bring you success.

WHERE: STILLWATER IN TEMPERATE REGIONS

WHEN: ALL YEAR BUT SPRING TO SUMMER IS BEST

WHAT: TROUT

HOW: CHIRONOMID IMITATION

HOOK: 10 TO 14 CURVED STANDARD SHANK
BODY: BLACK FLOSS WITH SILVER WIRE RIB AND SILVER HOLOGRAPHIC TINSEL ALONG BACK
THORAX: PEACOCK HERL WITH ORANGE FLOSS CHEEKS AND BLACK FLOSS BACK

Dry Gold-ribbed Hare's Ear

THIS ULTRA-SHAGGY FLY will work just about anywhere, but is particularly good during hatches of olives and especially suggests one that has died while trying to hatch. Trout can become ultra-selective when presented with rich feeding and will target in on just one stage of a hatch, but it can be tough to work out which one. Forget your exact copies and try this rough-and-ready fly, which is best fished in the surface film rather than on it. It is also very good on stillwaters, especially during a calm when fish are quietly rising and are easily spooked.

WHERE: WORLDWIDE IN RIVERS AND STILLWATER IN TEMPERATE REGIONS

WHEN: MOST OF THE YEAR BUT SPRING TO AUTUMN IS BEST

WHAT: TROUT, GRAYLING

HOW: SUGGESTS ALL MANNER OF INSECTS BUT PARTICULARLY THE SMALLER OLIVE MAYFLY

HOOK: 10 TO 16 STANDARD SHANK
TAIL: LONGISH CHEEK HAIRS FROM HARE'S MASK
BODY: HARE'S FACE OR EAR FUR RIBBED WITH FINE GOLD WIRE
WINGS: PAIRED STARLING OR GREY MALLARD
HACKLE: THE PICKED-OUT FIBRES OF HARE

Kite's Imperial

OLIVER KITE IS ONE OF THE VERY FEW ANGLERS to use purple in a trout fly. A master at observation, he chose this fly to represent many of the smaller olive mayfly species. It remains exceptionally effective both during – and long after – the hatch. A true chalk-stream angler, he epitomized the saying that a successful fly fisher should 'study to be quiet'. The views and attitude he held towards trout fishing evoked happy days of space and clean waters

WHERE: WORLDWIDE IN TEMPERATE REGIONS IN RIVERS AND STILLWATER

WHEN: SPRING AND SUMMER

WHAT: TROUT, GRAYLING

HOW: A BROADBAND PATTERN TO SUGGEST MANY OF THE SMALLER OLIVE MAYFLY SPECIES

HOOK: 14 TO 18 STANDARD SHANK FINE WIRE
TAIL: HONEY DUN COCK HACKLE FIBRES
BODY: NATURAL HERON HERL SPACED OVER A PURPLE THREAD
HACKLE: HONEY DUN COCK

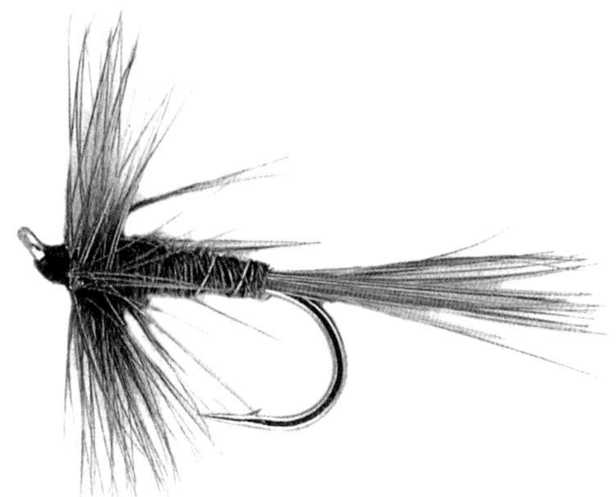

Temple Dog

A VERY INTERESTING VARIANT ON THE TUBE FLY PRINCIPAL for Atlantic salmon, which has become immensely popular on larger rivers. Tie it huge and you could do very well for taimen and other very large salmonids. Also use it as a lure for nile perch.

WHERE: RIVERS IN TEMPERATE REGIONS

WHEN: YEAR ROUND

WHAT: MOST MIGRATORY SALMONIDS AND TAIMEN

HOW: AN ATTRACTOR WITH MOBILITY

TAIL: SCARLET GLO-BRITE
BODY: YELLOW AND BLACK FLOSS RIBBED WITH FLAT GOLD TINSEL AND PALMERED YELLOW
HACKLE: WITH BLACK THROAT HACKLE
WING: PEACOCK WITH BLACK ARCTIC FOX OVER AND A FEW FIBRES CRYSTALHAIR AND FLASHABOU

The combination of colour with the offset wing design makes a mobile and provocative pattern which is especially effective in cold water situations where fish are torpid. Steelheaders use this pattern in British Columbia after fall floods.

Lunn's Particular

AN ALL TIME CLASSIC SPINNER PATTERN for evenings on limestone streams when the smaller upwings are egg laying. It sits very low in the surface film and mimics the dead or dying insect. Invented by Alfred Lunn whose family was deeply involved with the famed River Test for three generations. This is a beautiful fly contructed from simple and easily available materials.

WHERE: WORLDWIDE IN CHALK STREAMS (LIMESTONE WATERS)

WHEN: LATE SPRING TO AUTUMN

WHAT: TROUT, GRAYLING

HOW: IMITATES THE SPINNER STAGE OF AN OLIVE MAYFLY

HOOK: 14 STANDARD SHANK
TAIL: RED GAME COCK HACKLE FIBRES
BODY: STRIPPED HACKLE STALK OF RED GAME COCK
WINGS: MEDIUM DUN COCK HACKLE POINTS TIED SPENT
HACKLE: RED GAME COCK

Sparkle Gnat

THIS FLY IS VERY SIMILAR TO THE GRIFFITH'S GNAT (see page 293), but as with so many flies a minor variation makes a completely different fly. This relatively simple amendment by Charles Jardine was made when he realized that as chironomid pupae hatch they frequently do so with a half-stage when the pupal shuck remains attached. I think that this signals to a trout that the adult cannot easily escape and will be an easy meal, and hence the reason why they will often just select this stage. Try it on otherwise difficult fish in a calm, but also fish it in a big wind from a drifting boat.

WHERE: WORLDWIDE IN STILLWATER IN TEMPERATE REGIONS

WHEN: ALL YEAR BUT BEST FROM LATE SPRING TO AUTUMN

WHAT: TROUT, GRAYLING

HOW: SUGGESTS THE HATCHING STAGE OF CHIRONOMIDS

HOOK: 14 TO 18 STANDARD SHANK FINE WIRE
TAIL: THREE STRANDS OF FINE PEARL TWINKLE
BODY: SINGLE STRAND OF PEACOCK HERL PALMERED THROUGH WITH A GRIZZLE HACKLE

Inchworm

I BET THAT THIS INSECT, also known as measuring worm, has completely fooled many experts. The trouble is that when it decides to fall from its arborial home on its silken thread there is rarely any disturbance as it lands on water. Its life expectancy is then somewhat abrupt as almost all freshwater fishes will feast on it. The fly fisher has little to work on other than the sight of frantically feeding fish, but the main clue is that the activity takes place under overhanging vegetation, usually oak trees. Expect to take the most wily of brown trout with this fly.

WHERE: WORLDWIDE IN TEMPERATE ZONES AND WITH GOOD TREE COVER

WHEN: EARLY TO MID-SUMMER, ESPECIALLY ON WARM, DRY DAYS

WHAT: TROUT, GRAYLING, SMALLMOUTH BASS, BLUEGILL

HOW: CLOSE COPY OF THE INCHWORM, A SMALL, BRIGHT GREEN CATERPILLAR

HOOK: 14 TO 20 STANDARD SHANK FINE WIRE

TAIL AND BODY: TAKE A PIECE OF BRIGHT INSECT-GREEN SUEDE CHENILLE AND TIE IN AT THE HOOK BEND THEN AGAIN AT THE THORAX POSITION. MAKE A SLIGHT LOOP THEN TIE OFF

Tash Bung Fly

THIS IS REALLY NO MORE THAN A SIGHT INDICATOR WITH A HOOK, and was developed from competition fishing for trout where the modern skinny buzzer patterns are presented high in the water. The problem with so many indicators is that fish will frequently take them rather than the fly, so one with a hook solves that problem as well as following the rules of competitions which prohibit the use of separate indicators. Although amazingly popular and undeniably effective surely it's just bobber fishing?

WHERE: WORLDWIDE IN STILLWATER AND RIVERS

WHEN: ALL YEAR

WHAT: TROUT, GRAYLING AND OTHER FISH

HOW: HELPS YOU KNOW WHAT IS HAPPENING UNDER THE SURFACE

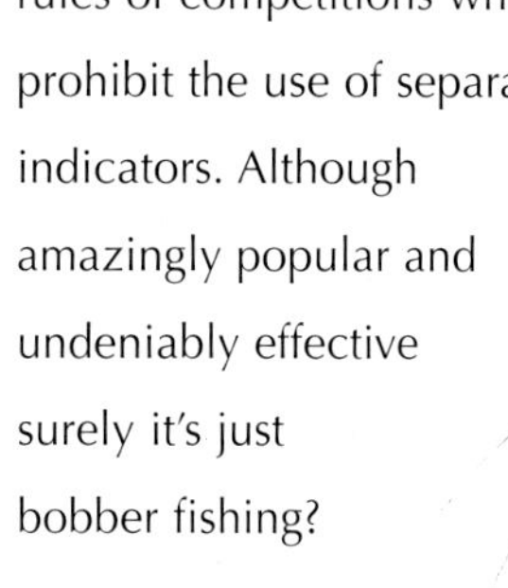

HOOK: 8 STANDARD SHANK
BODY: GLO BUG EGG YARN TIED AT HEAD AND TEASED OUT
HACKLE: COSMETIC TO KEEP THE YARN IN PLACE COLOURS CAN BE BLACK, WHITE AND ORANGE DEPENDING ON THE LIGHT

Woolly Worm

FLIES DON'T COME MUCH EASIER TO TIE than this one, and if you are fishing stocked trout or lightly used rivers or lakes you can bank on this pattern catching fish just about anywhere. There are more modern developments, but the Woolly Worm remains an exceedingly effective fly. Use it with a slow sink line or sink tip to search the lower layers when there's a bit of colour in the water. Olive, black, peacock and brown versions will cover other water situations. A very wide variety of fish can be induced to accept this as food.

WHERE: MOST FRESHWATER SITUATIONS

WHEN: ALL YEAR

WHAT: TROUT, SEA AND LAKE TROUT, GRAYLING, BASS, BLUEGILL

HOW: A GENERAL-PURPOSE ATTRACTOR PATTERN

HOOK: 6X TO 10X 4X SHANK
TAIL: RED WOOL
BODY: YELLOW CHENILLE WITH A PALMERED GRIZZLE COCK HACKLE AND GOLD WIRE RIB

Hern's Hatching Mayfly

A GREAT MANY FLY PATTERNS are simply variations on an already popular theme. In some cases the change can make a huge improvement. This is what happened when Tony Hern adapted an early Rivaz pattern to create a fly which is especially good for emergent stages of the larger upwinged species. Tony is one of the UK's foremost fishery managers, devises many new fly patterns, teaches fly tying and is ideally placed to observe how effective new flies can be as his pupils and clients put them to use. As good in stillwater as it is in rivers, this fly should be tried during the early stage of each day's hatch and is best positioned only just floating on the water.

WHERE: MOSTLY IN THE NORTHERN HEMISPHERE IN RIVERS AND STILLWATER THAT HAVE HATCHES OF THE LARGE MAYFLY

WHEN: BEST IN SPRING/SUMMER

WHAT: TROUT, GRAYLING, SMALLMOUTH BASS

HOW: SUGGESTS THE EMERGENT STAGE OF THE LARGER MAYFLY

HOOK: 10 STANDARD SHANK
TAIL: COCK PHEASANT CENTRE TAIL FIBRES
BODY: COCK PHEASANT CENTRE TAIL FIBRES RIBBED WITH FINE COPPER WIRE
WINGS: TIED WULFF STYLE WITH NATURAL DEER BODY HAIR
HACKLE: PALE OLIVE COCK

Peach Doll

WHEN THE PEACH DOLL came onto the competition scene on UK stillwaters it quickly became the dominant fly and some amazing catches were made with it. Then new patterns came along and the Peach Doll began to fade in popularity. Quite why it works so well is impossible to define, but even in water with totally wild fish it most certainly has its day, and you would be well advised to try one from time to time. Peach became the choice colour of the 1990s and has gradually given way to coral – I wonder what will be next?

WHERE: STILLWATER IN TEMPERATE AND SUBARCTIC REGIONS

WHEN: USUALLY IN THE WARMER MONTHS

WHAT: TROUT

HOW: SIMPLE ATTRACTOR LURE

HOOK: 12 TO 10 STANDARD SHANK
TAIL, BACK AND BODY: ALL PEACH WOOL

Bead Head Sparkle Caddis

WHERE: RIVERS, STILLWATERS IN TEMPERATE, SUBARCTIC REGIONS

WHEN: YEAR ROUND

WHAT: TROUT, GRAYLING, SMALLMOUTHS, BLUEGILLS

HOW: CADDIS PUPA IMITATION

HOOK: 10 TO 16 STANDARD SHANK
BODY: ANTRON WOOL
HACKLE: BROWN PARTRIDGE
COLLAR: PEACOCK HERL

BEAD HEADS WERE UNDENIABLY the hottest thing to have happened to fly fishing in the 1990s and they continue to evolve. In many instances it's just a way of adding weight, but nevertheless some patterns seem wedded to the bead as an integral part of their success. This is one such, and in freestone streams it's a real hottie that gets results. You need a variety of colours and sizes. Used when caddis are no longer hatching, it makes a great grayling fly in the winter months.

Mosquito Larva

MOSQUITOES ARE BECOMING THE SCOURGE OF THE WORLD, not only because of their nasty bite, but particularly as those species that carry malaria are increasing their range due to global warming. They need stagnant water or very slow-moving backwaters in order to breed, and, of course, blood. What makes them a prized fish food is their necessity to frequently come to the surface to breath. The wriggling action as they do so is very attractive to fish but then when the larvae hang in the surface tension to breathe they are easy meat.

WHERE: WORLDWIDE

WHEN: SPRING AND SUMMER

WHAT: TROUT, BLUEGILL, CARP

HOW: IMITATES THE LARVA OF THE MOSQUITO

HOOK: 12 TO 14 STANDARD SHANK
TAIL: GRIZZLE COCK HACKLE FIBRES
BODY: STRIPPED PEACOCK QUILL
THORAX: PEACOCK HERL
ANTENNAE: GRIZZLE HACKLE FIBRES

Gold Bead Daddy

WHERE: INTENDED FOR STOCKED TROUT IN STILLWATER BUT CAN HAVE SURPRISING RESULTS IN MANY LOCATIONS

WHEN: ALL YEAR BUT BEST WHEN DADDY-LONGLEGS (CRANE FLIES) ARE HATCHING IN AUTUMN

WHAT: BROWN AND RAINBOW TROUT

HOW: LOOKS JUST LIKE AN ADULT DADDY-LONG-LEGS

HOOK: 10 TO 14 STANDARD SHANK OR 2X NYMPH SHANK
HEAD: 2, 3 OR 4 MM (¾, 1 OR 1½ INCHES) GOLD BEAD
BODY: TAN RAFFINE
WINGS: CREE COCK HACKLE POINTS TIED SPENT
LEGS: SIX TO TEN COCK PHEASANT CENTRE TAIL FIBRES WITH TWO KNOTS PER FIBRE
HACKLE: RED GAME OR CREE COCK TIED SWEPT BACK

I ENTIRELY AGREE THAT THERE IS NO SUCH THING AS AN UNDERWATER, swimming, daddy-longlegs (crane fly), but try telling that to trout which absolutely love to eat this pattern! Best used on reared fish in stillwaters, but I have seen it slaughter trout in deep, clear pools on chalk streams and I have even seen migrating sockeye salmon move off station to take it. I think it must be something to do with the legs. Incidentally, rubber legs are even better than the knotted pheasant tail kind. Usually best fished deep with an erratic retrieve, it can also be very good on a slime line.

Halibut Ghost

THIS IS DEFINITELY A SERIOUS FLY. The monster flatfish, the Pacific halibut, is a very efficient predator and actively feeds on other fish, which makes it a prime target for fly fishermen. Just because it usually lives in very deep water with strong currents does not mean that there aren't times and areas where it can be successfully fly fished. I know Pacific halibut have been landed weighing over 45 kg (100 lbs) on fly gear using 15- to 17-weight sailfish rods, although having caught them on conventional tackle I think it must be like fighting with a bear to handle them on fly gear!

 **WHERE:** ALASKA AND BRITISH COLUMBIA

 **WHEN:** SUMMER

 **WHAT:** HALIBUT

 **HOW:** SUGGESTS A LARGE BAIT FISH

 **HOOK:** 5/0 SALTWATER O'SHAUGHNESSY
TAIL: WHITE BUCKTAIL
BODY: SILVER MYLAR TUBING WOUND OVER SHANK
WING AND HACKLE: WHITE MEGAHAIR TOPPED OVER WITH WHITE EVERGLO SYNTHETIC HAIR
HEAD: EPOXY OVER THE WHITE TYING THREAD. YOU CAN ADD EYES AS WELL

Hydropsyche Larva

WHERE: FREESTONE STREAMS IN THE NORTHERN HEMISPHERE

WHEN: ALL YEAR BUT BEST TOWARDS THE END OF THE YEAR

WHAT: GRAYLING, TROUT

HOW: CLOSE COPY OF A SPECIFIC CADDIS (SEDGE) SPECIES

HOOK: 8 TO 12 CURVED SHANK
TAIL: A PARTRIDGE FILOPLUME TRIMMED
BACK: BROWN SPECKLED TURKEY
BODY: A DIRTY YELLOW ANTRON OR SIMILAR
GILLS: OSTRICH HERL DOWN EACH SIDE DYED DIRTY YELLOW
RIB: TURNS OF CLEAR 1.8 KG (4 LB) NYLON AND FINE GOLD WIRE
LEGS: THREE CLUMPS OF DARK BROWN PARTRIDGE
TINT THE THORAX WITH A BLACK PANTONE PEN AND THE HEAD WITH YELLOW.

I HAVE INCLUDED THIS PERFECTION in fly tying from Oliver Edwards, an artist at the vice who knows just how far it is possible to take the art of fly tying and yet still make flies that catch fish. This particular caddis (sedge) lives in rough, freestone streams and is very much a grayling special. It comes into its own as the water cools and trout go out of season. It needs to be well-weighted and fished hard on the bottom.

Depth Charge Czech Mate

THIS IS AN EXTREMELY HEAVY VERSION OF THE CZECH NYMPH (see page 91) and uses a tungsten shot. I have included it because it can be essential for heavy-flowing rivers where you need to get the fly right down to the bottom and to take down other, more lightly dressed flies with it. Ideal for those reservoirs where trout are reared in cages. Massive bloodworm beds develop underneath the cages and the fly should be suspended a few centimetres (inches) off the bottom from an anchored boat using very fast-sinking lines. If fished well, grown-on fish will swallow this unusual offering.

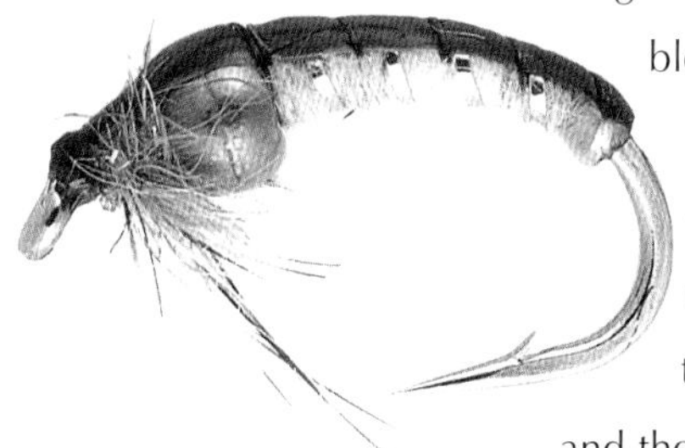

WHERE: FREESTONE RIVERS WITH HEAVY FLOW AND ALONGSIDE RESERVOIR CAGES

WHEN: ALL YEAR

WHAT: GRAYLING, TROUT

HOW: STONEFLY IMITATOR AND VERY SPECIALIZED RESERVOIR NYMPH

HOOK: 8 OR 10 CURVED SHANK HEAVY WIRE
BODY: OFF WHITE WOOL WITH ORANGE TAG AND A BROWN LATEX BACK RIBBED WITH OVAL GOLD TINSEL
THORAX: BLACK TUNGSTEN BEAD WITH A SPINNING OF HARE'S FUR

Sea Habit Green Machine

WHERE: SALTWATER, USUALLY TROPICAL OR SUBTROPICAL

WHEN: ALL YEAR

WHAT: REDFISH, STRIPED BASS, SNOOK, SEA TROUT, MACKEREL SPECIES

HOW: A HIGHLY SURFACE ACTIVE ATTRACTOR

HOOK: DEPENDS ON BODY SIZE BUT USUALLY 2/0 TO 4 STAINLESS STEEL PATTERN IS BUILT ON A PLASTIC TUBE BY MIXING WHITE AND CHARTREUSE FISHAIR THEN SURROUNDING BODY WITH MASSES OF CHARTREUSE SADDLE HACKLES, DARK BLUE HACKLES DARK OLIVE AND FINALLY CHARTREUSE BUCKTAIL AND BLUE CRYSTALFLASH. THE HEAD IS A CYLINDER OF CHARTREUSE FOAM WITH STICK-ON EYES

OFFSHORE FLY FISHING IS A SEPARATE ISSUE and this book only covers patterns that can be cast with conventional fly gear without the target fish being teased up to close quarters. However, some flies in suitable sizes will serve both functions, hence the amazing success of popper and banger style flies which really hit the right spots for many inshore saltwater species. To cast bulky flies like this you need a heavy fly line and a powerful rod.

Bitch Creek Nymph

NEVER UNDERESTIMATE THE EFFECTIVENESS OF RUBBER LEGS when added to many fly patterns. Poppers, crabs, squid, nymphs and daddy-longlegs (crane fly) can all be enhanced by the wiggle of rubber. This Montana Nymph variant is a popular and effective pattern for waters that aren't that rich in insect life. In the far northern and southern hemispheres, it is a summer standard for trout and grayling. Also well worth trying on lakes for stocked trout. I have even taken jaded Atlantic salmon from Irish rivers on this big nymph.

WHERE: WORLDWIDE IN FAR NORTHERN AND SOUTHERN HEMISPHERE RIVERS

WHEN: USUALLY BEST FROM LATE SPRING TO SUMMER

WHAT: TROUT, GRAYLING, LAKE TROUT

HOW: PERHAPS DUE TO THE WIGGLE OF THE RUBBER LEGS

HOOK: 4X TO 8 4X LONG SHANK
TAIL: TWO PIECES OF WHITE RUBBER
BODY: REAR TWO-THIRDS IS WOVEN WITH BLACK AND ORANGE CHENILLE
THORAX: BLACK CHENILLE WITH A RED GAME COCK HACKLE WOUND THROUGH
ANTENNAE: TWO PIECES OF WHITE RUBBER

Prince

THIS EVER-POPULAR, broad-spectrum nymph uses peacock herl for the body although a man-made substitute such as Micro-Brite is a tougher substitute. A nice little bug which catches just about anywhere. When well-weighted, is a great search pattern for deep pools. Grayling love it when drifted along the bottom, while fished unweighted around weed beds, it is a killer for crappies and bluegill. Try it late in the evening for migratory trout and char that have been in the river for a few weeks.

WHERE: WORLDWIDE IN RIVERS AND STILLWATER

WHEN: ALL YEAR

WHAT: TROUT (INCLUDING MIGRATORY), GRAYLING, CHAR, SMALLMOUTH BASS, BLUEGILL

HOW: A PATTERN THAT MEANS SOMETHING EDIBLE

HOOK: 14 TO 8 NYMPH 2X SHANK
TAIL: TWO BROWN GOOSE BIOTS
BODY: PEACOCK HERL RIBBED WITH FLAT GOLD TINSEL
HACKLE: TWO OR THREE TURNS OF RED GAME HEN
HORNS: TWO WHITE GOOSE BIOTS

Gold Ribbed Hare's Ear

FULLING MILL (THE MAJOR UK FLY TYING COMPANY) tell me that their biggest-selling fly worldwide is a size 12 Gold Ribbed Hare's Ear. It is an unbelievably effective pattern on any water where fish eat nymphs of the upwinged clan or stonefly family, which makes it a first fly for anywhere in the world. With a gold bead for weight and attractive glitter, it is a doubly effective river pattern for fast water. If I was confined to the use of just one fly then this would be it.

WHERE: WORLDWIDE IN RIVERS AND STILLWATER

WHEN: ALL YEAR

WHAT: TROUT, GRAYLING, SMALLMOUTH BASS, BLUEGILL, CARP, LAKE TROUT

HOW: SUGGESTS MANY FORMS OF AQUATIC LIFE, PARTICULARLY EPHEMERIDS AND CADDIS (SEDGE)

HOOK: 8 TO 18 STANDARD SHANK TO 2X NYMPH SHANK
TAIL: A FEW FIBRES FROM THE CHEEK OF A HARE'S FACE
BODY: DUBBED HARE'S FACE (FROM THE EARS FOR VERY SMALL PATTERNS)
THORAX: A FEW FIBRES OF ANY BROWN FEATHER AND THEN THE FUR PICKED OUT TO SUGGEST A FEW STRAGGLY LEGS

Grey Sockeye Nymph

SOCKEYE SALMON FEED ON PLANKTON in the ocean and are usually deemed uncatchable unless specifically foul hooked in the mouth – this may be skilful but it isn't fly fishing.

I have spent years working on ways to take sockeye salmon properly, and there is absolutely no doubt that they will take a fly. This can be infuriatingly difficult even when present in large numbers. Try this one at close range into the marching columns or with an indicator when the salmon are stacked prior to the next stage of their run up river.

WHERE: ALASKAN RIVERS AND SOME IN BRITISH COLUMBIA

WHEN: JULY

WHAT: SOCKEYE SALMON

HOW: A NON-SPECIFIC PATTERN

HOOK: 10 TO 6 STANDARD SHANK
TAIL: SHORT TUFT OF GREY MARABOU
BODY: DUBBING BRUSH OF GREY HAIR DRESSED THIN
HACKLE: GREY HEN TWO TURNS AND TIED SWEPT BACK

Roe Bug

ALL SPECIES EAT FISH EGGS, even their own, and some take them just to remove opposition for their own eggs.

This fly is excellent for all migratory salmonids especially Pacific species, and the tying technique using a manmade synthetic yarn called Glo Bug Yarn is certainly unusual. Presentation is often the key factor and the egg must dead drift with the current. This fly usually works at spawning time in stillwater, but rather puzzlingly it also works where only triploid (sexless female) fish are stocked so maybe the egg just appears to be edible rather than being seen as an egg as such.

WHERE: WORLDWIDE IN FRESHWATER, PRINCIPALLY IN RIVERS

WHEN: ALL YEAR, BUT BEST WHEN SPAWNING IS OCCURRING

WHAT: TROUT, SALMON (ESPECIALLY PACIFIC), CHAR, GRAYLING

HOW: IMITATES A FISH EGG

HOOK: 6 TO 16 SHORT SHANK WIDE GAPE 2 TO 4 PIECES OF GLO BUG
BODY: YARN TIED IN THE MIDDLE ON TOP OF HOOK THEN LIFTED UP WITH TIGHT WRAPS AROUND BASE AND TRIMMED WITH SCISSORS TO MAKE IT FLARE AROUND THE HOOK
NOTE: SIZE AND COLOUR CAN BE CRITICAL AND AN EGG SPOT USING A SMALL PIECE OF DIFFERENT COLOUR CAN ALSO BE A FACTOR.

Funneldun

NEIL PATTERSON LOOKED AT TROUT DRY FLIES as though he were a fish and concluded that the 'footprint' made in the surface film by a conventional dry fly tying did not match that of the natural and allowed the bend of the hook to project under the surface. By tying the hackle to sweep towards and having the tail slightly round the bend of the hook, he discovered that clipping a 'v' in the hackle would make the fly always land upside down and perfectly match the footprint of a natural insect.

WHERE: LIMESTONE (CHALK) STREAMS WORLDWIDE IN TEMPERATE REGIONS

WHEN: LATE SPRING THROUGH TO FALL

WHAT: TROUT, GRAYLING

HOOK: 14 TO 18 FINE WIRE UP EYE
TAIL: COCK HACKLE COLOUR TO MATCH THE HATCH
BODY: TYING THREAD COLOUR TO MATCH THE HATCH
THORAX: LIGHT COLOURED MINK UNDEFUR
HACKLE: COCK COLOUR TO MATCH THE HATCH

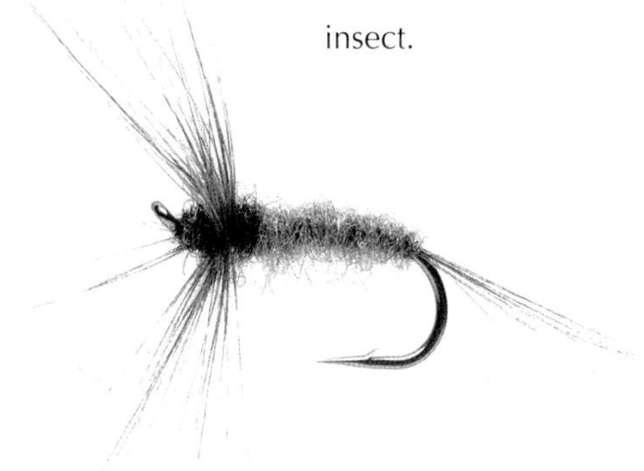

Sea Habit Tube Sardine

THIS STYLE OF TYING makes it easy to carry a wide range of sizes without the need for many hooks, so it is an economical method for the saltwater angler who needs many options for different bait fish. Trey Coombs ties four principal options – Ballyhoo, Anchovy, Flying Fish and Sardine. Used in different lengths these will serve for the various sizes of prey fish, depending on which age group is being exploited by the fish. Easy to cast, these super flies also work for many freshwater predators such as pike, walleye and lake trout.

WHERE: WORLDWIDE IN SALTWATER AND SOME FRESHWATER LOCATIONS

WHEN: ALL YEAR

WHAT: VIRTUALLY ANY PREDATORY FISH

HOW: EXCELLENT BAIT FISH IMITATION

HOOK: 1/0 TO 4 SHANK DEPENDING ON OVERALL SIZE BEING USED
BODY: A PLASTIC TUBE
WING: BUILT UP WITH WHITE FISHAIR AND PEARL FLASHABOU, TOPPED WITH SILVER AND OLIVE CRYSTAL HAIR, EMERALD AND MOSS GREEN FISHAIR WITH PEACOCK CRYSTAL HAIR OVER.HEAD IS PEARL MYLAR PIPING PAINTED GREEN ON TOP WITH A STICK ON EYE AND THEN A LAYER OF EPOXY

Wee Double

ANY TRADITIONAL WET FLY OR NYMPH can be tied in this way. It's an almost outdated way of adding weight, stability and extra hooking ability to very small flies. Where wild trout rarely grow to any great size but are caught in numbers, the double hook has a strong following. Mostly used in Scotland and Ireland. Competition anglers often use a larger double on their point fly to add weight. Quite useful for early season downstream wet fly tactics in freestone rivers.

WHERE: MOSTLY IN SCOTLAND AND IRELAND IN STILLWATER

WHEN: SPRING TO AUTUMN

WHAT: TROUT, SEA TROUT

HOW: FLASHY ATTRACTOR

HOOK: 14 TO 16 DOUBLE
TAIL: RED FEATHER FIBRES
BODY: FLAT GOLD TINSEL RIBBED WITH FINE GOLD WIRE
WING: GREY MALLARD
HACKLE: ORANGE COCK

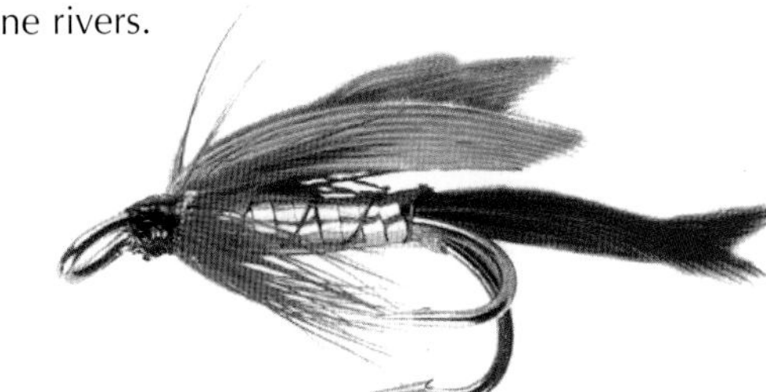

Two Egg Sperm Fly

THE NAME SAYS IT ALL – clearly this is a fly to be fished where spawning is taking place. All fish eat eggs and in some parts of the world this becomes a very important part of their diet. Cold climates with large runs of salmon will support char, trout, whitefish and grayling because they eat eggs. Although not actually feeding, salmon will also take eggs. I believe they do so because they see eggs as competition to their own. A couple of eggs with wriggling sperm attached drifting into their lie will be attacked.

WHERE: RIVERS IN SUBARCTIC REGIONS

WHEN: SUMMER THROUGH TO FALL

WHAT: RAINBOWS, GRAYLING, CHAR, THE PACIFIC SALMON SPECIES

HOW: SUGGESTS FISH EGGS AT SPAWNING TIME

HOOK: 4 TO 6 STANDARD SHANK OR SALMON IRON
TAG: FLAT GOLD TINSEL
TAIL: YELLOW COCK HACKLE FIBRES
BODY: HOT ORANGE CHENILLE, FLAT GOLD TINSEL THEN HOT ORANGE CHENILLE
WING: WHITE MARABOU AND PEARL CRYSTAL FLASH
HACKLE: HOT ORANGE COCK

Polar Chub Bucktail

QUITE AN OLD PATTERN, but this is one of those flies that is an all-time standard. To make it really effective you need to use the original tying material. Nothing else is quite like polar bear fur, and fortunately it is still legally obtainable. A marvellous bait fish fly, especially when the smolt run takes place in salmon rivers. Also excellent for the smelt feeders of Lake Taupo in New Zealand. Whenever you need a small lockfish imitation this is the one to reach for.

WHERE: WORLDWIDE IN FRESH- AND SALTWATER

WHEN: ALL YEAR DEPENDING ON LOCATION

WHAT: ALL PREDATORY SPECIES

HOW: SUGGESTS A SMALL BAIT FISH

HOOK: 2 TO 8 4X SHANK
TAIL: WHITE POLAR BEAR HAIR
BODY: OVAL SILVER TINSEL
WINGS: WHITE, OLIVE AND BROWN POLAR BEAR HAIR
CHEEKS: JUNGLE COCK
HEAD: PAINTED BROWN ON TOP AND OLIVE UNDER

Bead Bloodworm

FISH THAT FEED ON BLOODWORM – the larval stage of the chironomid – can very quickly put on weight. What is often not appreciated is that bloodworm will often leave their sediment home and free swim many metres (yards) in the water. Fish expect to see them in the open and will eat them in very large numbers. I have taken large rainbow trout under rearing cages in lakes which have been stuffed to the gills with bloodworm. This pattern works best fished 'on the drop' or with a very slow retrieve.

WHERE: WORLDWIDE IN STILLWATER AND SOME SLOWER-FLOWING RIVERS

WHEN: ALL YEAR, NOT JUST WHEN CHIRONOMIDS ARE HATCHING

WHAT: ALL TROUT SPECIES, BASS, CRAPPIES, CARP

HOW: IMITATES THE LARVAL STAGE OF THE CHIRONOMID

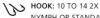

HOOK: 10 TO 14 2X NYMPH OR STANDARD SHANK OR CURVED SEDGE HOOK

TAIL: ABOUT 10 FIBRES OF DEEP RED MARABOU

BODY: TRANSLUCENT, BLOOD RED GLASS BEADS RIBBED THROUGH WITH MARABOU FIBRES

Foam Beetle

NEVER UNDERESTIMATE THE IMPORTANCE OF TERRESTRIALS. Many upland trout will have beetles in their stomach contents no matter what insects are hatching. This is a morsel that few fish will turn down, no matter how rich their environment, and at times there can be so many beetles landing on water that fish will become preoccupied with them. If you aren't sure what to fish in mid-summer, but can see single spasmodic rises, then the chances are that the fish are taking beetles drifting on the wind. Use this fly on a long leader and be patient.

WHERE: WORLDWIDE IN FRESHWATER LAKES AND RIVERS AND OCCASIONALLY IN ESTUARIES

WHEN: USUALLY SUMMER

WHAT: TROUT, GRAYLING, SMALLMOUTH BASS, BLUEGILL

HOW: SUGGESTS MANY SPECIES OF BEETLE

HOOK: 10 TO 16 STANDARD SHANK
BACK: STRIP OF BLACK ETHAFOAM
BODY: DUBBED BLACK RABBIT UNDERFUR
HACKLE: SINGLE TURN BLACK HEN
HEAD: BLACK ETHAFOAM

Cicada

SOME INSECTS DEMAND SPECIFIC IMITATIONS because they have very localized occurrence and are so different to anything else that a precise copy is essential. This pattern came from Clark Reid in New Zealand and can be used in South Africa and many southern states of the US, as well as in Paraguay and Chile. It will also double up as a grasshopper pattern and may be used as a stonefly or even a surface attractor for stillwater trout. Fish it to land with a plop and give it an occasional twitch.

WHERE: SUBTROPICAL REGIONS WORLDWIDE

WHEN: SUMMER

WHAT: TROUT, SMALLMOUTH AND LARGEMOUTH BASS

HOW: COPIES THE NATURAL CICADA

HOOK: 8 TO 10 2X SHANK
BODY: CLOSE-CLIPPED OLIVE DEERHAIR
WINGS: PEARL CRYSTAL HAIR WITH SYNTHETIC SHIMAZAKI FLY WING
COLLAR AND HEAD: OLIVE DEERHAIR
EYES: BLACK NYLON OR BEADS

Dahlberg Diver

A BRILLIANT IDEA FROM AMERICAN fly innovator, Larry Dahlberg, was to design a fly that fishes like a floating plug. It has since proven to be very good for peacock bass and, when used in large sizes, for taimen and many other predatory species. The idea is that the buoyant deerhair head is cut in such a way that when retrieved the fly is forced under the water – but pause, and up it pops again. Try this one for trout in summer when the weed growth gets bad, or for small tarpon in backwaters.

WHERE: WORLDWIDE IN STILLWATER, BOTH FRESH- AND SALTWATER

WHEN: ALL YEAR BUT BEST IN WARM WATER

WHAT: SMALLMOUTH, LARGEMOUTH AND PEACOCK BASS, TROUT, TAIMEN

HOW: AN AGGRESSIVE, SURFACE-ACTIVE DIVING LURE

HOOK: 2 TO 6 4X SHANK
BODY: BLACK FLOSS
WING AND HACKLE: BLACK MARABOU MIXED WITH BLACK BUCKTAIL, PEARL FLASHABOU AND GRIZZLE SADDLE HACKLES
HEAD: BLACK DEERHAIR TRIMMED TO SHAPE

Bristol Hopper

THIS FLY EVOLVED DURING THE PERIOD when emerger fishing for hatching chironomids and competition fishing from drifting boats became popular. The teams centred around Bristol in the west of England were then the strongest force and produced many world class anglers. Using ragged seal's fur bodies and short straggly legs to fish a fly right in the surface film, they found that trout would readily accept this rough and ready tying when feeding on emergers. Various colours are used throughout the year. The straggly legs are definitely an important feature.

WHERE: WORLDWIDE IN STILLWATER IN TEMPERATE REGIONS

WHEN: SPRING TO AUTUMN

WHAT: TROUT

HOW: SUGGESTS THE HATCHING STAGE OF THE CHIRONOMID

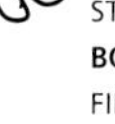
HOOK: 12 TO 16 STANDARD SHANK
BODY: SEAL'S FUR WITH FINE FLAT PEARL TINSEL RIB
LEGS: SIX SHORT, SINGLE KNOTTED PHEASANT TAIL FIBRES
HACKLE: MATCHING COLOUR COCK TIED SLOPING BACK. GINGER, ORANGE, CLARET AND BLACK ARE BEST

Bloom Fly

DAPHNIA (THE FRESHWATER FLEA) forms an extremely important element in the diet of trout weighing up to 1.8 kg (4 lbs) in large stillwaters. In the warmer months, daphnia occurs in huge swarms and trout will really pack on the weight. You only have to see the effect of feeding daphnia to tropical freshwater fish at home to appreciate how ambitious this food form really is. This little pink special was born at Hanningfield Reservoir in eastern England and works extremely well once the depth at which the fish are feeding is located.

WHERE: STILLWATER IN TEMPERATE AND SUBTROPICAL REGIONS

WHEN: WARMER MONTHS ARE BEST

WHAT: TROUT

HOW: MAYBE SUGGESTS A CLUSTER OF DAPHNIA

HOOK: 12 OR 14 STANDARD SHANK
TAIL: PEACH MARABOU
BODY: PINK CHENILLE WITH FLAT PEARL TINSEL RIB
HACKLE: WHITE HEN

CDC Loopwing Emerger

THIS STYLE OF TYING holds a fly in the surface and gives the impression of a fly struggling to hatch. This particular tying is marvellous for most of the smaller olive ephemerids and I use it on stillwaters when pond and lake olives are coming off. As time goes on I believe we will see less and less 'traditional' dry flies being used and much more of this emerger style. It's not a difficult tying technique to master but try buying bulk CDC instead of pre-selected packs. That way you get more choice of feather size.

WHERE: RIVERS AND LAKES TEMPERATE REGIONS

WHEN: SPRING THROUGH TO FALL

WHAT: TROUT, GRAYLING

HOOK: 18 TO 12 FINE WIRE STANDARD SHANK
TAIL: RED GAME COCK HACKLE FIBRES
BODY: OLIVE TYING THREAD WITH THINLY SPUN HARES EAR DYED OLIVE
WING: SINGLE LARGE CDC FEATHER TIED LOOP STYLE

Marabou Damsel

WHERE: MOST STILLWATER EXCLUDING THE HIGH ARCTIC AND MANY SLOW AREAS OF RIVERS

WHEN: ALL YEAR BUT BEST IN SUMMER

WHAT: TROUT, GRAYLING, LAKE TROUT, SMALLMOUTH AND LARGE MOUTH BASS, BLUEGILL

HOW: SUGGESTS THE LARVAL STAGE OF THE DAMSEL FLY

HOOK: 8 TO 14 2X NYMPH OR STANDARD SHANK
TAIL: BUNCH OF OLIVE MARABOU FIBRES
BODY: TWISTED AND WOUND OLIVE MARABOU FIBRES
THORAX: SAME AS BODY PLUS OLIVE FEATHER FIBRE OVER TO MAKE THORAX CASE
EYES: TWO SMALL GREEN GLASS BEADS THREADED ON THICK MONO

FISH THAT LIVE IN STILLWATER or slow-flowing rivers know all about the larvae of the damsel nymph as it is a major food item in all its sizes. They occur in staggering numbers in summer, especially when the water is rich enough and alkaline. Although the natural damsel is a slim and fragile-looking creature, the marabou fibres in the fly which give movement, the olive colouring and the eye effect all combine to make trout believe this is the real thing. A close copy is not necessarily best!

Blue Flash Damsel

MANY SPECIES OF DAMSEL FLY have blue adults and it has long been known that tyings of the larval form are particularly effective when a touch of blue is included in the dressing. In 1998, a number of tiers had the good idea of using damsel nymphs with marabou tails and a bit of Crystalflash. This excellent version is the pick of the bunch. I sell hundreds of them every season. This is a great fly to give a newcomer to get them hooked on fly fishing.

WHERE: STILLWATER AND SLOW RIVERS IN TEMPERATE REGIONS

WHEN: EARLY SUMMER TO AUTUMN IS BEST

WHAT: TROUT, PERCH, SMALLMOUTH AND LARGEMOUTH BASS, BLUEGILL

HOW: DAMSEL NYMPH IMITATION

HOOK: 12 TO 8 2X SHANK
HEAD: GOLD BEAD
TAIL: OLIVE MARABOU WITH 6 STRANDS OF ROYAL BLUE CRYSTALFLASH
BODY: OLIVE CHENILLE WITH PALMERED OLIVE HEN HACKLE AND BLUE TINSEL RIB

Coachman

THIS OLD FAVOURITE, can be used with confidence for sea-run brown trout by day or night, freshwater and sea-run cutthroat steelheads of the Great Lakes, or the migrating rainbows and brown trout in New Zealand. As an attractor wet fly, the Coachman is usually best fished in the top few feet of water with either a floating or a slow sinking line. Don't be tempted to use a stiff wing fibre as this fly works best with the original tying. A variation of this fly has a grey fibre wing and is called the Leadwing Coachman.

WHERE: WORLDWIDE IN RIVERS OR LAKES

WHEN: ALMOST ANY TIME BUT DUSK IS BEST IN STILLWATER, WHILE IN RIVERS A LITTLE COLOUR IN THE WATER HELPS

WHAT: TROUT, SEA-RUN CUTTHROAT, STEELHEAD, SEA TROUT

HOW: A BASIC ATTRACTOR, WHICH RELIES ON THE WHITE WING

HOOK: 8 TO 16 STANDARD SHANK
BODY: PEACOCK HERL
HACKLE: RED GAME COCK TIED FALSE
WINGS: WHITE SATIN FEATHER FROM UNDER A MALLARD WING

Yellow Humpy

A FANTASTIC FLOATER FOR ROUGH STREAMS, the Yellow Humpy is capable of bringing up surprisingly large fish that really ought to know better. Originating in the western USA it is now in common use throughout the world as a standard dry fly. Deerhair is not the easiest of materials to work with and many tiers use white calf body for the wings, allegedly to aid sighting the fly! However, the original calls for the wings to be the turned-back tips of the deerhair used for the body.

WHERE: WORLDWIDE IN FREESTONE STREAMS AND MOST RIVERS

WHEN: ALL YEAR BUT BEST FROM SPRING TO AUTUMN

WHAT: TROUT, GRAYLING, CUTTHROAT, SMALLMOUTH AND LARGEMOUTH BASS, BLUEGILL

HOW: A NON-SPECIFIC DRY FLY WITH GREAT FLOATABILITY

HOOK: 8 TO 14 STANDARD SHANK
TAIL: MOOSE MANE FIBRES
BODY: YELLOW ANTRON WOOL WITH DEERHAIR ALONG THE BACK
WINGS: TIPS OF THE DEER TIED BACK INTO TWO BUNCHES
HACKLE: GRIZZLE COCK

Flesh Fly

ALMOST ALL FISH will happily eat both the eggs and flesh of their kin. Indeed, in many river environments it is an important part of the nutrition cycle. The death after spawning of Pacific salmon is a vital part of nature's regeneration system in what are otherwise almost barren waters. This pattern is intended for rainbow trout in Alaska, but I have seen miniature versions work under fish cages in lakes where trout expect to feed on rotting carcasses. Like so many of the patterns in this book you should think about options other than the obvious.

WHERE: RIVERS IN ALASKA AND BRITISH COLUMBIA AND PERHAPS CHILE

WHAT: PRIMARILY RAINBOW TROUT BUT MOST SPECIES WILL TAKE IT

WHEN: BEST FROM LATE JULY TO SEPTEMBER

HOW: A SPECIFIC IMITATION OF ROTTING SALMON FLESH

HOOK: 1/0 TO 4 LONG SHANK STANDARD SALMON WITH GENEROUS UNDER-RIBBING OF LEAD WIRE
BODY: TWO-TONE RABBIT DYED PEACH, CUT CROSSWAYS AND WOUND ALONG SHANK WITH TWO TUFTS OF RED AND ORANGE MARABOU MIXED IN

Cat's Whisker

WHILE DEVELOPED FOR STOCKED RAINBOW and brown trout fisheries, the mix of white and fluorescent green has a fatal attraction for many wild trout and other predatory species. There is, of course, nothing living in freshwater that resembles this fly, but nevertheless it works by inciting curiosity and aggression. The lovely name came from its originator, David Train of England, who used some long, white whiskers from his cat to keep the marabou fibres in place (although the lack of white cat's whiskers means this is now largely unused). Try the fly in miniature form up to large long shank versions and in its numerous colour variants.

WHERE: STILLWATER THROUGHOUT THE WORLD WHERE TROUT ARE STOCKED, PLUS SOME WILD LOCATIONS TOO

WHEN: ALL YEAR

WHAT: RAINBOW AND BROWN TROUT AND SOME OTHER SALMONIDS

HOW: A STRAIGHT ATTRACTOR PATTERN

HOOK: 12 STANDARD SHANK TO 6 4X LONG SHANK
TAIL: TUFT OF WHITE MARABOU
BODY: FLUORESCENT GREEN CHENILLE
WING: WHITE MARABOU

Diawl Bach

THERE MAY BE VERY LITTLE TO THIS FLY but looks can be deceptive and this nondescript pattern is utterly deadly when fished in stillwaters for rainbow and brown trout. It is very commonly used as one of a three-fly combination for competition fishing when trout may be pulled in by other patterns only to take this bland and inoffensive nymph. It works best when fished really deep to just under the surface and as a point or single fly on a floating line for clear water trout in summer. The Diawl Bach (Welsh for 'little devil') is a real confidence-booster and has many variants using coloured pearl or holographic ribbing.

WHERE: STILLWATER IN TEMPERATE AND SUB-ARCTIC REGIONS

WHEN: ALL YEAR BUT BEST IN WARMER MONTHS

WHAT: TROUT

HOW: RESEMBLES MANY KINDS OF NYMPHS

HOOK: 10 TO 16 STANDARD SHANK
TAIL: RED GAME COCK HACKLE FIBRES
BODY: PEACOCK HERL
HACKLE: RED GAME COCK FIBRES TIED BEARD STYLE

Olive Suspender

USING A POLYSTYRENE BALL OR A PIECE OF ETHAFOAM ensures that the fly stays very firmly in the surface. Nowadays, it may seem an old-fashioned way of achieving an emerger presentation, but it still takes a lot of beating in rough water on a flat calm where you can't risk scaring a fish with repeated casting. I like this tying in many nymph patterns because it can often fool a fish into thinking that this is a dead or dying insect sitting lifeless in the surface, it is rarely refused. Everything likes an easy mealticket at times and this style gives a fish just that.

WHERE: RIVERS AND STILLWATERS WORLDWIDE TEMPERATE REGIONS

WHEN: SPRING TO AUTUMN

WHAT: TROUT, GRAYLING, SMALLMOUTH BASS, BLUEGILLS

HOW: IMITATES A DEAD OR DYING INSECT

HOOK: 10 TO 14 STANDARD SHANK TO 2X SHANK
TAIL: OLIVE COCK HACKLE
BODY: OLIVE SEAL'S FUR GOLD WIRE RIB
HACKLE: OLIVE COCK TIED PARACHUTE AROUND A POLY BALL

Fry Feeder Tandem

TIED AS A PIKE FLY and very clearly intended to be a bait fish it is also very good indeed for the larger, resident trout in lakes. These big fish are usually fish eaters and a fly of this size fished with a fast-sinking shooting head can bring a few surprises. If you are not averse to trolling a fly, it can be even better and will outfish spoons and plugs for lakers. One of the best flies I know for Nile Perch and most saltwater species. If you fish for pike be brave and cast around structure and weeds while trying to do a fluttery, sink and draw retrieve but be very careful when you lift off to recast, as the take can come at the very last second.

WHERE: STILLWATERS, RIVERS AND SALTWATER WORLDWIDE

WHEN: YEAR ROUND

WHAT: PIKE AND PREDATORS

HOW: IT'S A FISH IMITATION

HOOKS: SIZE 2 4X SHANK WIDE GAPE TIED TANDEM WITH 50LB MONO
BODY: PEARLY MYLAR TUBE
WING: MIX OF PEARL FISHAIR AND CRYSTALFLASH WITH PALE BLUE AND GREEN CRYSTALFLASH OVER THE TOP
THEN RED FISHAIR UNDER
HEAD: STICK ON PRISMATIC EYE THEN THE WHOLE FIRST HOOK COVERED WITH SOFTBODY AND MOULDED TO SHAPE

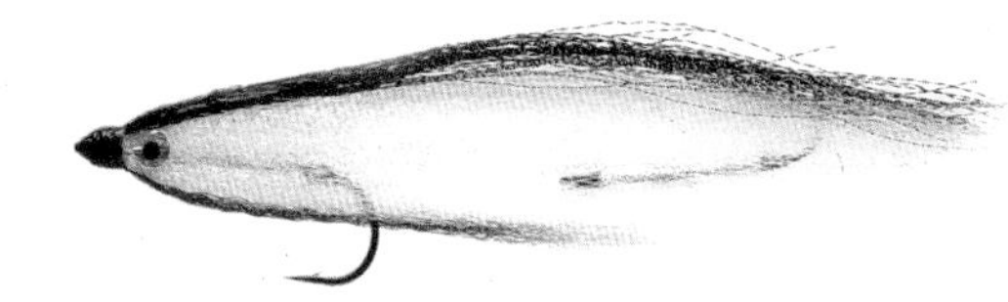

Comet Waddington

THIS STYLE OF FLY DRESSING makes for a very long body, much like a tube fly, and is very popular as an early spring or late autumn fly on large, Atlantic salmon rivers when fished with fast-sinking lines in heavy water. The damage from such a hook can be severe so it isn't recommended if the requirement is to release a proportion of the catch. Comets are undeniably effective for salmon but I don't know why they are taken by the fish.

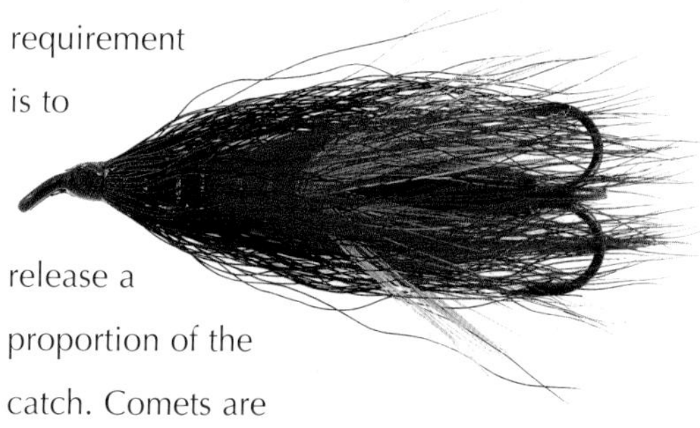

WHERE: SALMON RIVERS IN THE NORTHERN HEMISPHERE

WHEN: SPRING AND AUTUMN OR AT HIGH WATER

WHAT: ATLANTIC SALMON AND LARGE SEA TROUT

HOW: A LARGE, HEAVY LURE (FOR BIG AREAS OF WATER) WHICH PROVOKES A STRIKE FROM THE FISH

HOOK: 5 TO 7.5 CM (2 TO 3 INCH) WADDINGTON OR TUBE WITH SIZE 8 TO 4 TREBLE
TAIL: YELLOW BUCKTAIL TIED AROUND THE SHANK
BODY: REAR IS RED FLOSS AND FRONT IS BLACK FLOSS WITH AN OVAL GOLD TINSEL RIB
HEAD: BLACK BUCKTAIL TIED TO ENVELOP THE PRECEDING MATERIAL
MID-BODY HACKLE: RED BUCKTAIL TIED TO ENVELOP THE PRECEDING MATERIAL

Cockroach

CHICO FERNANDEZ tied this tarpon fly and it produced a 31.5 kg (70 lb) fish on my first ever try, fishing out from Marathon in Florida. I was mightily impressed by this beautiful fish, which has the wonderful name Megalops Atlanticus – perfect for this fly fishing monster. Many tarpon flies are quite gaudy, but this one is bland and inoffensive and is dependent on the presentation being correct so that quiet cruisers will follow and suck it in without getting aggressive.

WHERE: TROPICAL SALTWATER

WHEN: ALL YEAR

WHAT: TARPON AND OTHER FISH

HOW: BAIT FISH IMITATION

HOOK: 3/0 STAINLESS O'SHAUGHNESSY
TAIL: GRIZZLE COCK SADDLE HACKLES
COLLAR: GREY SQUIRREL
HEAD: BLACK WITH YELLOW AND BLACK EYE AND EPOXY

Peter Ross

THE PETER ROSS IS THE UK'S EMBLEM OF THE FLY DRESSERS GUILD, a worldwide organization that seeks to unite fly tiers from around the world. This traditional wet fly is a beautiful blend of many materials creating a pattern that is visually appealing to both us and the trout. Trout love it, especially in broken water where wild-bred fish can be expected. As a search pattern it excels and makes a very good point fly on a three-fly cast, but can also be used for migratory brown trout or for stillwater trout, which sometimes feed on sticklebacks.

WHERE: IN FREESTONE STREAMS, NON-FERTILE LAKES, AND RIVERS THAT HAVE MIGRATORY BROWN TROUT (SEA TROUT)

WHEN: USUALLY BEST EARLY AND LATE IN THE SEASON AND OFTEN VERY GOOD IN ROUGH WEATHER OR WHEN THE WATER IS A LITTLE COLOURED

WHAT: BROWN, CUTTHROAT, RAINBOW AND SEA TROUT

HOW: A NON-SPECIFIC PATTERN THAT CAN SUGGEST "FOOD" TO TROUT.

HOOK: 6 TO 14 STANDARD SHANK
TAIL: GOLDEN PHEASANT TIPPETS
BODY: REAR HALF IS FLAT SILVER TINSEL; FRONT HALF IS RED WOOL. BOTH SECTIONS ARE THEN RIBBED WITH SILVER WIRE
WING: TEAL FLANK FEATHER
HACKLE: BLACK HEN

Freight Train

I WONDER IF WE WILL EVER DISCOVER why steelhead and other salmonids love purple flies? I hope not as some of the mystique will then be gone. For now, we can accept that purple is a killer at times. This is Randall Kaufmann creation is typical of traditional wet flies tied large to attract steelhead. The chrome-bright summer steelhead of one salt year (a salt year is a year spent in the sea) will take the biggest of flies, and this fly tickled through the runs can bring really hard pulls as the fish hit at speed.

WHERE: PACIFIC NORTHWEST, ALASKA, THE GREAT LAKES, KAMCHATKA AND SOUTH AMERICA

WHEN: ALL YEAR BUT BETTER WHEN THE WATER IS COLD

WHAT: STEELHEAD

HOW: AN ATTRACTOR

HOOK: 1 TO 6 SALMON IRON
TAIL: PURPLE COCK HACKLE FIBRES
BODY: REAR QUARTER FLUORESCENT FIRE ORANGE THEN QUARTER FLUORESCENT RED WOOL THEN BLACK CHENILLE ALL RIBBED WITH FINE OVAL SILVER
HACKLE: PURPLE HEN
WING: WHITE CALF TAIL AND PEARL CRYSTALFLASH

Chernobyl Crab

THERE WAS A TIME WHEN THE ULTRA SMART Permit was thought to be impossible to catch on a fly, but then Del Merkin made a really good crab imitation which worked and soon new patterns came along. This one, once again a Borski pattern, is relatively simple to tie and also works well. Permit on fly is one on my list of wants before I'm too old.

WHERE: TROPICAL SEAS AROUND THE EQUATOR, MOSTLY IN SHALLOW WATER

WHEN: BEST OUT OF THE HURRICANE SEASON

WHAT: PERMIT AND MANY OTHER FLATS' DWELLERS SUCH AS BONEFISH AND REDFISH. ALSO TRY IT FOR BARRAMUNDI IN CLEAR WATER

HOW: IT LOOKS LIKE A CRAB

HOOK: HOOK 4 TO 3/0 SALTWATER O'SHAUGHNESSY
TAIL: WHITE CALF TAIL WITH PEARL CRYSTALFLASH AND BROWN HACKLE TIPS
BODY: CLIPPED DEERHAIR WITH PALMERED BROWN HACKLE
EYES: LEAD DUMBBELLS PAINTED BLACK AND YELLOW
NYLON WEED GUARD IS 20 MASON

Braided Barracuda Fly

BARRACUDA, THE LEAN, MEAN, KILLING-MACHINE of saltwater requires an unusual fly to make it strike. The retrieve should be as rapid as you can make it. Make sure you use a wire leader, as these aggressive fish can slice another fish in half with ease. Barracuda accelerate so fast that it just isn't possible to see them. I love it when you spook one on the flats and it just disappears leaving a puff of silt. It is great fun to fight on fly gear, and will make leaps with a high speed run known as 'greyhounding'.

WHERE: TROPICAL SALTWATER

WHEN: ALL YEAR

WHAT: BARRACUDA

HOW: SUGGESTS A NEEDLEFISH

HOOK: 2/0 LONG SHANK O'SHAUGHNESSY
TAIL: BRAIDED NYLON
BODY: NYLON WITH EPOXY RESIN OVER AND INCORPORATING A STICK ON A DOLL'S EYE. VARIANTS ARE WHITE/GREEN AND FLUORESCENT GREEN.

Crippled Mayfly Suspender

HOW OFTEN HAVE YOU FISHED a mayfly hatch only to have your very best presentations refused? Observation is the key, and it's likely that the fish are only taking the crippled or stillborn insects which have failed to hatch. This pattern is a real winner that can be presented exactly where the trout expects to find it. Well worth carrying a few for stillwaters too, and dropped into a sticky slick area next to the bank it will take those ultra-cautious bankside cruisers as long as you resist the impulse to recast – let the fish find the fly.

WHERE: LIMESTONE RIVERS AND STILLWATER IN TEMPERATE REGIONS

WHEN: LATE SPRING TO EARLY SUMMER

WHAT: TROUT

HOW: COPIES A FAILED MAYFLY HATCH

HOOK: 12 2X CURVED SHANK
TAIL: COCK PHEASANT CENTRE TAIL FIBRES
BODY: CREAM ANTRON YARN WITH DARK BROWN FLOSS RIB
LEGS: COCK PHEASANT CENTRE TAIL FIBRES
THORAX: CREAM ANTRON YARN WITH WHITE ETHAFOAM BACK
WINGS: WHITE RAFFENE

Mac Salmon

WHERE: RIVERS IN WESTERN USA

WHEN: EARLY TO MID SUMMER

WHAT: TROUT

HOW: SPECIFIC IMITATION OF THE SALMON FLY (A HUGE STONEFLY)

DRESSING: HOOK SIZE 6 OR 4 2XSHANK

HOOK: SIZE 8 TO 4 4X SHANK
BODY: YELLOW FOAM CYLINDER TIED TO SHOW SEGMENTS
WING: PRECUT BLACK LACEWING OVER STRANDS OF PEARL CRYSTALFLASH
LEGS: BLACK RUBBER HEAD,HACKLE,
OVERWING: ELK HAIR

THIS IS AN UPDATED VERSION of the famous imitation created by Dave Whitlock for the Salmon Fly hatch. Commonplace for western USA anglers but when seen first time by visitors it's a frighteningly huge insect and this imitation is also a monster. I bought this one at Kaufmann's Streambourne in Oregon and can only vouch for its effectiveness by recommendation from good friends in Montana as I have yet to fish a hatch of this fly.

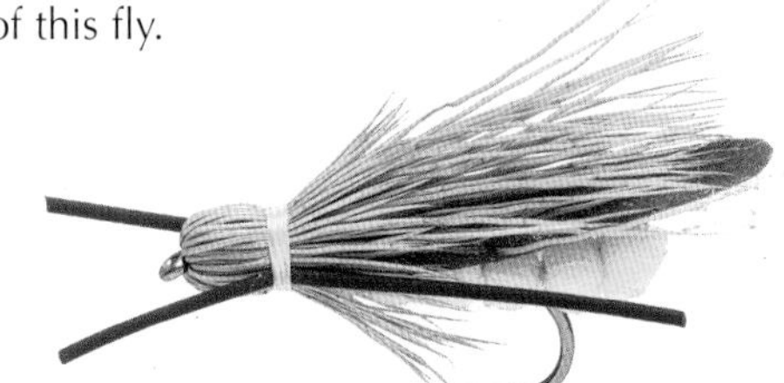

Ultra Shrimp

ANOTHER INCREDIBLE PATTERN from Bob Popovics, the master of epoxy resin fly dressing. Shrimps are an important food item in the sea and imitations will catch just about any fish that swims. This pattern is so realistic that fish will accept it without so much as a second glance. The strike must be immediate as the fish will often reject it on feeling the hardness of the artificial. Occasionally it is used for fresh-run salmon and sea trout in rivers, and for sea trout in Swedish and Norwegian fjords.

WHERE: WORLDWIDE IN SALTWATER AND SOME RIVERS

WHEN: ALL YEAR

WHAT: MOST SPECIES

HOW: ACCURATELY REPRESENTS A SHRIMP

HOOK: 1/0 TO 4 SALTWATER O'SHAUGHNESSY
TAIL: TAN ULTRA HAIR AND COPPER CRYSTALFLASH WITH BURNT MONO EYES (BLACK)
BODY SAME MATERIALS AS TAIL WITH EPOXY BUILT OVER AND A RIB OF TAN THREAD AND A PALMERED TAN HACKLE AND TAN ULTRA HAIR OVER HOOK EYE

Grasshopper

THERE ARE LOSTS OF INGENIOUS GRASSHOPPER PATTERNS but Dave Whitlock's has proved itself time and again. High summer is the time for this pattern, when the naturals frequently land in streams bordered by open grassland and the biggest, smartest fish in the river will be on the lookout for them. The mid west USA, Argentina, New Zealand and Australia all have hopper feeders and the technique is to drop the fly onto the water with a distinct plop. It is also a good pattern for species other than trout and its a wonderfully exiting way to fish.

WHERE: TEMPERATE REGIONS WORLDWIDE

WHEN: HIGH SUMMER

WHAT: TROUT, BASS, CARP

HOW: GRASSHOPPER IMITATION

HOOK: 12 TO 8 2X SHANK
TAIL: RED CALF TAIL
BODY: YELLOW FLOSS WITH CLIPPED PALMERED RED GAME COCK HACKLE
WINGS: DARK TURKEY
LEGS: BUNCHES OF KNOTTED PHEASANT TAIL FIBRES
HEAD: DEER HAIR

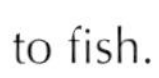

Cuda Fly

BARRACUDA CAN BE TOUGH to catch unless you have the right fly. This is much like the tube patterns used by spin casters, and must be fished incredibly fast to get the barracuda to strike. Hold the rod held under your casting arm, and retrieve hand over hand as quickly as possible. The take is usually so violent that there is little need to strike, just hold on and keep your feet clear of the loose line as it streaks off through the rings.

WHERE: TROPICAL SALTWATER

WHEN: ALL YEAR

WHAT: SPECIFICALLY BARRACUDA

HOW: SUGGESTS BARRACUDA'S FAVOURITE FOOD, THE NEEDLEFISH

HOOK: 3/0 SALTWATER O'SHAUGHNESSY TIED TANDEM WITH WIRE BRAID
TAIL HOOK: GREEN EVERGLOW TUBE FRAYED OUT
BODY: GREEN EVERGLOW TUBE
THROAT: RED MARABOU
HEAD: THREAD WITH PAINTED EYE OR DOLL'S EYE AND EPOXIED ALL OVER

Ginger Quill

THE MANY UPWINGED SPECIES are very important to limestone waters and occur to a lesser degree just about anywhere in freshwater. There is no doubt that trout in particular are very keen to feed on them, and taking a fish on a dry imitation is just about the nicest way to fly fish. The Ginger Quill makes a very good broad-based imitation of smaller ephemerids and can be relied upon to succeed if you are unsure as to which exact insect is hatching or you don't have a wide range of specific patterns. I particularly favour a fly with a strongly marked body and choose my stripped quill carefully.

WHERE: WORLDWIDE IN STILLWATER AND RIVERS IN TEMPERATE REGIONS

WHEN: BEST IN SPRING AND SUMMER

WHAT: TROUT, GRAYLING, CHAR

HOW: AN ALL-PURPOSE IMITATION OF SMALLER EPHEMERID

HOOK: 12 TO 18 STANDARD SHANK FINE WIRE
TAIL: GINGER COCK HACKLE FIBRES
BODY: A STRIPPED PEACOCK EYE QUILL (VARNISH OR SUPERGLUE FOR STRENGTH)
WING: GREY MALLARD WING QUILL SLIPS
HACKLE: GINGER COCK

Floating Snail

ON WATERS WHERE SNAILS are abundant, expect the trout to be big. Eaten at any time of the year, snails are pushed to the top of the menu when they rise to the surface to migrate. So many are eaten that the trout's stomach is almost filled to bursting. In these situations it is a good idea to have the Floating Snail ready.

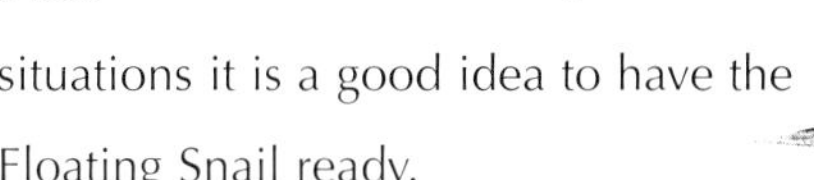

WHERE: WORLDWIDE IN STILLWATER IN TEMPERATE REGIONS

WHEN: SUMMER ONLY

WHAT: TROUT

HOW: SNAIL IMITATION

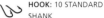

HOOK: 10 STANDARD SHANK
BODY: BLACK DEERHAIR TRIMMED

Woodward Alevin

HAVE YOU EVER WATCHED AQUARIUM FISH eat newly hatched fry of all species, including their own? Just about everything will eat baby fish, that's why fish lay thousands of eggs knowing that a few will make it through to adults while the rest become part of the food chain. I love this pattern and have caught many different species with it. Best for trout and char in spring and summer on spawning streams, you can try it for grayling in autumn in Europe. This is a pattern that should make you think about for its many possible applications.

WHERE: WORLDWIDE IN FRESHWATER WHEREVER FISH SPAWN

WHEN: USUALLY BEST FROM SPRING TO AUTUMN

WHAT: TROUT, CHAR, GRAYLING, WHITEFISH AND MANY OTHER SPECIES OF FISH

HOW: PERFECT BABY FISH IMITATION

HOOK: 8 TO 12 STANDARD SHANK
BODY: FINE PEARL BRAID
WING: TWO OLIVE COCK HACKLES WITH A COUPLE OF FIBRES OF OLIVE CRYSTALHAIR
EGG SACK: PEACHY KING GLO BUG WITH TINY AMOUNT OF RED
HEAD: SMALLEST PEARL BEADS THREADED ON BLACK NYLON AND TIED WITH OLIVE

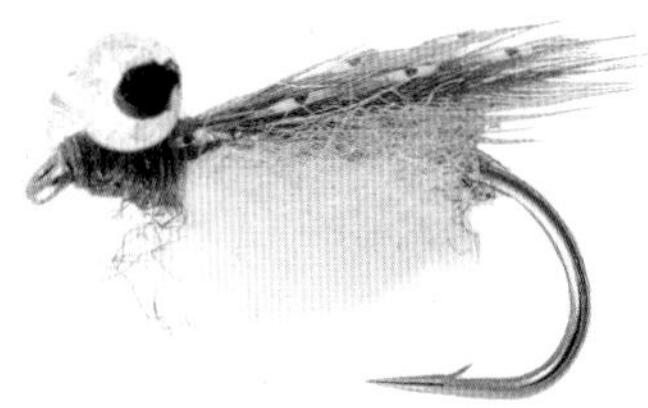

Tups Indispensable

TUPS INDISPENSABLE IS ONE OF THE BEST PATTERNS to replicate the hatch of the Pale Watery and suggests any pale ephemerid. It is also a first-rate pattern for rough streams as a search fly to induce a rise from fish that aren't rising to a specific hatch, but will come up for an opportunistic snack. There was a time when obtaining a good honey dun hackle was very difficult, but genetic hackles have solved that problem. The other requirement to tie this fly, namely wool from a ram's scrotum, can easily be substituted unless you are a stickler for tradition!

WHERE: LIMESTONE STREAMS BUT ALSO ANY RIVERS

WHEN: SPRING TO MID-SUMMER IS BEST

WHAT: TROUT, GRAYLING

HOW: VERY GOOD SUGGESTION OF PALE WATERY

HOOK: 14 TO 20 STANDARD SHANK FINE WIRE
TAIL: HONEY DUN COCK HACKLE FIBRES
BODY: 2/3 PALE YELLOW FLOSS AND 1/3 BLEND OF NATURAL, CRIMSON AND PALE YELLOW SEAL'S FUR TO GIVE A PINKISH TINGE
HACKLE: HONEY DUN COCK

Green Butt Stick

THIS IS ONE OF THOSE SIMPLE LITTLE FLIES that takes trout year after year. It is excellent on the richer, lowland reservoirs where the feeding is good and seems to work in just about any conditions. Many competitions have been won with this simple fly, although inexplicably its position on a three-fly cast can at times but quite critical. Orange, pearl and red tags are options but, as with so many flies, it is the fluorescent green tag that seems to be the most attractive.

WHERE: WORLDWIDE IN STILLWATER IN TEMPERATE REGIONS

WHEN: ALL YEAR

WHAT: TROUT

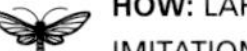

HOW: LARVA AND PUPA IMITATION

HOOK: 10 TO 14 STANDARD SHANK
TAG: FLUORESCENT GREEN FLOSS
BODY: PEACOCK HERL ALL RIBBED WITH FINE OVAL SILVER TINSEL
HACKLE: RED GAME COCK SPARSE AND TIED BACK

Walker's Killer

WHEN I FISHED IN THE DRAKENSBURG REGION in South Africa some years ago, I was overawed by the bewildering variety of bird and insect life I saw there. To a fly fisher the most fascinating thing to see in the rivers was the abundance of freshwater crabs scuttling among the rocks. Walker's Killer is an outstanding crab imitation which has a strong following in other parts of the world as an imitation of those creatures that spend their lives creeping about on the bottom of lakes and rivers.

WHERE: PRIMARILY RIVERS IN SOUTH AFRICA BUT TRY IT ANYWHERE

WHEN: ALL YEAR

WHAT: TROUT, YELLOWFISH, BASS

HOW: A GREAT CRAB IMITATION

HOOK: 4 TO 10 4X SHANK
TAIL: BLACK SQUIRREL TAIL
BODY: RED CHENILLE
WING: STRIPPED PARTRIDGE HACKLE FEATHERS TIED ALONG EACH SIDE IN THREE SETS

Iron Blue

WHERE: PREDOMINANTLY ENGLISH CHALK STREAMS BUT MANY OTHER RIVERS WORLDWIDE HAVE A SIMILAR HATCH

WHEN: LATE SPRING TO AUTUMN

WHAT: TROUT AND GRAYLING

HOW: GOOD COPY OF BAETIS NIGER AND MANY OTHER SMALL DARK FLIES

HOOK: 16 TO 18 STANDARD SHANK LIGHT WIRE
TAIL: IRON BLUE COCK HACKLE FIBRES
BODY: A FEW TURNS OF BRIGHT RED THREAD AND THEN MOLE DUBBING
HACKLE: IRON BLUE COCK HACKLE
WINGS (OPTIONAL): VERY DARK BLUE DYED STARLING

FISH A CHALK STREAM during the latter stage of the mayfly hatch and you may well be fooled by a hatch of iron blues. This tiny fly must be unbelievably tasty as trout will switch to it rather than the much larger and more meaty mayfly. It's a classic case of needing to be observant and watching what the fish are actually feeding on. This fly can also work very well many months after the hatch has ended, and is either so tasty that fish remember it or is just a really good general-purpose pattern. As is so often true in fishing, if you aren't sure what to use then fish small and dark!

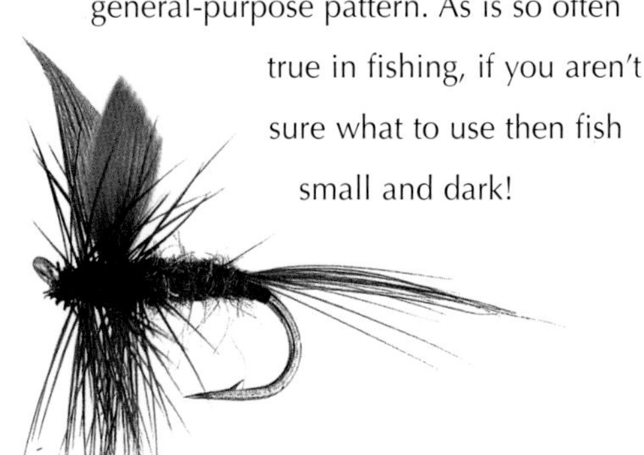

Magic Minnow

I KNOW WHAT YOU ARE THINKING – there just isn't enough dressing on this fly to make it worth a try. However, simplicity is frequently the best option in fly fishing and this super little fish pattern from Jack Gartside is a clear winner when bonefish are chasing fry on the flats. It swims high in the water, has a slim silhouette, a bit of silvery flash and a hint of scales, which combined together is enough to convince most bonefish that it has another snack lined up. Try to cast well ahead of cruisers to strip the fly across and away from them. If a fish follows don't stop the retrieve until you see it take the fly.

WHERE: TROPICAL SALTWATER FLATS

WHEN: ALL YEAR

WHAT: BONEFISH, REDFISH, SEA TROUT

HOW: RESEMBLES A BABY BAITFISH

HOOK: 4 OR 6 STAINLESS O'SHAUGHNESSY
BODY: FLAT SILVER MYLAR IN TWO LAYERS AND SUPERGLUED
WING: A SILVER MALLARD FLANK FEATHER FOLDED AND TIED LOW

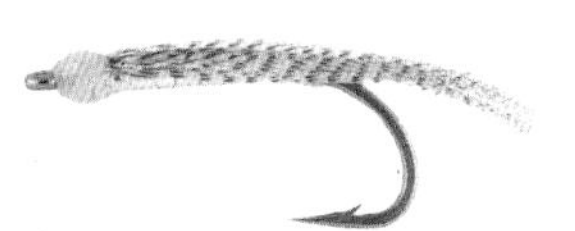

March Brown

THE NATURAL WHICH THIS PATTERN IS TIED TO IMITATE is an unusual fly in that it occurs only in rough streams. Hatches in spring but often for a very limited time and in specific places. This wet fly works just about anywhere, including stillwaters. It is so buggy looking that trout simply love it. I suspect that it might often be taken for a hoglouse, which is an extremely common stillwater crustacean. The March Brown has many variants along the same bland theme. With a silver body, it makes a super fry or corixa imitation.

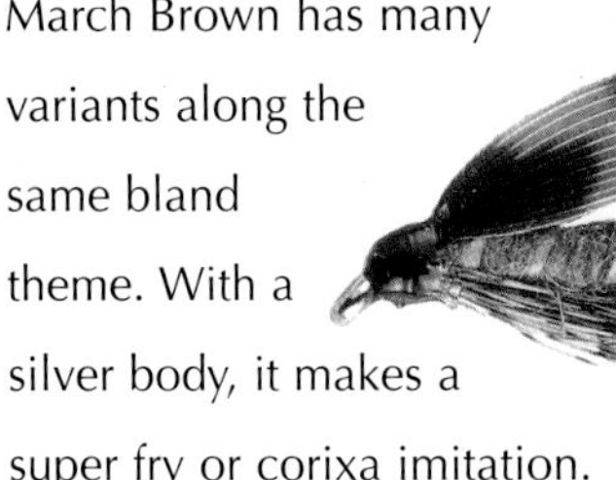

WHERE: WORLDWIDE ON STILLWATERS AND FREESTONE STREAMS IN TEMPERATE REGIONS

WHEN: TRULY BEST IN SPRING BUT GOOD ALL YEAR

WHAT: BROWN TROUT, SEA TROUT, RAINBOWS, SMALLMOUTH BASS

HOW: IMITATES AN EPHEMERID BUT IS ALSO GENERAL PURPOSE

HOOK: 8 TO 14 STANDARD SHANK
TAIL: BROWN PARTRIDGE HACKLE FIBRES
BODY: YELLOW WOOL WITH HARES EAR DUBBED OVER AND A GOLD WIRE RIB
HACKLE: BROWN PARTRIDGE
WING: HEN PHEASANT SECONDARY WING FIBRES

Gum Beetle

AN EXTREMELY IMPORTANT BUG FOR TASMANIA and eastern Australia where the many gum trees are host to a wide variety of beetles. These beetles drift onto the lakes in enormous numbers and the trout become totally preoccupied with them, so woe betide you if you don't have a suitable imitation. You can use this pattern just about anywhere as a summer search pattern and it works on rivers, too. Trout are great opportunists and will rarely turn down the chance of a good snack, and when beetles occur in large numbers trout most definitely know what they are.

WHERE: SPECIFICALLY TASMANIA AND AUSTRALIA BUT ALSO WORLDWIDE

WHEN: SUMMER

WHAT: TROUT

HOW: IMITATION OF A GUM BEETLE

HOOK: 10 TO 12 STANDARD SHANK
BACK: EITHER RED OR YELLOW ETHAFOAM
BODY: AMBER SEAL'S FUR OR ANTRON
HACKLE: RED GAME OR FURNACE HEN

Montana Nymph

AN OLD FAVOURITE TO IMITATE THE LARGE STONEFLY NYMPH of streams in the western USA, it is equally effective where this species does not occur and is also a big hit on stocked

stillwaters. This is a good example of how a pattern tied to imitate a specific insect becomes an excellent general-purpose pattern and then in turn spawns innumerable variants. Flies with long marabou tails, Fritz, Crystalflash and gold beads are also sometimes called Montana nymphs, but this is the original and has stood the test of time.

WHERE: ORIGINALLY FOR WESTERN USA STREAMS BUT WORKS WORLDWIDE IN RIVERS AND STILLWATER

WHEN: ALL YEAR BUT OF COURSE ESPECIALLY GOOD DURING STONEFLY HATCH

WHAT: TROUT, GRAYLING, SMALLMOUTH BASS AND MANY FRESHWATER SPECIES

HOW: AN EXACT IMITATION NOW EFFECTIVE AS A GENERAL-PURPOSE NYMPH/ATTRACTOR

HOOK: 6 TO 12 2X NYMPH SHANK
TAIL: THREE BLACK COCK HACKLE TIPS
BODY: BLACK CHENILLE
THORAX: YELLOW CHENILLE WITH BLACK COCK HACKLE PALMERED THROUGH AND BLACK CHENILLE OVER TOP.

Octopus

A TREMENDOUS FLY on the great Irish loughs at Mayfly time when, if conditions are right, the water is covered in hatching fly and there is always the chance of raising one of the really big browns. I was given this fly by Tony, Pawson, who once won the World Fly Fishing Championship for England and is still a very active angler at well past 80. Most classic Irish patterns rely on the use of seal's fur in the dressing to achieve a straggly effect and there's no doubt that it creates a wonderful illusion of life. Try this fly on waters where wild trout live in the spring on warm days with a strong breeze.

WHERE: LARGE STILLWATERS IN TEMPERATE REGIONS

WHEN: SPRING TO SUMMER

WHAT: TROUT AND OCCASIONAL GRILSE

HOW: EXCELLENT ON LARGE STILLWATERS WHEN THE BIGGER MAYFLY HATCH

HOOK: 10 TO 8 2X SHANK
BODY: GOLDEN OLIVE SEAL'S FUR
TAIL: YELLOW GLO-BRITE FLOSS
HACKLE: PALMERED GOLDEN PHEASANT YELLOW BODY AND THEN SOFT RED GAME LONG IN FIBRE

Transparant Red

ANTS ARE A HIGHLY COMPLEX COMMUNITY CREATURE which survive everywhere and at times will make sudden mass migrations. When this happens they will often have huge casualties at river crossings and the fish take advantage of these incidents. I first saw this when I fished the Murrumbidgee in Australia. While I did quite well with a hatched emerger pattern, I wish I had been sensible enough to have a few of this super pattern in my box. Just don't get bitten by the real thing!

WHERE: WORLDWIDE RIVERS AND STILLWATERS APART FROM ARCTIC REGIONS

WHEN: USUALLY LATE SUMMER

WHAT: TROUT, GRAYLING, CUTTHROAT, SMALLMOUTH BASS, BLUEGILL

HOW: COPIES A RED ANT VARY THE COLOUR FOR SPECIES IF BROWN OR BLACK

HOOK: 12 TO 16 STANDARD SHANK
BODY: RED TYING THREAD WITH EPOXY OVER
HACKLE: RED COCK

Waller Waker

LANI WALLER'S NAME IS synonymous with steelhead in British Columbia, and he is undoubtedly a master with the skated dry fly. This special fly was clearly created for maximum surface effect. It's actually quite an art to master the intricacies of working the 5-metre (15-foot) rods still popular with steelheaders who love the control these long double-handers give in. It's strange how migratory fish will come to skaters in some countries and in just some river systems, but not in others.

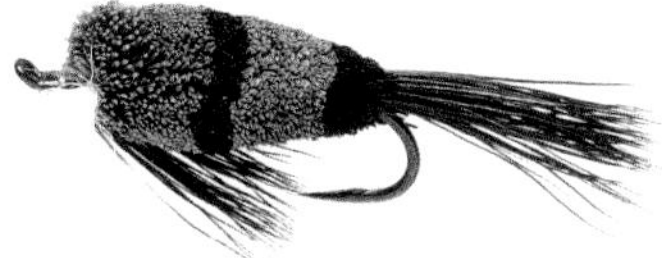

WHERE: PACIFIC NORTHWEST, ALASKA, THE GREAT LAKES AND SOUTH AMERICA

WHEN: ALL YEAR BUT BEST WHEN WATER IS OVER 4°C (40°F)

WHAT: STEELHEAD AND ATLANTIC SALMON

HOW: THE SURFACE DISTURBANCE ATTRACTS AN ATTACK FROM THE FISH

HOOK: 1 TO 6 LOW WATER SALMON IRON
TAIL: DARK MOOSE BODY
BODY: RUST BROWN AND BLACK DEERHAIR SPUN AND CLIPPED
WINGS: WHITE ELK OR CALF TAIL
THROAT: DARK MOOSE BODY

Rubber Band Worm

THIS IS AN UPDATED VERSION OF A FLY USED BY BILL SIBBONS at Damerham in the UK in the early 1970s after watching bloodworm in clear water lakes leaving the bottom and swimming many metres (feet) from their home among the silt and detritus. Bloodworm, the larval stage of chironomids, occur too in slower, silty sections of rivers and all fish know how good they are to eat. Expect a take as the fly sinks immediately after casting. Failing that, use a very slow retrieve to keep this pattern well down in the water. It usually is most effective in 3 metres (10 feet) of water.

WHERE: WORLDWIDE IN LAKES AND SLOW-FLOWING SECTIONS OF RIVER

WHEN: ALL YEAR

WHAT: TROUT, GRAYLING, CARP, SMALLMOUTH AND LARGEMOUTH BASS, BLUEGILL

HOW: SUGGESTS LARVAL STAGE OF CHIRONOMID

HOOK: 8 TO 12 CURVED SHANK

BODY: A RED RUBBER BAND WOUND OVER FLUORESCENT RED TYING THREAD AND CUT SO A SECTION PROJECTS AT EACH END

Slider

THIS FLY WOULD NOT BE OUT OF PLACE in many river situations but Tim Borski invented it as a flats pattern for bonefish where it passes as a shrimp, crab or more likely as a goby. Certainly it will catch while left static and that makes me think a bonefish sees it as a goby out sunning itself. However, it is also useful to add turbulence as an attractor from the deerhair head which also cushions impact when landing on the water. Bones which are skittish and sometimes picky fish should always be tried with alternative patterns like this.

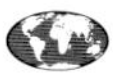

WHERE: TROPICAL SALTWATER FLATS
WHEN: YEAR ROUND
WHAT: BONEFISH, PERMIT

WHEN: ALL YEAR

WHAT: BONEFISH

HOW: A GENERAL PURPOSE PATTERN

DRESSING: HOOK SIZE 2 STAINLESS O' SHAUGHNESSY
TAIL: TAN POLAR FUR MARKED WITH PANTONE TO GIVE BARRED EFFECT PLUS A FEW FIBRES ORANGE CRYSTALFLASH
HACKLE: SOFT GRIZZLE HACKLE TRIMMED UNDERSIDE
HEAD: DEERHAIR WITH LEAD DUMBBELL EYES

Green Tail Damsel

FIRST USED TO MY KNOWLEDGE IN THE 70S as a variant of the Demoiselle (see page 221) in lakes coloured by clay run off. Fluo green is a real 'hot' colour for trout and when later tried in clear water it worked just as well. The tail is out of proportion to the body but that seems to make it all the better. Figure eight retrieve on an intermediate line using search tactics near weedbeds in the warmer months is a great way to 'bag up' on stocked stillwaters.

WHERE: LAKES WORLDWIDE IN TEMPERATE AREAS

WHEN: USUALLY THE WARMER MONTHS BUT IT'S A YEAR ROUND FLY

WHAT: TROUT, BASS, BLUEGILLS

HOW: TURNS A DAMSEL PATTERN INTO A LURE

HOOK: SIZE 12 TO 8 2X SHANK
TAIL: FLUO GREEN WOOL
BODY: TWO PARTS OF AMBER AND DARK OLIVE SEAL'S FUR RIBBED OVAL GOLD TINSEL
HACKLE: PARTRIDGE DYED OLIVE

Green Peter

THIS IRISH FLY COPIES A SPECIES OF LARGE CADDIS (SEDGE) which hatches at last light on large limestone lakes. It is very important to mirror the size and shape at the natural flies at this time of day – colour is less important – and many successful anglers are adamant that the wing of this fly should lie close to the body to present a solid outline. This is a big, active fly and skating the artificial fly is a very good way to entice a take when there's a little breeze. If it goes flat calm, which it often does as darkness comes, try giving your fly an occasional twitch.

WHERE: LARGE LIMESTONE LAKES THROUGHOUT EUROPE

WHEN: MID-SUMMER

WHAT: TROUT

HOW: SUGGESTS A SPECIFIC LARGE CADDIS FLY (SEDGE)

HOOK: 6 TO 8 2X SHANK
BODY: GREEN OLIVE OR DARK OLIVE SEAL'S FUR RIBBED WITH GINGER COCK HACKLE AND FINE OVAL GOLD TINSEL
WING: OAK TURKEY OR SIMILAR DARK SPECKLED FEATHER. CLIP THE BODY HACKLE TO LET THE WING SIT LOW
HACKLE: GINGER OR RED GAME COCK

Sand Shrimp

AN ALL-PURPOSE SHRIMP PATTERN which is intended for snag-free, sandy bottoms where it can be twitched along to kick up little puffs of sediment and pull fish in for a look. It's good for most saltwater and brackish situations and although it might be thought of as essentially a flats' fly for tropical waters. It is very good for many flatfish species in colder waters where it can be used as a search fly in slightly coloured water. I know of European saltwater fly rodders who do well with this one for plaice and flounders as well as estuary sea trout and bass.

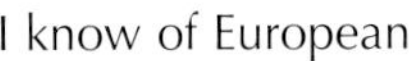

WHERE: WORLDWIDE IN SALTWATER

WHEN: ALL YEAR

WHAT: ALL SPECIES IN SHALLOW WATER AREAS

HOW: LOOKS LIKE A (WEIGHTED) SHRIMP

HOOK: 8 TO 4 STAINLESS O'SHAUGHNESSY
TAIL: TWO GRIZZLE COCK HACKLE POINTS WITH STRANDS OF PEARL CRYSTALFLASH
BODY: TAN RABBIT DUBBING AROUND PAINTED YELLOW/BLACK LEAD EYES THEN TAN RABBIT AGAIN WITH PEARL LITE BRITE AND A PALMERED GRIZZLE COCK HACKLE

Flash Fly

IF YOU EVER INTEND TO FISH FOR SALMON in British Columbia or Alaska then make sure you have a few of these flies in the box. Pacific salmon (apart from sockeye) are usually very aggressive when they enter freshwater and will hit glitzy flies really hard. They don't come much brighter than the Flash Fly and it really does get the fish going. It is so exciting to watch a freshly arrived pod of coho when this fly swims through the pool. It is as though every fish wants to destroy the fly – so don't fish with light tippets.

WHERE: BRITISH COLUMBIA, ALASKA, KAMCHATKA AND THE GREAT LAKES

WHEN: FROM JUNE TO OCTOBER DEPENDING ON THE RUN

WHAT: CHINOOK, COHO, CHUM, HUMPBACK SALMON, STEELHEAD

HOW: AN OUT-AND-OUT ATTRACTOR

HOOK: 1/0 TO 4 SALMON IRON
TAIL: SILVER FLASHABOU
BODY: SILVER BODYWRAP
WING: SILVER FLASHABOU OVER BLUE GOAT
HACKLE: HOT ORANGE COCK SADDLE

White Moth

THIS CAN BE AN ALL-PURPOSE DRY FLY for waters where you need to do a bit of prospecting and I also like it for dull, overcast days. Its principal use is in the evening when whitish moths will often flutter onto the water if it is calm (there is a small white moth which comes off oak trees in the UK), especially if it is dank and chilly and when other flies have ceased to hatch. At times this pattern has caught some quite good fish for me, but nothing will beat the riser I finally hooked against a weed bed which turned out to be a 60 cm (2 foot) eel!

WHERE: WORLDWIDE IN STILLWATER IN TEMPERATE REGIONS

WHEN: EVENINGS DURING THE WARMER MONTHS

WHAT: TROUT, BASS, BLUEGILL

HOW: IT LOOKS LIKE A WHITE MOTH

HOOK: 10 TO 16 STANDARD SHANK
BODY: WHITE POLYPROPYLENE
HACKLE: WHITE COCK PALMERED THROUGH BODY THEN BUILT UP AT HEAD
WINGS: WHITE GOOSE OR DUCK FIBRES

Net Crab

A 21ST-CENTURY CRAB PATTERN which is mercifully easy to cast, looks absolutely deadly and really does work. It has to be one of the ultimate permit flies, but in colour variations will work for many saltwater species in a great many locations (it's not just the warm-water species that take flies). European bass are great crab eaters and in estuaries or harbours this pattern will do very well. Brackish species such as barramundi will eat this crab too, and it will help to open out many more saltwater fly fishing destinations including less-exotic home waters.

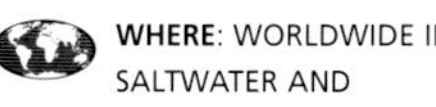

WHERE: WORLDWIDE IN SALTWATER AND BRACKISH WATER

WHEN: ALL YEAR

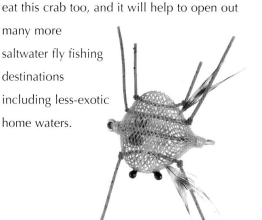

WHAT: PRIMARILY PERMIT AND BONEFISH, BUT ALSO NUMEROUS SALTWATER SPECIES

HOW: CRAB IMITATION

HOOK: 2 STAINLESS O'SHAUGHNESSY
BODY: PLASTIC MESH TUBE FORCED TO SHAPE BY TYING TO BEND
EYES: BLACK-TIPPED MONO SUPERGLUED IN WITH LEAD DUMBBELLS
LEGS: GLITTER ROUND RUBBER KNOTTED AND SUPERGLUED IN
CLAWS: GRIZZLE COCK SUPERGLUED TO SHAPE AND POSITION

Serendipity

SEGMENTATION AND THE STRAGGLE OF DEER HAIR make this an altogether odd pattern which serves well as a chironomid pupa on stillwater and slower rivers for most people, but not for me. It's an odd thing in fishing, but if you don't have faith in a fly or lure then you somehow transmit that down through the rod and will fail. The frustrating thing is that I like the look of this fly and have seen it do very well, even though why it works with a gold bead head is a bit of a conundrum. There are lots of colour options but use orange if you aren't sure which to choose.

WHERE: STILLWATER AND SLOW-FLOWING RIVERS IN TEMPERATE REGIONS

WHEN: WARMER MONTHS ARE BEST

WHAT: TROUT, GRAYLING, SMALLMOUTH BASS, BLUEGILL

HOW: AN ALL-PURPOSE NYMPH AND A GOOD CHIRONOMID PUPA

HOOK: 12 TO 20 CURVED STANDARD SHANK
BODY: Z-LON TWISTED LIKE A ROPE
HEAD: DEER HAIR

Pond Olive Nymph

AS I WRITE IT IS EARLY APRIL IN SOUTHERN ENGLAND and this beautiful little stillwater ephemerid is hatching on the lakes close to my shop. If I can only persuade customers to buy this nymph instead of some gaudy lure they will be taking their first steps to becoming a genuine fly fisher. You can safely use this wonderful fly on any stillwater when the situation calls for a small olive pattern or a general-purpose nymph.

WHERE: STILLWATER IN TEMPERATE REGIONS

WHEN: SPRING TO EARLY SUMMER

WHAT: TROUT

HOW: CLOSE COPY OF THE POND OLIVE NYMPH

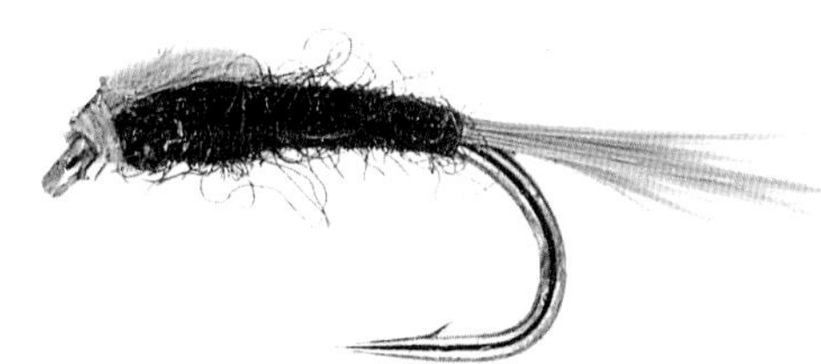

HOOK: 14 WET FLY
TAIL: OLIVE COCK HACKLE FIBRES
BODY: DARK OLIVE SEAL'S FUR WITH FINE GOLD WIRE RIB
WING CASE: PALE OLIVE GOOSE FIBRES

Sherry Spinner

THIS FLY IMITATES THE EGG-LAYING STAGE of the blue winged olive. It's one of those peculiar little flies that many anglers never try because they think it's just too old-fashioned. But, if you are on a limestone river at dusk and being beaten by freely rising fish, you had best become a traditionalist and tie on a Sherry Spinner. It uses that favourite dry fly hackle, the honey dun, but I have a suspicion that it is the careful blend of seal's fur that gives this fly the edge.

WHERE: LIMESTONE RIVERS IN TEMPERATE ZONES, USUALLY IN THE NORTHERN HEMISPHERE

WHEN: LATE SPRING AND SUMMER

WHAT: TROUT, GRAYLING

HOW: SPECIFIC IMITATION OF EGG-LAYING STAGE OF BLUE WINGED OLIVE MAYFLY

HOOK: 14 TO 16 STANDARD SHANK FINE WIRE
TAIL: HONEY DUN COCK HACKLE FIBRES
BODY: SHERRY COLOUR SEAL'S FUR WITH FINE GOLD WIRE RIB
WING: TWO BLUE DUN HACKLE POINTS TIED SPENT
HACKLE: HONEY DUN COCK

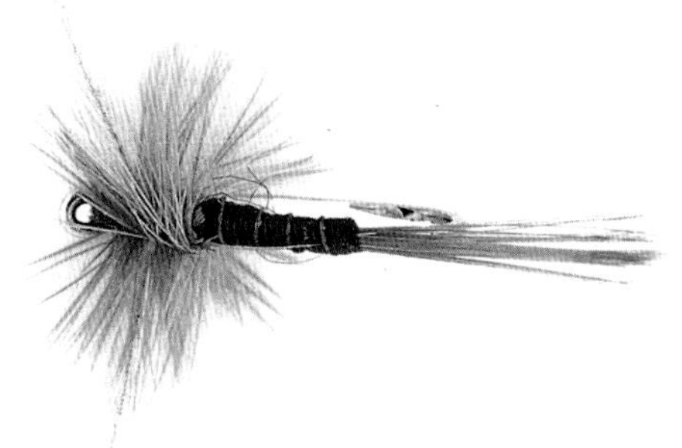

Egg-Sucking Leech

THE EGG-SUCKING LEECH REALLY does work for just about any predatory fish where salmonids are expected to spawn, and will tempt anything from a grayling to the mighty king salmon. It is best fished close to the bottom with fast-sinking lines in rivers, but it also works well when retrieved in virtual slacks, which can be a very exciting way to fish king and silver salmon and chum. This is really a fly for Pacific seaboard fishes, but it can also be adapted as a trout lure. It also works in miniature versions in New Zealand's streams during the spawning runs. Black and purple are the main colour options but a white version is popularly known as the 'lawyer fly'!

WHERE: THE RIVERS OF THE PACIFIC NORTHWEST THROUGH TO ALASKA, BUT TRY IT ELSEWHERE TOO

WHEN: JUNE TO LATE AUTUMN WHEN EGGS ARE LIKELY TO BE PRESENT

WHAT: ALMOST ANY SALMONID SPECIES

HOW: HAS THE BULK, COLOUR AND MOVEMENT OF AN EGG

HOOK: 1/0 TO 6 LONG SHANK STANDARD SALMON
TAIL: GENEROUS AND LONG TUFT OF BLACK MARABOU
BODY: BLACK CHENILLE WITH OVAL SILVER TINSEL RIB
HACKLE: PALMERED BLACK COCK
HEAD: FLUORESCENT ORANGE OR PINK CHENILLE

Pink Shrimp

ALTHOUGH I BELIEVE THAT FISH SEE COLOUR, what they think of when they see a pink shrimp in freshwater I cannot imagine. However, note how the Killer Bug (see page 219) uses a wool that looks pinkish when wet and is a marvellous shrimp imitation. Perhaps there is a reaction is provoked by the colour pink as it appears edible. Pink has been the 'in' colour for European grayling anglers for the past few years. Try this shrimp either in slightly coloured water or on very bright days.

WHERE: WORLDWIDE IN STILLWATER AND RIVERS IN TEMPERATE REGIONS

WHEN: ALL YEAR

WHAT: TROUT, GRAYLING, SMALLMOUTH BASS, BLUEGILL

HOW: SHAPED LIKE A GAMMARUS (SHRIMP)

HOOK: 12 TO 18 BENT SHANK
TAIL: FLUORESCENT PINK HACKLE FIBRES
BODY: FLUORESCENT PINK ANTRON WITH A BACK OF PEARL FLASHABOU COVERED WITH CLEAR PLASTIC AND RIBBED WITH CLEAR MONO
ANTENNAE: FLUORESCENT PINK HACKLE FIBRES

Black and Orange Firefly

YOU CAN MAKE ANY PATTERN OF FLY into a Firefly by adding a tiny plastic tube containing an isotope. These permanent lights come in a range of colours such as green, orange or blue, and have a very long lifespan. There is no doubt that we can perceive the tiny pinprick of light under dark conditions and my own belief is that this can be an added benefit to a fly by attracting a fish to strike. Migratory fish will often pick out the fly armed with an isotope when others on the same case are ignored.

WHERE: WORLDWIDE IN FRESH- AND SALTWATER

WHEN: BEST AT TIMES OF POOR LIGHT

WHAT: PROBABLY ANY SPECIES BUT KNOWN TO WORK ON MIGRATORY SALMONIDS

HOW: IMITATES A FIREFLY

HOOK: 8 DOUBLE SALMON
TAIL: MINIATURE ISOTOPE
BODY: BLACK FLOSS WITH OVAL GOLD RIB
WING: ORANGE AND BLACK SQUIRREL TAIL
HACKLE: HOT ORANGE COCK SADDLE FIBRES

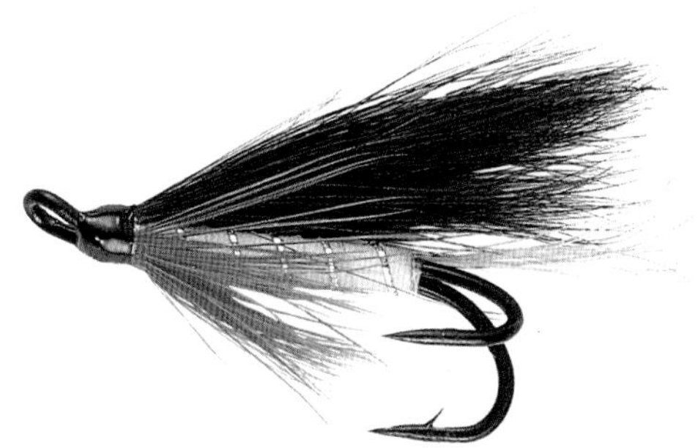

Slow Water Caddis

THERE IS A GROUP OF CADDIS (SEDGE) called needle flies because of their very slim wing profile. Typically they live in – and emerge from – the quieter parts of rivers. The adults have a curiously exaggerated skittering motion on the water surface after hatching which can make trout, grayling and smallmouth bass go mad as they try to catch them. Experiment with your fishing by trying the areas of rivers not necessarily deemed to be the best, and this will often mean fishing the hatch of the needle flies.

WHERE: WORLDWIDE IN RIVERS IN TEMPERATE REGIONS

WHEN: LATE SPRING TO AUTUMN

WHAT: TROUT, GRAYLING, SMALLMOUTH BASS

HOW: COPY OF THE ADULT NEEDLE FLY (CADDIS)

HOOK: 14 TO 18 2X SHANK
BODY: GREY RABBIT DUBBING
HACKLE: BLUE DUN COCK
WING: GREY HEN SADDLE FEATHER TIED VERY LOW AND SLIM

The Red Hook

I HAD HEARD OF THE DATSUN, a size 10 2X hook painted with red Datsun car-body paint, when a friend quietly told me that he had an improved version and that I should try it. I did, but with little success until I was shown how to fish it. Takes are usually as the fly falls through the water or with the slowest of slow retrieves. You just need the confidence to fish this fly and they take it so well that converting takes to the hooked fish is easy. What puzzles me is that the hook is invariably found in the upper jaw.

WHERE: STILLWATER IN TEMPERATE REGIONS

WHEN: ALL YEAR

WHAT: TROUT

HOW: NYMPH ATTRACTOR

HOOK: 10 TO 6 2X SHANK
BODY: RED FLOSS RIBBED WITH FLAT PEARL TINSEL AND THEN LAYERS OF SUPERGLUE

Epoxy Pearl Squid

THE MANY SPECIES OF SQUID and one of the most important items in the oceanic food chain, and when they come up from the deep to spawn, squid will trigger feeding frenzies like you have never seen. Fished off reefs, rock ledges or from boats, a squid pattern can take most fish species, and this pattern is much less bulky than those used out in blue water for oceanic species. Use the specialist heavy sinking tip fly lines and you can get this fly out a reasonable distance and work it back deep. As the light fails, fish it higher in the water and even up on the surface around dock lights at night.

WHERE: WORLDWIDE SALTWATER LOCATIONS

WHEN: YEAR ROUND BUT PEAK ACTIVITY CAN BE VERY SEASONAL

WHAT: MOST PREDATORY SPECIES

HOW: SPECIFIC SQUID IMITATION

HOOK: SIZE 1/0 TO 4/0 SALTWATER O'SHAUGHNESSY
TAIL: WHITE SCHLAPPEN FEATHERS MIXED WITH PEARL CRYSTAL FLASH AND MAGIC MARKER PEN SPOTS
BODY: EITHER EPOXY OR SOFT BODY WITH PEARL FLAKES MIXED IN AND COLOUR SPOTS PLUS AN EYE EFFECT

Superglue Buzzer

THIS ONE SIMPLE FLY transformed the scene of fishing stillwater with chironomid imitations and is an outstanding killer of both brown and river trout. I sometimes teach on stillwaters where I confiscate all the regular flies and give the group a few of this fly. By sticking with it and fishing it at two speeds – dead slow and stop, anglers who always use gold beads, Fritz and marabou lines suddenly become adept at fishing more imitative flies.

WHERE: WORLDWIDE IN STILLWATER AND SLOW-FLOWING PARTS OF RIVERS

WHEN: ALL YEAR, BUT BEST FROM SPRING ONWARDS

WHAT: TROUT

HOW: COPIES PUPAL STAGE OF CHIRONOMID

HOOK: 10 TO 14 CURVED SHANK
BODY: BLACK FLOSS WITH FINE SILVER WIRE RIB
THORAX: BLACK FLOSS WITH ORANGE PAINTED SIDES SUPERGLUED ALL OVER TO GIVE A SHINY, HARD EFFECT

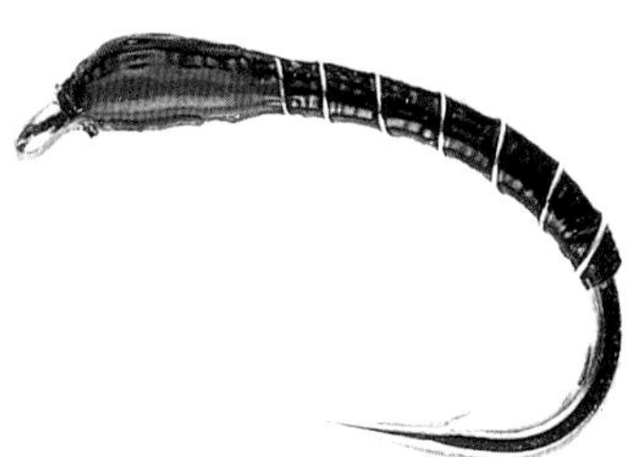

Silver Banger

CAST THIS POPPING LURE where you suspect there are trevally, and strip it fast across the surface so that it spits, bubbles and gurgles its way through the water, and hold on tightly for one almighty heave as you hook-up. This is as close as you will get to proper fly fishing for sailfish when a number have been teased up to the boat, or you can cast to surface cruisers in flat calms. You need a good casting arm to work this fly for long, but it is guaranteed excitement when you can get fish to attack, and the spluttering surface action seems to drive them wild.

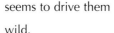

WHERE: TROPICAL AND SUBTROPICAL SALTWATER

WHEN: ALL YEAR

WHAT: TREVALLY, STRIPED BASS, SAILFISH, BLUEFISH

HOW: GENERAL WAKE ATTRACTOR

HOOK: 4/0 STAINLESS O'SHAUGHNESSY
TAIL: WHITE BUCKTAIL
BODY: PEARL FRITZ
HEAD: ETHAFOAM CYLINDER WITH SILVER SPARKLE LAYER AND LARGE BLACK AND SILVER EYE

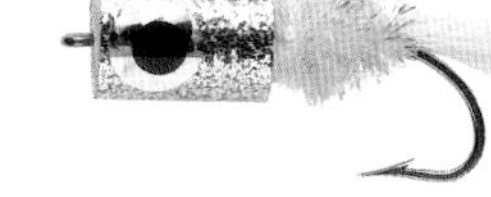

Blue Winged Olive

WHEN YOU READ CLASSIC ANGLING LITERATURE the decline of the blue-winged olive is so frequently emphasized that by rights it should be long gone. In fact, its populations are cyclical. It is a wonderful little mayfly whose hatch guarantees good sport. Perhaps it's because we want it to hatch every day that we think it is always in decline. This tying is a subtle delight for the fly tier and will work on all limestone streams where this fly occurs. Marvel at the chance to witness this beautiful fly and be grateful that trout love to eat it.

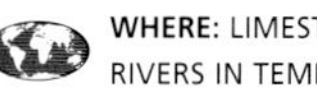

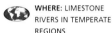

WHERE: LIMESTONE RIVERS IN TEMPERATE REGIONS

WHEN: USUALLY EARLY TO LATE SUMMER

WHAT: TROUT, GRAYLING

HOW: BLUE-WINGED OLIVE IMITATION

HOOK: SIZE 20 TO 14 STANDARD SHANK FINE WIRE
TAIL: DARK DUN HACKLE FIBRES
BODY: MUSKRAT UNDERFUR MIXED WITH DYED OLIVE HARE
HACKLE: DARK DUN COCK HACKLE
WINGS: BLUE DUN HACKLE TIPS TIED UPRIGHT

Dragonfly Larva

LIKE SOMETHING FROM A HORROR FILM this huge larva stalks its prey and grabs them with an underslung, telescopic jaw and proceeds to eat them alive before turning into a creature of exquisite beauty. Drab, squat and slow-moving the dragonfly larva is a very tasty morsel for a fish and they really do relish eating them. Fish the imitation slow and deep among bottom detritus and you will invariably get good solid takes. Fish hiding in weeds will pounce on this fly if dropped into holes in the weed – I think they expect to see the larva fall from the weed as they make their way to the air to hatch.

WHERE: WORLDWIDE IN FRESHWATER

WHEN: ALL YEAR BUT BEST IN SUMMER

WHAT: TROUT, SMALLMOUTH AND LARGEMOUTH BASS, BLUEGILL, PIKE, CARP (IN FACT JUST ABOUT ANY FISH THAT SWIMS)

HOW: IMITATES THE LARVA OF THE DRAGONFLY

HOOK: 6 TO 12 2X SHANK
TAIL: TWO DYED OLIVE GOOSE BIOTS
BODY: BROWN ANTRON OR WOOL RIBBED WITH GREEN THREAD
THORAX: BROWN ANTRON WITH DARK BROWN FEATHER FIBRE WING CASE
HACKLE: BROWN PARTRIDGE
HEAD: PEACOCK HERL INCLUDING RED BEAD EYES ON NYLON

Gosling

YOU MIGHT NOT BELIEVE IT AT FIRST but this pretty fly imitates the largest of the mayfly species. It was created in Ireland for the large limestone loughs and designed to be fished wet or just struggling in the surface. During intense hatches of fly, try to be on Lough Sheelin at peak time, when the number of flies is so immense that an artificial fly needs to stand out and be counted. A mayfly pattern with orange has always been a good choice for such occasions, and the Gosling is as good as you can get, particularly if the seal's fur body is picked out and roughed up.

WHERE: LIMESTONE STILLWATER IN TEMPERATE REGIONS

WHEN: EARLY SUMMER

WHAT: TROUT AND EVEN ATLANTIC SALMON WHEN PASSING THROUGH STILLWATER

HOW: SUGGESTS A HATCHING OR DROWNING LARGE MAYFLY

HOOK: 8 TO 10 2X SHANK
TAIL: COCK PHEASANT CENTRE TAIL FIBRES
BODY: GOLDEN OLIVE SEAL'S FUR RIBBED WITH GOLD WIRE
HACKLE: ORANGE COCK HACKLE WITH LONG FIBRES SPECKLED MALLARD BODY FEATHER

Mosquito

CHOOSE TO FISH ANYWHERE IN THE SUBARCTIC in summer and you will know all about mosquitoes. In the tropics, too, they cause great problems when the wind drops, but fish eat them and we can use an imitation! Most smaller game fish will eat adult mosquitoes and this is the fly to use. I would love to be able to score one back on mosquitoes for the thousands of bites I have suffered, but must settle for using an imitation to do the thing I love best – catching fish on fly gear.

WHERE: THE TROPICS, THE SUBARCTIC AND ANYWHERE NEAR STAGNANT WATER WHERE MOSQUITO BREED

WHEN: EARLY SUMMER IN THE ARCTIC BUT JUST ABOUT ANY TIME IN THE TROPICS

WHAT: ALL TROUT, GRAYLING, PAN FISH

HOW: ALTHOUGH A SPECIFIC IMITATION IT'S ALSO A GOOD GENERAL PATTERN

HOOK: 12 TO18 STANDARD SHANK
TAIL: GRIZZLE COCK HACKLE FIBRES
BODY: ALTERNATE DARK AND LIGHT MOOSE MANE
WING: GRIZZLE HEN HACKLE TIPS
HACKLE: GRIZZLE COCK

Pete's Olive Taddy

ANOTHER DAMSEL NYMPH IMITATION, but this one is based on the Taddy principle which uses the longest possible marabou fibres with a lightly weighted standard shank hook to get the wiggle effect that trout find so irresistible. I have been tying this fly since the mid-1970s and find that stocked trout and grown-on fish take it well in the summer months. It was mostly down to this particular fly that in five consecutive years I came in the top three in the European Open, and first twice in the UK Small Fisheries Championships.

WHERE: STILLWATER IN TEMPERATE REGIONS

WHEN: SPRING TO AUTUMN

WHAT: TROUT

HOW: BASIC DAMSEL COLOUR WITH WIGGLE

HOOK: 8 TO 10 STANDARD SHANK
TAIL: LONG BUNCH OF OLIVE MARABOU
BODY: OLIVE RAYON CHENILLE
HACKLE: OLIVE HEN

Goddard Sedge

LEGENDARY ENGLISH FLY FISHER JOHN GODDARD developed this pattern along with fishing companion Cliff Henry and it quickly became a standard adult sedge (caddis) imitation. Looked at from below, this fly has the wing and body outline of a sedge complete with straggly legs and feelers. Vary the underbody colour and most groups of caddis can be suggested. Tied with clipped deerhair it is virtually unsinkable and thus perfect for skating or slowly retrieving in a breeze. Larger versions are good for steelhead in rivers. Clip the hackle and you have a good dry fly for carp, especially when fished around reed beds or lily pads.

WHERE: WORLDWIDE IN RIVERS AND STILLWATER

WHEN: BEST FROM EARLY SUMMER TO AUTUMN

WHAT: TROUT, GRAYLING, CHAR, LAKE TROUT, BASS, CRAPPIES

HOW: MARVELLOUS IMITATION OF ADULT CADDIS (SEDGE)

HOOK: 6 LOW-WATER SALMON TO 12 2X NYMPH TO 12 STANDARD SHANK
BODY: CLIPPED NATURAL DEERHAIR CUT TO GIVE BODY EXTENSION AND SHAPED TO ROOF PROFILE
UNDERBODY: SEAL'S FUR OR SIMILAR LAID ALONG AS DUBBING ROPE
HACKLE: RED GAME COCK WITH HACKLE STALK USED AS FEELERS

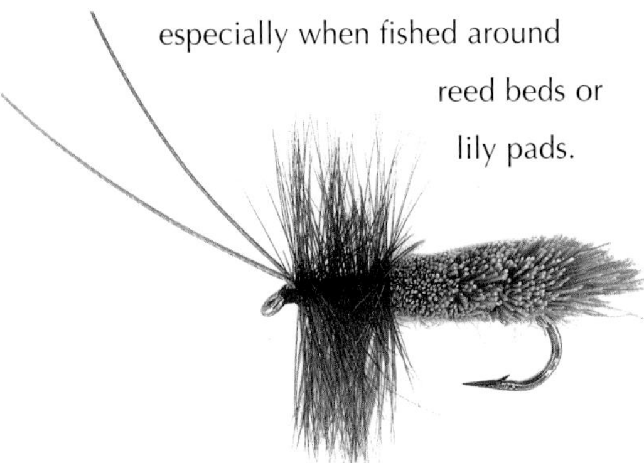

Balloon Caddis

ROMAN MOSER HAS CONTRIBUTED so much to modern fly-fishing and tying that it is impossible to say which was his best idea! Roman worked hard on river caddis patterns before creating this highly buoyant emerger capable of floating on the roughest of streams. It is also easily seen, especially as the light fades. A 'must-have' fly for both river and stillwater fishers.

WHERE: RIVERS AND STILLWATERS IN TEMPERATE REGIONS

WHEN: LATE SPRING THROUGH FALL

WHAT: TROUT, GRAYLING

HOW: CADDIS IMITATION

HOOK: SIZE 10 TO 14 STANDARD SHANK
BODY: OLIVE ANTRON
WING: ELK HAIR
THORAX: YELLOW ETHAFOAM

Pike Bomber Chartreuse

THE BIG, BUOYANT HEAD makes this a killing lure for the warmer months when predators lie up in cover or weed beds to strike out at unsuspecting prey. In the colder months, fish it on a fast-sinking fly line and retrieve it very slowly close to the lake bed where its bulk will kick up all sorts of fuss and arouse a semi-torpid fish into attack mode. However, I guess it's the surface take which is the most exciting for fly fishers, and I love fishing clear water when you can watch a pike coil itself into a spring just prior to its attack.

WHERE: WORLDWIDE IN STILLWATER AND RIVERS

WHEN: ALL YEAR

WHAT: PIKE, WALLEYE, LAKE TROUT, PEACOCK BASS, NILE PERCH, DORADO

HOW: ATTRACTOR LURE

HOOK: 4/0 FINE WIRE PIKE
TAIL: CHARTREUSE BUCKTAIL
BODY: WHITE TYING THREAD
WING: WHITE AND BLACK BUCKTAIL
COLLAR: BLACK COCK SADDLE
HEAD: SHAPED BLACK ETHAFOAM WITH YELLOW-AND-BLACK EYE

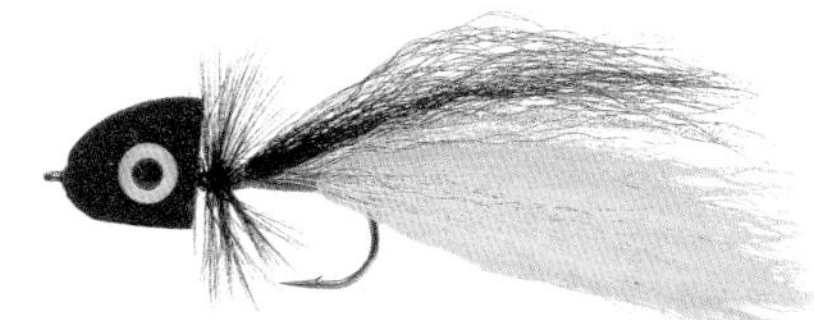

Sedge Pupa

THIS IS AN EXCELLENT REPRESENTATION of an emerging sedge (caddis) and works equally well in waters running or still. Allowed to sink then draw to the surface in a long sweep or twitched along just under the surface, expect trout to take very firmly. Fish too light a leader at your peril. Orange, olive or cream are the most useful options. Look for areas where the natural are hatching. Used as part of a three fly cast for trout in large stillwaters, this pattern is a pupa imitation to rely on.

WHERE: RIVERS OR STILLWATERS IN TEMPERATE AND SUB ARCTIC REGIONS

WHEN: LATE SPRING THROUGH TO FALL

WHAT: TROUT, GRAYLING

HOW: SUGGESTS A HATCHING SEDGE (CADDIS)

HOOK: 14 TO 8 2X SHANK
BODY: BUFF TO CREAM SEAL FUR OR OSTRICH HERL RIBBED WITH FLAT OR SILVER
THORAX: BUFF CONDOR HERL SUBSTITUTE WITH WING CASE OVER
HACKLE: LIGHT FURNACE (GREENWELL) HEN

Whit's Sculpin

WHERE: TEMPERATE AND ARCTIC REGIONS WORLDWIDE, MOSTLY IN RIVERS

WHEN: ALL YEAR

WHAT: TROUT, CHAR, GRAYLING, LAKE TROUT, PIKE, WALLEYE, LARGEMOUTH AND SMALLMOUTH BASS

HOW: PERFECTLY COPIES A SCULPIN (BULLHEAD)

HOOK: 2 TO 8 4X SHANK
BODY: LIGHT OLIVE WOOL OR YARN RIBBED WITH OVAL GOLD TINSEL
GILLS: RED WOOL DUBBING
TAIL AND BACK: TWO DYED OLIVE GRIZZLE HACKLES TIED DOWN MATUKA-STYLE
FINS: DYED OLIVE PARTRIDGE OR MALLARD BREAST
COLLAR AND HEAD: DYED OLIVE DEER HAIR WITH A BAND OF BLACK

THERE IS NO FINER IMITATION OF SCULPIN than this one by master fly dresser, Dave Whitlock. Sculpins are a prime food item for resident fish in rivers, and be prepared to use an imitation if you want to catch a really big fish one day. I often fish this fly in very small streams with a split shot a couple of feet (metres) away to drop it into holes under banks and structures. It is fascinating to watch a trout cruise from cover and stalk the sculpin before the attack, seemingly losing all its in-built caution for a moment. Bass, grayling and pike all eat sculpin, so make sure you have some of these flies.

Spent Mayfly

TIED TO SUGGEST THE DEAD or dying mayfly lying motionless on the surface the Spent Mayfly is particularly used within the UK and Ireland where the hatch of this giant among ephemerids is regarded as a very special event. When the adult dies after mating it lies on the water surface in the spent position, but tying an artificial that sits just right isn't easy. This one, which uses ultra-modern materials, is an absolute godsend for the last moments of light in early summer when the biggest and smartest trout come up to feed. Be very careful with your presentation and if on rivers, be sure to get any drag on the fly on the leader.

WHERE: LIMESTONE RIVERS AND STILLWATER IN TEMPERATE REGIONS

WHEN: LATE SPRING AND EARLY SUMMER

WHAT: TROUT

HOW: IMITATES THE FINAL STAGE IN THE LIFE OF A MAYFLY

HOOK: 10 AND 12 2X SHANK
TAIL: COCK PHEASANT CENTRE TAIL FIBRES
BODY: CREAM OR OFF-WHITE ANTRON YARN WITH TWO BANDS OF DARK BROWN FLOSS
WINGS: TIED SPENT WHITE ANTRON YARN
THORAX: BROWN ANTRON WITH A FEW BROWN PARTRIDGE HACKLE FIBRES UNDER

Mayfly Cripple Callibaetis

THE MORE OBSERVANT YOU CAN BECOME the more you will notice that surface-feeding fish can be ultra-selective as to which stage of the hatch they prefer to feed on. This is much more common in limestone waters where the hatches can be immense and the fish don't need to look far for their next meal. Very often, the period of selective feeding may happen without any apparent cause, and what was previously working is now ignored. That's the time to try crippled patterns which suggest a hatching failure.

WHERE: WORLDWIDE IN RIVERS AND LAKES, BUT MOST COMMONLY IN LIMESTONE RIVERS

WHEN: SPRING TO AUTUMN

WHAT: TROUT, GRAYLING, CUTTHROAT

HOW: SUGGESTS A MAYFLY THAT HAS FAILED TO HATCH

HOOK: 14 TO 18 STANDARD SHANK FINE WIRE
TAIL AND BODY: GREY MARABOU
THORAX: GREY ANTRON
WING: GREY DEER
HACKLE: GRIZZLE COCK

Teeny Nymph

DEVISED BY OREGON'S JIM TEENY, this one fly in its many colours and formats accounts for all of Jim's fish and it is truly an amazing fly. Made entirely from the centre tail feather of a cock pheasant, this nymph can mean a number of things to all fish. Of course, you must believe that it will work and that is Jim's great forte in that he has absolute confidence in his ability to make a fish accept his fly, and he never gives up. Simple as it may be, this fly will work for nearly every fish.

WHERE: WORLDWIDE IN FRESH- OR SALTWATER

WHEN: ALL YEAR

WHAT: ALL SPECIES OF FISH

HOW: IN DIFFERENT COLOURS AND SIZES IT IS TAKEN FOR MANY THINGS

HOOK: 14 TO 8 STANDARD SHANK
BODY: COCK PHEASANT CENTRE TAIL
FALSE HACKLES: TIPS OF CENTRE TAIL FIBRES
VARIANT FLY
HOOK: 3/0 TO 14 SALTWATER TO 2X NYMPH TO STANDARD SHANK
TAIL, BODY, HACKLE AND WING: COCK PHEASANT CENTRE TAIL FIBRES (MAY BE BLEACHED OR DYED) ADD A FEW FIBRES OF CRYSTALFLASH FOR EXTRA EFFECT

Stoat's Tail

AS YOU MIGHT IMAGINE, this old-fashioned salmon and sea trout fly should be made with the tip of a stoat's tail (the UK has a stoat with a black tip on its tail). However, nowadays it is perfectly acceptable to use black squirrel hair as real stoat's hair is become increasingly hard to find. Innovative UK salmon fisher Richard Waddington said that for salmon all you need is a black fly in a range of sizes, and with his enviable record it would be hard to disagree. Certainly this fly is a necessity in any migratory fish fly box wherever in the world they may run.

WHERE: WORLDWIDE IN RIVERS AND STILLWATER WHEREVER SALMONIDS LIVE

WHEN: ALL SEASON

WHAT: ALL SALMON AND TROUT SPECIES ALTHOUGH MOSTLY KNOWN FOR ATLANTIC SALMON, SEA TROUT

HOW: THE PERFECT, SIMPLE BLACK FLY WHICH CAN MEAN ALL THINGS TO FISH

HOOK: 6 TO 12 STANDARD SALMON IRON OR 6 TO 12 DOUBLE
TAIL: GOLDEN PHEASANT CREST
BODY: BLACK FLOSS WITH OVAL SILVER TINSEL RIB
HACKLE: BLACK COCK HACKLE FIBRES
WING: BLACK SQUIRREL (NATURAL OR DYED)

Teal, Blue and Silver

COMPARE THIS FLY TO THE CIVIL WAR FLY (see page 286) and you will see how it evolved from this sea trout classic. A beautiful, traditional wet fly which, when well-tied, looks just like a tiny fish. Very effective for newly-arrived sea trout, sea-run cutthroats, steelhead and grilse, but oddly not so good for char and Pacific salmon. The barred effect of the wing suggests the motted backs of many small bait fish, and blue with silver is a small-fish combination that always attracts. Good for sea trout in the sea off the Swedish and Norwegian coasts, I have also caught pollack and small cod on this little attractor.

WHERE: WORLDWIDE IN RIVERS WHERE MIGRATORY TROUT, SALMON AND CUTTHROAT OCCUR

WHEN: ANY TIME OF THE YEAR WHEN IN SEASON AND USUALLY LOWER IN THE RIVER

WHAT: SEA TROUT (MIGRATORY BROWN TROUT) SEA-RUN CUTTHROAT AND FIRST-YEAR ATLANTIC SALMON

HOW: SUGGESTS ALL MANNER OF SMALL BAIT FISH, PARTICULARLY MACKEREL

HOOK: 12 TO 6 STANDARD TO 2X SHANK OR IN TANDEM FORMAT

TAIL: GOLDEN PHEASANT TIPPETS

BODY: FLAT SILVER TINSEL WITH SILVER WIRE RIB

HACKLE: KINGFISHER BLUE TIED FALSE

WING: TEAL, PINTAIL OR WIDGEON FLANK TIED PAIRED OR ROLLED

Skykomish Sunrise

THIS FABULOUS NAME FOR A STEELHEAD FLY instantly conjures up images of the perfect dawn on a Pacific Northwest river with a run of chrome-bright steelhead flashing in the runs as they feel the warming rays of light. Red flies like this one are often best in late summer and autumn, but just having it on the leader inspires confidence in me. Of course, other species will take this fly but it is primarily a pattern that deserves to be used for steelhead, that most mystical of fish.

WHERE: RIVERS OF THE PACIFIC NORTHWEST, ALASKA, KAMCHATKA, THE GREAT LAKES AND CHILE

WHEN: ALL YEAR DEPENDING ON THE RUN

WHAT: STEELHEAD

HOW: AN ATTRACTOR THAT MAYBE REMINDS FISH OF OCEANIC FOOD

HOOK: 2/0 TO 8 SALMON IRON
TAG: FLAT SILVER TINSEL
TAIL: MIXED RED AND YELLOW HACKLE FIBRES
BODY: RED CHENILLE OR RED DUBBING WITH FINE OVAL SILVER RIB
HACKLE: RED AND YELLOW COCK HACKLE WOUND TOGETHER
WING: WHITE CALF TAIL OR POLAR BEAR

Zug Bug

THIS SIMPLIFIED LITTLE nymph can be relied on to catch fish just about anywhere. Tied huge it can be a dragonfly larva, small it can be a shrimp, and indeed its great attraction is that it can be just about anything to a fish. I like the Zug Bug as a caddis (sedge) larva imitation in rough streams littered with mossy rocks. The little brown trout of acid moorland streams was one of the fish I pitted my wits against with this fly.

WHERE: WORLDWIDE IN STILLWATER OR RIVERS

WHEN: ALL YEAR

WHAT: TROUT, GRAYLING, CHAR, CUTTHROAT, SMALLMOUTH AND LARGEMOUTH BASS, BLUEGILL

HOW: A GENERAL-PURPOSE NYMPH

HOOK: 6 TO 12 STANDARD SHANK
TAIL: PEACOCK SWORD
BODY: PEACOCK HERL RIBBED WITH FLAT SILVER TINSEL
HACKLE: RED GAME HEN
WING: WOODDUCK OR BRONZE MALLARD

Mrs Simpson

UNLESS YOU HAVE EVER FISHED where crayfish (yabbies) or freshwater crabs occur you would assume that this fly was something of an oddball, whereas in fact it is an extremely effective imitation of these freshwater crustaceans. Make no mistake, trout love to eat these creatures and grow very big on them. The only snag is that a lot of the feeding takes place at night, and I'm sure this is one of the reasons why the large brown trout in fly-only lakes are so seldom caught. A pattern not to be ignored wherever trout swim. It is a first choice fly in New Zealand, Australia and Africa.

WHERE: WORLDWIDE IN TEMPERATE REGIONS, MOSTLY IN STILLWATER

WHEN: ALL YEAR BUT BEST AT NIGHT

WHAT: TROUT

HOW: SUGGESTS A CRAB OR CRAYFISH

HOOK: 6 TO 10 2X SHANK
TAIL: BLACK SQUIRREL TAIL FIBRES
BODY: RED OR YELLOW CHENILLE
WINGS: TWO PAIRS OF COCK PHEASANT RUMP FEATHERS TIED FLAT ALONG THE SIDE OF THE HOOK

Swannundaze sedge pupa

THE SWANNUNDAZE SEDGE PUPA was invented in 1970 by Taff Price, the much-travelled UK angler and entomologist. Taff realized that synthetic materials were enhanced by an underbody of DFM fluorescent materials. Used as a point fly during early evening when the sedges (caddis) begin to hatch, this pattern will consistently catch fish. It is particularly good when you fish it with a sink-and-draw motion.

I have also done well with this fly when trickled across the gravelly run in a river or a clean gravel lake bed.

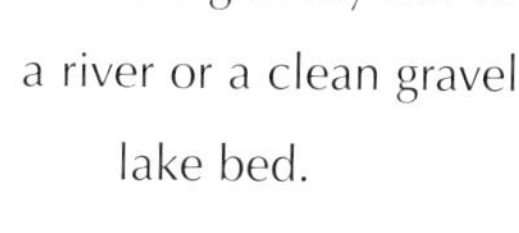

WHERE: WORLDWIDE IN RIVERS AND STILLWATER, BUT PROBABLY BEST IN TEMPERATE REGIONS

WHEN: LATE SPRING TO AUTUMN

WHAT: TROUT, GRAYLING, LAKE TROUT, WHITEFISH

HOW: ADMIRABLY SUGGESTS THE PUPAL STAGE OF SEDGE (CADDIS)

HOOK: 8 TO 10 CURVED SHANK SEDGE HOOK
BODY: FLUORESCENT DFM FLOSS WITH OPEN SPIRALS OF SWANNUNDAZE OVER AND THEN RIBBED WITH PEACOCK HERL
FEELERS: TWO PEACOCK CENTRE TAIL FIBRES
THORAX: SEAL'S FUR WITH PHEASANT CENTRE TAIL FIBRES OVER THE BACK
HACKLE: BROWN PARTRIDGE

Whiskey Fly

RAINBOW TROUT OFTEN HAVE a fatal fascination for orange flies, especially when the water temperature starts to climb above 5°C (40°F). Definitely a stillwater fly by preference, the Whiskey Fly works well when fished slowly among the ever-moving daphnia clouds in large stillwaters. As a chase pattern, it will really gets rainbow trout going when stripped fast. In autumn they will often attack the fly with the sides of their bodies as often as with their mouth.

WHERE: STILLWATER IN TEMPERATE REGIONS

WHEN: ALL YEAR BUT BEST IN WARMER WATER

WHAT: TROUT

HOW: A HIGHLY VISIBLE ATTRACTOR

HOOK: 6 TO 12 2X OR STANDARD SHANK
TAG: FIRE ORANGE TYING THREAD
BODY: FLAT SILVER TINSEL RIBBED WITH TYING THREAD
WING: HOT ORANGE SQUIRREL OR CALF HAIR
HACKLE: HOT-ORANGE COCK HACKLE FIBRES TIED FALSE

The Big Bug

I FIRST USED THESE ULTRA-HEAVY RIVER NYMPHS during the World Championships in 1991 on New Zealand's North Island when I fished the Rangitaiki river. Although they hurt when you make a casting mistake, they do their job and sink like stones in deep, fast water. The actual bed of a river can be a relatively quiet haven for fish even if the upper layers are ripping. At its best in places where lack of space prohibits the use of a fast-sinking line to get the fly down to the fish's feeding level.

WHERE: WORLDWIDE IN RIVERS IN VERY FAST, DEEP, POCKET WATER

WHEN: WHENEVER CIRCUMSTANCES DEMAND

WHAT: TROUT, GRAYLING, STEELHEAD

HOW: IT'S A WAY OF PRESENTING IN DIFFICULT CIRCUMSTANCES

HOOK: 8 TO 10 2X SHANK VERY HEAVILY LEADED
BODY: BROWN WOOL OR ANTRON RIBBED WITH COPPER WIRE
HACKLE: BROWN PARTRIDGE

Yellow Matuka

THIS PARTICULAR TYING STYLE developed in New Zealand prevents the wing from wrapping around the hook and creates a more solid profile. Original Matukas were tied with a special feather, but any good-quality hen hackle is fine and saves a rare bird from further persecution. Matuka-style tyings are used a lot in stillwater and as river lures. Learn to tie one well and it will make a fly that swims on an even keel.

WHERE: WORLDWIDE IN RIVERS AND STILLWATER

WHEN: ALL YEAR

WHAT: TROUT, BUT JUST ABOUT ANY OTHER FRESHWATER SPECIES

HOW: SMALL FISH OR LEECH IMITATION

HOOK: 8 TO 10 4X SHANK
TAIL AND BACK: PAIR OF HEN DARK GREENWELL HACKLES
BODY: YELLOW FLOSS
RIB: OVAL GOLD TINSEL THROUGH THE HACKLE FEATHERS
HACKLE: HEN GREENWELL

Pete's Black Taddy

THE TADPOLE STYLE OF TYING evolved in the 1960s when I was trying to imitate a swimming damsel nymph for a small stillwater and Terry Griffiths was looking for a big water lure with lots of wiggle. We both came to the conclusion that the only way to achieve our aims was to combine maximum marabou length, a short shank hook and a minimal amount of weight. Retrieve it in fast figure of eight twists on short, jabbing pulls.

WHERE: WORLDWIDE IN LAKES AND PONDS

WHEN: ALL SEASON BUT REMEMBER TO HAVE LOTS OF COLOUR VARIATIONS

WHAT: BROWN AND RAINBOW TROUT AND MOST STILLWATER PREDATOR

HOW: RELIES ON THE SINUOUS WIGGLE OF THE MARABOU TO ATTRACT

HOOK: 8 TO 12 STANDARD SHANK, LIGHTLY WEIGHTED
TAIL: LONGEST POSSIBLE BUNCH OF MARABOU FIBRES
BODY: SPECKLED FLUORESCENT GREEN AND BLACK CHENILLE
HACKLE: BLACK HEN

Spot on Shrimp

GAMMARUS SPECIES (COMMONLY KNOWN as scuds or shrimps) carry their eggs under their body. The Spot on Shrimp tying is a common way of imitating this habit but, more importantly, it gives a lift to the fly by making it stand out from the crowd. You can do this with metal or plastic beads and even fluorescent options.

WHERE: RIVERS AND STILLWATERS IN TEMPERATE REGIONS

WHEN: YEAR ROUND

WHAT: TROUT, GRAYLING,SMALLMOUTHS, WHITEFISH, YELLOWFISH

HOW: SUGGESTS GAMMARUS SPECIES

HOOK: 8 TO 14 CURVED SHANK
TAIL: FEW STRANDS OF PARTRIDGE HACKLE
BODY: DUBBED ANTRON WITH LATEX SHELL BACK RIBBED WITH WIRE BEAD IN THE MIDDLE
HACKLE: FIBRES OF PARTRIDGE TIED UNDER AS LEGS

Crustaceans are extremely popular as food for many species and often occur in huge numbers. That's when close copy imitations may not be the best option and this 'spot on' pattern is the one to use.

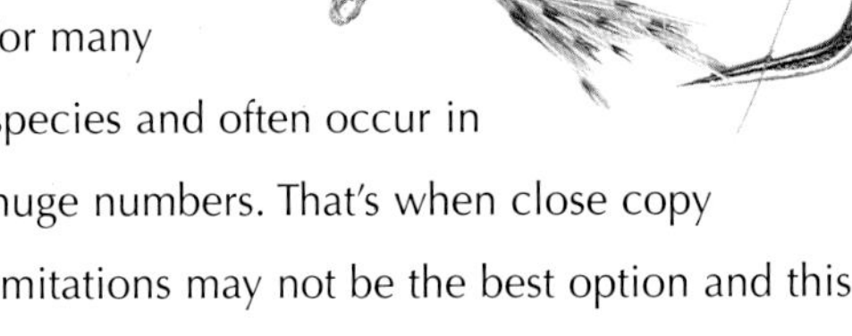

Turd Fly

SOME FLY PATTERNS have almost mystical names, while others carry the name of what they imitate. In this case, I really don't want to know how it originated, but if you fish for bonefish in the Bahamas you will soon be glad that you have a Turd Fly with you. With ever-increasing pressure on bonefish flats, the fish are becoming smarter, but this little beauty will sort them out. It's small, lands lightly, blends in well and does not arouse suspicion. Make a good cast with a finer than normal tippet and you will have a very good chance of having this fly taken.

WHERE: TROPICAL SALTWATER FLATS

WHEN: ALL YEAR

WHAT: BONEFISH

HOW: A SUPERB SMALL SHRIMP IMITATOR

HOOK: 8 STAINLESS O'SHAUGHNESSY
TAIL: BUFF MARABOU AND A FEW STRANDS OF YELLOW CRYSTALFLASH
BODY: BUFF/TAN CHENILLE WITH SMALL SILVER BEAD CHAIN EYES

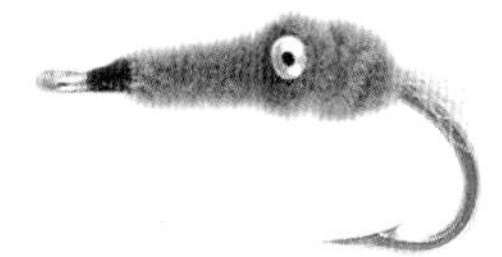

Watson's Fancy

A FANTASTIC WET FLY for wild brown trout, it's a really good-looking pattern, too. This was my first commercial fly tying order – 150 at size 14 – and after that I knew how to tie this fly properly! Use it wherever stillwater or rivers have a peaty satin and try to cover as much ground as possible because you will be fishing for wild fish which, although opportunist feeders, will not take repeated presentations. It's good too for sea trout and in larger sizes has fooled quite a few Atlantic salmon. I like to fish it as the tail fly to a three-fly cast

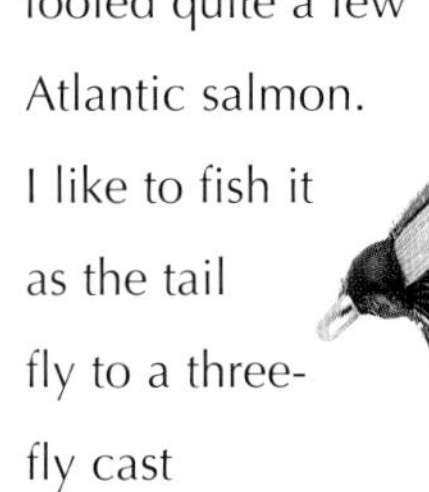

WHERE: WORLDWIDE IN NATURAL LAKES AND ROUGH STREAMS

WHEN: BEST DURING SPRING AND AUTUMN

WHAT: BROWN, SEA AND CUTTHROAT (ESPECIALLY SEA-RUN) TROUT, ATLANTIC SALMON

HOW: A GENERAL-PURPOSE PATTERN WITH THE KEY COLOUR INGREDIENTS

HOOK: 8 TO 14 STANDARD SHANK
TAIL: A GOLDEN PHEASANT TOPPING
BODY: REAR HALF BLACK FLOSS OR WOOL; FRONT HALF RED FLOSS OR WOOL. ALL RIBBED WITH FINE OVAL SILVER TINSEL
WING: BLACK CROW
HACKLE: BLACK HEN TIED AS A BEARD
CHEEKS: SMALL JUNGLE COCK

Sunk Lure

TANDEM HOOK RIGS ARE NOT AS COMMON as they once were due thanks to a growing habit among migratory anglers to return their catch and restrict their tying to single barbless hooks. Where you occasionally take a fish to eat then the tandem enables the use of comparatively small hooks on an overall long pattern which keeps it light, and thus gives it better movement. This is a Hugh Falkus special for night work on sea trout (migratory brown trout) and can be deadly on relatively fresh fish in deep pools.

WHERE: RIVERS IN TEMPERATE REGIONS

WHEN: SPRING THROUGH TO FALL

WHAT: MIGRATORY SALMONIDS PARTICULARLY SEA TROUT

HOW: SUGGESTS A SMALL FISH OR SAND EEL

HOOK: 8 2X SHANK TANDEM RIG
BODY: FLAT SILVER TINSEL WITH SILVER WIRE RIB
WING: FOUR PALE BLUE COCK HACKLES WITH PEACOCK HERL OVER
HACKLE: BLUE COCK TIED BEARD STYLE
HEAD: RED VARNISH

Thorax Pale Morning Dun

THE LITTLE PALE EPHEMERID which hatches in the mornings can spark off a feeding period which is immensely frustrating unless you are armed with the right artificial. The Pale Watery can be an afternoon fly of importance to the chalkstream angler. This clipped hackle style of tying with feather fibre wings makes a fly which is easy to see and which sits right in the surface film. Change the colours but keep the style and you can tie a host of highly effective dry flies.

WHERE: WORLDWIDE IN LIMESTONE RIVERS IN TEMPERATE REGIONS

WHEN: SPRING AND SUMMER

WHAT: TROUT, GRAYLING

HOW: SUGGESTS A SMALL, PALE MAYFLY

HOOK: 14 TO 20 STANDARD SHANK FINE WIRE
TAIL: LIGHT DUN COCK HACKLE FIBRES
BODY: PALE YELLOWISH GREEN ANTRON
WING: LIGHT GREY TURKEY FLAT OR CDC
HACKLE: LIGHT DUN WOUND THROUGH THORAX AND CLIPPED

Snipe and Purple

ORIGINATING IN THE NORTH OF ENGLAND, this is a simple, sparse fly for use in shallow, rough streams where food is scarce and the fish are quick and smart. It must suggest all manner of food items, but with quick water and using the across-and-down style of fishing, you won't give the fish much time to make up their mind whether to take or not. Opportunist feeders are frequently best taken with minimalist patterns and the unusual use of purple makes this a fly to use as a searching pattern where you aren't sure what to try or what species of fish may be present.

WHERE: WORLDWIDE IN FREESTONE STREAMS

WHEN: ALL YEAR BUT SPRING IS USUALLY BEST

WHAT: TROUT, GRAYLING

HOW: GENERAL-PURPOSE WET FLY WHICH LOOKS JUST LIKE A DROWNED INSECT

HOOK: 12 TO 16 STANDARD SHANK
BODY: PURPLE THREAD OR FLOSS TIED THIN
HACKLE: SINGLE TURN OF A FEATHER FROM THE SHOULDER OF A SNIPE

Swimming Frog

MORE INGENUITY GOES INTO MAKING FROGS, either for spin or fly fishers, than any other amphibian food form. Large predators go crazy and lose all those accumulated years of caution for a mad attack when they see one of these.

This fantastic combination tying of coloured deer hair and rubber legs often goes into fishing hats rather than where it should be. You should try it for species you might not otherwise credit with being frog eaters. Usually best in warmer water as in high summer. Try it for perch, trout and even the mighty taimen.

WHERE: TROPIC AND TEMPERATE REGIONS WORLDWIDE

WHEN: SUMMER

WHAT: LARGEMOUTH, SMALL MOUTH BASS, PIKE, PERCH, TROUT, LAKE STRIPERS, TAIMEN

HOW: FROG IMITATION

HOOK: SIZE 2 6X SHANK
TAIL: GRIZZLE HACKLES DYED ORANGE AND GREEN WITH LONGER FIBRES OF FIRST BODY STAGE OR ORANGE DEERHAIR
BODY: SUCCESSIVE SECTIONS OF DYED DEERHAIR WITH RUBBER LEGS AND EYES

Jonah

JOHN JONES OF BUDE IN CORNWALL, UK, taught me to tie flies back in 1958. He has a marvellous sense of proportion for hackled wet flies and is definitely at home when tackling wild brown trout. This is John's best-known creation. I had my first ever grayling with it from the River Tamar, Cornwall. That fish stuck with me and the grayling remains my favourite species. With the Jonah I have caught both trout and grayling worldwide.

WHERE: WORLDWIDE IN FREESTONE STREAMS AND REMOTE LAKES IN TEMPERATE REGIONS

WHEN: BEST IN SPRING AND EARLY SUMMER AND AGAIN IN AUTUMN WHEN THERE IS A CHILL IN THE AIR

WHAT: TROUT AND GRAYLING

HOW: AN IMPRESSIONIST PATTERN, PERHAPS OF A BEETLE OR PUPA

HOOK: 10 TO 14 STANDARD SHANK
TAIL: NEON MAGENTA DFM WOOL
BODY: BRIGHT GREEN TINSEL WITH A SILVER WIRE RIB
HACKLE: BLACK HEN, THREE TURNS

Stimulator

WHERE: WORLDWIDE PRINCIPALLY IN RIVERS BUT IN STILLWATER TOO

WHEN: SPRING TO SUMMER IS BEST

WHAT: TROUT, GRAYLING, SMALLMOUTH AND LARGEMOUTH BASS, ATLANTIC SALMON, STEELHEAD. IN VERY LARGE SIZES HAS FOOLED TAIMEN

HOW: SUGGESTS STONEFLY AND CADDIS (SEDGE) AS WELL AS GENERAL IMPRESSIONIST PATTERN

HOOK: 4 TO 16 2X SHANK SEDGE HOOK (CURVED)
TAIL: ELK HAIR
BODY: YELLOW ANTRON PALMERED WITH RED GAME COCK AND COUNTER-PALMERED WITH FINE GOLD WIRE
WING: ELK HAIR
HEAD: SEAL'S FUR, YELLOW ORANGE WITH PALMERED COCK GRIZZLE HACKLE

A MAGNIFICENT MULTI-PURPOSE FLOATING PATTERN from the fertile mind of Randall Kaufmann, whose Pacific west coast USA stores are a fly fisher's heaven. This is a very good pattern during stonefly hatches or for searching rough water streams, or in smaller sizes as a caddis (sedge) pattern. In latter years it has become popular with stillwater anglers. Cast it out and let it drift with just an occasional twitch and be prepared for some explosive takes.

Toddler

THOSE LUCKY ENOUGH TO FISH for grayling in lakes can do a lot worse than use this fly on the drafter. This is another pattern from Hans Van Klinken, and is a very good imitation of a northern stonefly larva for rivers and stillwater. It also serves extremely well as an imitation of a hoglouse. I use it wherever waters are clear and unfertile with limited fishing times due to extreme weather and short seasons. I also find it very good in stillwater areas up to 6 metres (20 feet) deep.

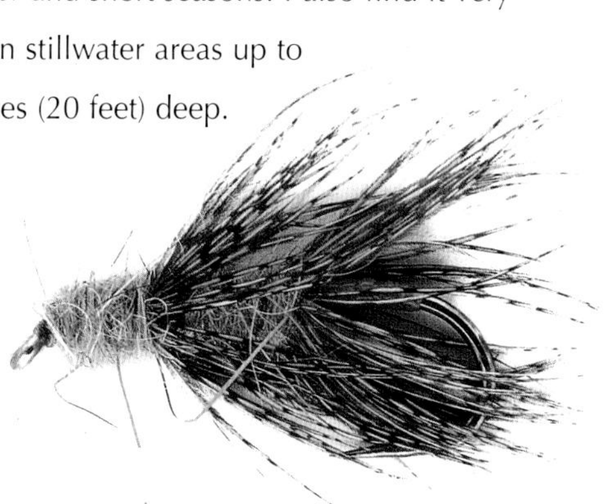

WHERE: WORLDWIDE IN STILLWATER AND RIVERS, PARTICULARLY TOWARDS THE ARCTIC REGIONS

WHEN: ALL YEAR WHEN THE WATER IS OPEN FOR FISHING

WHAT: TROUT, GRAYLING, CHAR, LAKE TROUT

HOW: SUGGESTS STONEFLY LARVA OR HOGLOUSE

HOOK: 10 TO 12 2X SHANK

REAR OF BODY: FLUORESCENT GREEN FLOSS WITH FINE POLYRIB

BODY: HARE'S EAR DUB WITH FINE POLYRIB

HACKLES: TWO SEPARATE STAGES WITH BUNCHES OF BROWN PARTRIDGE FEATHER TIED TO THE SIDES TO GIVE A NARROW PROFILE

Troth Bullhead

I WAS INTRODUCED TO THIS PATTERN of Al Troth's in the early 1970s when fishing on a very clear stillwater in southern England. A slow retrieve coupled with an intermediate sinking line brought immediate success. Before the advent of large over-wintered cock rainbows and radical changes in stocking facilities, this was the fly that these aggressive males could hardly resist.

WHERE: WORLDWIDE IN STILLWATER AND RIVERS IN TEMPERATE REGIONS

WHEN: ALL YEAR

WHAT: TROUT, SMALLMOUTH AND LARGEMOUTH BASS, LAKE TROUT, LANDLOCKED STRIPED BASS

HOW: SUGGESTS A BAIT FISH

HOOK: 3/0 TO 6 4X SHANK
TAIL: WHITE MARABOU WITH BLACK OSTRICH FROM THE SHELLBACK
BODY: CREAM RABBIT FUR DUBBED WITH BLACK OSTRICH SHELLBACK
COLLAR: RED DEER HAIR
HEAD: DEERHAIR
THE PATTERN IS USUALLY TIED WEIGHTED

Soldier Palmer

THIS IS A OLDER, TRADITIONAL PATTERN, and could indeed date back to the first fly tied for trout. Some of the old flies are still some of the best. Probably ideally fished as a dropper and at short range so it can be dibbled in the surface prior to recasting, this is an impressionist fly that means anything to trout and many other species. A firm favourite for Scotland and Ireland on the large stillwaters there, it has numerous variants and the principal of a palmered hackle and seal's fur body can be used in any colour combination, although red, claret and ginger are probably best.

WHERE: WORLDWIDE IN TEMPERATE REGIONS, USUALLY IN STILLWATER

WHEN: ALL YEAR BUT BEST FROM SPRING TO AUTUMN

WHAT: TROUT, SEA TROUT, GRAYLING, CHAR, BLUEGILL, SMALLMOUTH BASS

HOW: AN ALL-PURPOSE SURFACE-ACTIVE PATTERN

HOOK: 8 TO 16 STANDARD SHANK
TAIL: RED FLOSS OR WOOL
BODY: RED SEAL'S FUR WITH A PALMERED RED GAME COCK HACKLE

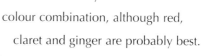

Teir Wing Caddis

WHERE: RIVERS AND STILLWATERS IN TEMPERATE REGIONS

WHEN: LATE SPRING THROUGH FALL

WHAT: TROUT, GRAYLING

HOW: SEDGE IMITATION

DRESSING: HOOK 8 TO 14 STANDARD SHANK AND 2X
BODY: DUBBED ANTRON WINGS CLUMPS OF CDC

I'M SURE IT WAS PETER GATHERCOLE who first publicized this method of tying CDC feathers in series along a hook shank. Carefully chosen for size, they create the perfect 'roof shape' silhouette of an adult caddis and by using a suitably coloured antron dub, you can imitate any caddis species. An updated version of John Goddard's sedge, this certainly lands lightly, which makes it a great fly for spooky river trout. I have also used this style with white CDC to make a super moth for late evening work. This works well when retrieved over a calm surface.

Thunder Creek Red Fin

A VERY CLEVER TYING STYLE, developed by Keith Fulsher, which uses the body fibres to make a bulbous head. With a painted eye this can then become a very realistic bait fish. It is tough, casts well and does not tangle. You can make up any colour combination to imitate whichever bait fish you know to be present. I like a brown or olive fly with a white belly for minnows, and have often seen brown trout stalk this fly across the tail of a pool before rushing in to grab it as it reaches the shallows.

WHERE: WORLDWIDE IN FRESH- OR SALTWATER

WHEN: ALL YEAR

WHAT: ALL PREDATORY SPECIES OF FISH

HOW: A BAIT FISH IMITATION

HOOK: 4 TO 10 4X SHANK
BODY: RED FLOSS WITH FLAT SILVER TINSEL RIB
BACK: BROWN BUCKTAIL
BELLY: WHITE BUCKTAIL
HEAD: FORMED BY TYING BACK THE BUCKTAIL THEN PAINTING A YELLOW AND BLACK EYE

The Wretched Mess

CHARLES JARDINE IS THE UK'S PRE-EMINENT ANGLER and such a good friend that he gave me a whole box of his dry flies when all my tackle was stolen. In that selection were two Wretched Mess flies. I used them so often and they were so good on small stillwaters that the hooks were polished from taking so many fish. I even bent them back again after they were straightened out just so I could still use the fly. Finally I made myself some more, and I strongly suggest that you do the same!

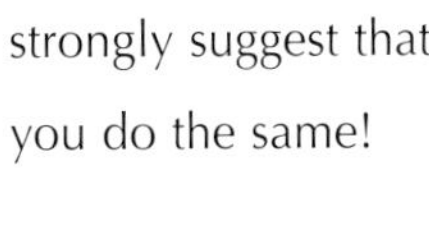

WHERE: WORLDWIDE IN STILLWATER IN TEMPERATE REGIONS AND SOME RIVERS

WHEN: LATE SPRING TO AUTUMN

WHAT: TROUT, GRAYLING, SMALLMOUTH AND LARGEMOUTH BASS, BLUEGILL

HOW: AN EMERGER PATTERN FOR CHIRONOMID HATCHES

HOOK: 12 TO 18 STANDARD SHANK
TAG: DUBBED BRIGHT ORANGE SEAL'S FUR
BODY AND THORAX: A DUB OF HARE'S MASK
WING: WHITE CDC WITH TWO FIBRES OF PEARL CRYSTALHAIR
HACKLE: GINGER CREE COCK WOUND THROUGH THORAX

Pheasant Tail Nymph

IF EVER THERE WAS A FLY YOU COULD rely upon to be accepted and known throughout the world it is this one. Any guide in any language will know the PTN. For trout it is a hugely important pattern to have in your armoury. As a basic representation of an ephemerid or small stonefly it reigns supreme, but only when tied in the correct proportions. In my fly tying classes this is the one fly that really tests the tier's ability to grasp the true meaning of proportions. It shouldn't be attempted until the tier has a good grasp of the fundamentals.

WHERE: WORLDWIDE IN ANY FRESHWATER SITUATION

WHAT: ANY INSECT EATING SPECIES

WHEN: YEAR ROUND

HOW: NON SPECIFIC INSECT LARVA IMITATION

HOOK: SIZE 18 STANDARD SHANK THROUGH TO SIZE 4 4X SHANK

TAIL, BODY, WING CASE AND THORAX: COCK PHEASANT CENTRE TAIL FIBRES

HACKLE: RED GAME HEN TIED FALSE OR TIPS OF FEATHER FROM WING CASE

Trico Polyspinner

HATCHES OF TRICO CAN BE IMMENSELY FRUSTRATING because as they occur in such vast numbers, no matter how good your imitation is, it is only one among thousands. It's now that the good fly fisher scores because you need a really good pattern (this one is excellent), and first-class presentation. Study the fish, be very accurate and put your fly in the chosen fish's view. This fly is also known as Caenis or the Fisherman's Curse because when the trico is hatching it is a demanding time to be fishing.

WHERE: WORLDWIDE IN RIVERS AND STILLWATER IN TEMPERATE ZONES

WHEN: USUALLY IN SUMMER AND PARTICULARLY IN THE EVENING

WHAT: TROUT, GRAYLING

HOW: CLOSE COPY OF SPENT STAGE OF TRICO SPECIES

HOOK: 18 TO 26 STANDARD SHANK FINE WIRE
TAIL: DUN MICRO-FIBETS SEPARATED
ABDOMEN: WHITE RABBIT UNDERFUR
THORAX: BLACK RABBIT UNDERFUR
WINGS: WHITE POLYPROPYLENE YARN TIED SPENT

Orange Butt Tarpon

A CREATION OF TIM BORSKI'S, this excellent tarpon fly is not unlike a cockroach. Use it for smaller, backwater tarpon and be ready to set the hook well. Many saltwater patterns, especially for tarpon, are now tied on circle hooks because of the better-than-average hook-up ratio. This is a great pattern for redfish, sea trout and tiger fish, and for snook in the early morning. It is even worth a try for peacock bass.

 **WHERE:** TROPICAL SALT- AND FRESHWATER

 **WHEN:** ALL YEAR

 **WHAT:** TARPON, REDFISH, SEA TROUT, SNOOK, TIGER FISH, PEACOCK BASS

 **HOW:** AN ATTRACTOR PATTERN

 **HOOK:** 1/0 OR 2/0 SHANK
TAIL: TAN POLAR FIBRE WITH PANTONE PEN STRIPING AND TOPPED WITH ORANGE CRYSTALHAIR
BODY: HOT ORANGE CHENILLE
COLLAR: GREY SQUIRREL TAIL

Terry's Coral Taddy

WHERE: STILLWATER IN TEMPERATE AND SUB-ARCTIC REGIONS

WHEN: ALL YEAR BUT SUMMER IS BEST

WHAT: TROUT, PERCH, PIKE, LARGEMOUTH AND SMALLMOUTH BASS

HOW: COLOUR AND MOVEMENT ARE THE KEY ATTRACTIONS

HOOK: 10 STANDARD SHANK
TAIL: CORAL MARABOU WITH TWO STRANDS OF PEARL FLASHABOU
BODY: CORAL FRITZ
HACKLE: CORAL HEN
HEAD: BLACK TUNGSTEN BEAD

AT ONE TIME PEACH WAS *THE* HOT COLOUR. As the tadpole variants evolved it became inevitable that coral would also be a big hit. Terry Griffiths makes this little beast and in stocked waters it can sometimes have every fish in the lake chasing after it. Even difficult and wise fish will lose all their caution and chase a Coral Taddy. Most effective when daphnia are around in the warmer waters of summer, it can be a decisive colour change at any time of year.

The Blob

THIS UNUSUAL FLY CAME ABOUT in 2001 from the competitive scene where drifting boats fish on lakes for trout to International Rules. The total hook length cannot be more than 1.5 cm (5/8 inch) and the total fly length no more than 2.4 cm (15/16 inch), while no weight may be used other than the hook itself. The Blob is cast in front of the boat and retrieved very quickly at varying depths, using varying density lines, until the fish are found. Undeniably effective, and in many colour variations, what the fish think it is remains a mystery.

WHERE: PECULIAR TO THE UK RESERVOIR SCENE BUT WOULD UNDOUBTEDLY WORK ELSEWHERE

WHEN: SEEMS BEST IN MIDSUMMER BUT COLOUR VARIANTS WORK FROM SPRING TO AUTUMN

WHAT: RAINBOW AND BROWN TROUT

HOW: SOMEHOW IT MUST INVOKE CURIOSITY OR AGGRESSION

HOOK: 10 TO 8 STANDARD SHANK
TAIL: TUFT OF ORANGE MARABOU FIBRES
BODY: DOUBLE LAYER OF ORANGE FRITZ
WING: A FEW FIBRES OF PEARL CRYSTALFLASH

Pink Thing

RECKONED TO BE THE BEST-EVER barramundi fly, the Pink Thing was developed by Graham White in Darwin, Australia, in the early 1980s. The concept of the fly is to create something that can be detected in murky estuarine water. The heavy hackling at the head makes a lot of disturbance in the water to pull in the fish. Then the hot pink hits them and the whole thing looks so good that they just have to eat it. It is important to get the bead chain eyes to the front to get the diving action. This is a feature of flies for attracting coho, who like the same action.

WHERE: TROPICAL AND SUBTROPICAL SALTWATER AND ESTUARIES

WHEN: ALL YEAR

WHAT: PRINCIPALLY BARRAMUNDI, BUT MANY OTHER SALTWATER SPECIES

HOW: AND OUT AND OUT ATTRACTOR WITH LOTS OF UNDERWATER VIBRATIONS

HOOK: 2/0 TO 4/0 STAINLESS O'SHAUGHNESSY
TAIL: SIX WHITE COCK SADDLES A FEW STRANDS OF SILVER FLASHABOU
BODY: WHITE BUCKTAIL IN TWO SECTIONS SILVER FLASHABOU WITH TWO GRIZZLE COCK HACKLES
COLLAR: FOUR COCK SPADE HACKLES IN HOT PINK WOUND TIGHT
HEAD: SILVER BEAD CHAIN

Club Sandwich

THIS FLY GAINED FAME by winning the Jackson Hole One Fly Competition. It is hard to know whether this is model making or fly tying but it's no different than fishing a popper, for example, on fly gear and this one will never sink.The deadly combination of multi-layered foam and rubber legs seems to make wild trout lose all caution. You will have to fish this fly to believe in it!

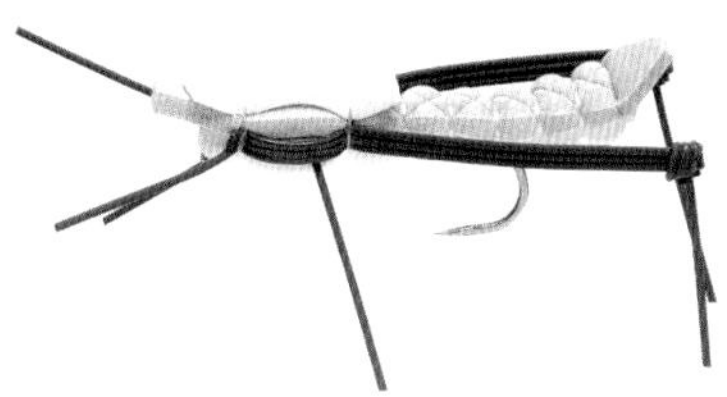

WHERE: TYPICALLY IN WESTERN USA RIVERS BUT LARGELY UNTRIED ELSEWHERE

WHEN: THE WARMER MONTHS WHEN FISH ARE MORE METABOLICALLY ACTIVE

WHAT: TROUT, AND MOST LIKELY BASS AND MAYBE MANY OTHER PREDATORY SPECIES

HOW: IT MUST SUGGEST SOME FOOD FORMS OR IS JUST SIMPLY ATTRACTIVE

DRESSING: CAREFUL CONSTRUCTION OF MULTI LAYERED FOAM SHEETS WITH KNOTTED RUBBER LEGS

Silhouette Mayfly

COME THE LAST WEEK OF MAY through the first week of June and the chalkstreams of England will be alive with hatching fly for the annual mayfly carnival. This huge insect (*Ephemera Vulgata* or *Danica*) has a lifespan of only one day and yet its various stages can induce a trout to feed very heavily and provide great sport. The Silhouette Mayfly sits very low in the water and is an excellent imitation of the hatching stage, which is frequently the only stage a feeding trout will choose to eat.

WHERE: BELGIUM, ENGLAND, FRANCE, IRELAND, SCOTLAND, SLOVENIA

WHEN: MAY TO JUNE

WHAT: TROUT, GRAYLING

HOW: EMERGENT STAGE OF EPHEMERA EANICA

HOOK: 10 OR 12 2X SHANK
TAIL: 3 SEPARATED BLACK HAIRS
BODY: OFF WHITE ANGORA WOOL WITH A DARK BROWN RIBBING
HACKLE: BLUE DUN COCK CLIPPED UNDER THE HOOK
WING: BUNCH OF CDC FEATHERS

Simon's Hover Crab

BRILLIANT USE OF FOAM to construct a model crab which can be cast on fly gear. One of the toughest things in fly tying is to make something which not only looks like the real thing but also behaves in the right way too. This tying produces a lifelike crab that drifts back to the seabed just like the real thing. Simon Becker deserves to be awarded some sort of honour by saltwater fly-fishers for this clever creation.

WHERE: SALTWATER TROPICAL FLATS AND TEMPERATE AREAS TOO

WHEN: YEAR ROUND

WHAT: PERMIT, BONEFISH, TARPON, REDFISH, STRIPERS

HOW: CRAB IMITATION

DRESSING: HOOK 4 TO 1/0 SALTWATER O' SHAUGHNESSY
BODY: 2MM (1/16 INCH) FLAT FOAM
LEGS AND CLAWS: KNOTTED SILICONE LEGS
EYES: PLASTIC BEAD CHAIN
UNDERBODY: SOFTEX AND FABRIC PAINT

Deep Flea

THIS IS A SMART WAY of imitating many varieties of sand and tube worms which spend most of their lives with their heads poking out of their burrow. Any that are slow to react to a predator are quickly snapped up. Designed by Rick Ruoff and intended to be fished hard on the bottom with the hook facing up it is particularly good on moving and mudding bonefish. This is a good fly for many species of flatfish and works well in muddy estuaries away from the tropics.

WHERE: TROPICAL FLATS BUT SHOULD BE EFFECTIVE ELSEWHERE

WHEN: YEAR ROUND

WHAT: BONEFISH

HOW: IMITATES SAND AND TUBEWORMS

HOOK: SIZE 4 STAINLESS O' SHAUGHNESSY. FISH THIS FLY HOOK POINT UP
BODY: TAN MOHAIR
HACKLE/WING: TWO CREE HACKLES WITH WHITE CALF TAIL AND WHITE CRYSTALHAIR
EYES: CHROMED LEAD BARBELLS

Crazy Charlie

BONEFISH ANGLERS owe a great deal to Bob Nauheim, who first tied this pattern to deceive the timid bonefish. These saltwater speed merchants have become a highly-prized trophy for fly fishers throughout the tropics and their habit of cruising the flats (vast areas of shallow, warm water) makes for an intensely visual and exacting style of fly fishing. Everything must be right – the fly, the cast, the presentation, the retrieve and the strike, but the rewards are enough to keep even the world's greatest anglers coming back for more.

WHERE: TROPICAL SALTWATER

WHEN: WARMER MONTHS

WHAT: BONEFISH

HOW: SUGGESTS A SHRIMP

HOOK: SIZE 2 TO 6. FISH THIS FLY HOOK POINT UP
TAIL: SHORT BUNCH OF PEARL CRYSTAL HAIR
BODY: SILVER MYLAR OVERWRAPPED WITH CLEAR MONO
WING: BUNCH OF WHITE CALF TAIL
EYES: BEAD CHAIN OR LEAD EYES
HEAD: WHITE

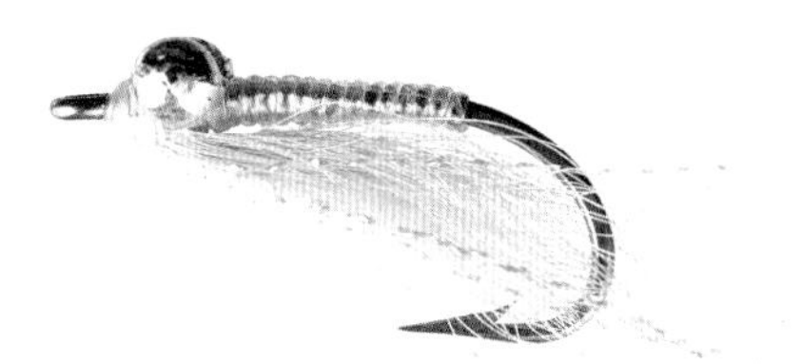

Wiggle Worm

BONEFISH WILL EAT WHATEVER IS ON OFFER, and sand worms are an especially tasty treat. Bill Sullivan tied this worm imitation that relies on the plastic wiggle tail so favoured by freshwater bass anglers to create the wiggling pulse of a worm. Cast the worm into an area where the fish cannot see it land and then just twitch the fly into life as the fish swims into viewing range. Tie it in tan, white and pink.

WHERE: TROPICAL SALTWATER FLATS

WHEN: YEAR ROUND

WHAT: BONEFISH

HOW: SAND WORM IMITATION

HOOK: SIZE 2 TO 6 STAINLESS O' SHAUGHNESSY
TAIL: PINK WAPSI SILI TWISTER TAIL
BODY: PINK CHENILLE
EYES: BEAD CHAIN

Glossary

Anadromous
Species of fish which migrate up rivers from the sea to breed.

Barbless
A hook with the barb removed or flattened, essential for catch and release.

Bucktail
A strong hair used for making larger flies.

Buzzer
A common term for the larval stage of the chironomid.

CdC
Abbreviation for 'Cul du Canard', the little fluffy feathers from a duck's preen gland which are naturally waterproof.

Chalk Stream
UK term for a limestone river.

Chironomid
A group of insects which have three life stages. These non-biting midges are called 'buzzers' by fly fishers.

CITES
Convention on International Trade in Endangered Species – an international body which governs the movement and usage of rare and endangered species.

Crystal Flash
A very popular tinsel material, fine and krinkled giving movement and flash.

Czech Nymph Style
A technique whereby short range casts in rivers allow for perfect dead drift and very close line control.

Combat Fishing
A term for large numbers of anglers fishing very close together.

Daphnia
Often called 'water fleas', these algae eaters can occur in vast swarms and make great food for filter feeders.

Dapping
A technique for presenting a fly in or on the surface with no line being seen by the fish.

Dropper
An additional fly on a leader, can be tied inline or as a spur.

Dry Fly
Any pattern which sits on the surface of the water.

Emerger
An imitation or a natural fly which is half in the surface of the water and half out.

Epoxy
A twin pack material which sets clear and is used to make bodies or heads of flies.

Ethafoam
A closed cell foam material which can never sink.

False hackle
Hackle fibres tied into the hook gape as a bunch.

Figure Eight
A retrieve style which gives a smooth, steady movement to the fly.

Flashabou
A flat tinsel used in wings for maximum flash.

Freestone
A rocky and usually shallow river with rich underwater fauna

Fritz
A chenille made from tinsel.

Fry
A common term for the young of fish species.

Fulling Mill
UK-based fly-tying company with factory in Kenya and colossal world wide distribution.

Hackle
Feather which is wound around hook shank.

Hi D
An abbreviation for 'High Density' which refers to the sink rate of a fly line

I G F A
International Game Fish Association, which administers the line class and all tackle world records for fly as well as bait/lure.

International Rules
The set of rules for competition fishing.

Isotope
A small, plastic sheath containing a chemical which permanently glows.

Jungle Cock

A pheasant from India which has a highly unusual, waxy, neck feather.

Kola

An area of northern Russia which has become of the last great strongholds of the Atlantic salmon.

Kype

Hook on the lower jaw of the mature male salmon.

Lateral Line

The line of scales midway along each side of most fishes which can detect vibration and pressure changes in water.

Limestone

Refers to a water type which has a high pH, both river or stillwater.

Lough

A large lake in Ireland. In Scotland they are called lochs.

Lure

A pattern which is not really imitative – it deceives or attracts curiosity or aggression.

Marabou
A highly mobile feather fibre originally from Marabou Stork and now from the common turkey.

Marrow Spoon
A tool for samplin the stomach contents of a dead fish.

Matuka Style
A technique whereby the wing of a fly is bound to the hook using the ribbing material

Nymph
A tying which suggests the larval stage of aquatic life

pH
Affects water productivity. This means that the higher the pH, the more insect and fish life it supports, the lower and more acid the pH, the more infertile the water tends to be.

Polar Fibre
A synthetic material which is tough, highly mobile, very fine and quickly absorbs water.

Schlappen
A large hackle feather with a broad fibre web often used as wings in saltwater flies.

Sculpin
A small, bottom dwelling fish with a big head and large pectoral fins, often called a bullhead.

Sediment
Accumulated detritus on the bed of lakes and rivers.

Slime line
Common usage term for clear, slow sinking lines with mono cores.

Teeny Lines
The group term for the fast sinking sink tips devised by Oregon's Jim Teeny.

Terrestrials
Insects which originate on land but fall onto water. Examples of these include Hawthorn, Ant, Daddy Long-Legs and Beetles.

Tube Fly
A type of fly where the materials used to make it are wound onto a tube (plastic, aluminium or brass), a leader is threaded through and a treble hook tied on.

Tundra
A region of the arctic which has a short but very intense summer season

Waddington

A fly type which is tied to a metal shank and which uses a small treble hook.

Wet Fly

Refers to any fly fished below the surface, but specifically to the older group of winged and hackled wet flies, such as Butcher, Dunkeld and Peter Ross.

Index

Acknowledgements

Author's acknowledgements

I am grateful to Barry Unwin and Ian Mackenzie of Fulling Mill Ltd and Orvis UK for providing the flies for the photographs and for their support throughout this project. Some flies are tied by myself, others by Peter Gathercole and Terry Griffiths, while special flies were contributed by Greg Wos in numerous saltwater patterns. Thanks guys, I value your friendship and envy your skills.